The Just War Tradition

I0807897

American Ideals and Institutions Series

Robert P. George, series editor

Published in partnership with the James Madison Program in American Ideals and Institutions at Princeton University, this series is dedicated to exploring enduring questions of political thought and constitutional law; promoting the canon of the Western intellectual tradition as it nourishes and informs contemporary politics; and applying foundational Western principles to modern social problems.

Also available in the **American Ideals and Institutions Series**:

Marriage: The Dream That Refuses to Die
by Elizabeth Fox-Genovese

In Defense of Religious Liberty
by David Novak

The Naked Public Square Reconsidered: Religion and Politics in the Twenty-First Century
edited by Christopher Wolfe

A Time to Speak: Selected Writings and Arguments
by Robert H. Bork

Living Constitution, Dying Faith: Progressivism and the New Science of Jurisprudence
by Bradley C. S. Watson

Western Civilization at the American Crossroads: Conflicts over the Nature of Science and Reason
by Arthur Pontynen and Rod Miller

The Just War Tradition

An Introduction

David D. Corey and J. Daryl Charles

ISI BOOKS

Wilmington, Delaware

Copyright © 2012 by David D. Corey and J. Daryl Charles
Paperback edition, February 2018

All rights reserved. No part of this publication may be reproduced or transmitted in any form or by any means, electronic or mechanical, including photocopy, or any information storage and retrieval system now known or to be invented, without permission in writing from the publisher, except by a reviewer who wishes to quote brief passages in connection with a review written for inclusion in a magazine, newspaper, broadcast, or online publication.

Library of Congress Cataloging-in-Publication Data

Corey, David D.
The just war tradition : an introduction / David D. Corey and J. Daryl Charles.
p. cm.
Includes bibliographical references and index.
ISBN 978-1-61017-150-2
1. Just war doctrine. 2. War—Religious aspects—Christianity. 3. War (Philosophy) I. Charles, J. Daryl, 1950– II. Title.
BT736.2.C59 2011
172'.42—dc23

2011049835

Published in the United States by:

ISI Books
Intercollegiate Studies Institute
3901 Centerville Road
Wilmington, Delaware 19807-1938
www.isibooks.org

Manufactured in the United States of America

To our children

Anna and John

Melody, Jesse, and Ian

Contents

1

Tradition and the Just War

On March 9, 2003—just ten days before American and coalition forces began operations in Iraq—former president Jimmy Carter wrote an impassioned editorial in the *New York Times*.[1] To Carter, it seemed that the Bush administration's plan to wage war in Iraq was a repudiation of the time-honored just war tradition. Carter explained: A just war should always be a "last resort," but other options still existed in Iraq. A war's weapons should "discriminate between combatants and noncombatants," but American bombs do not adequately discriminate. A war's violence should be "proportional to the injury suffered," but Iraq never directly injured the United States. War should be authorized by a "legitimate authority," but the UN Security Council (the relevant authority, according to Carter) did not approve the war. And finally, the war's results must be a "clear improvement upon what exists," but we had no reason for such hope in 2003. The conclusion for Carter was simple: war in Iraq would be unjust according to the just war tradition.

Less than a month earlier, Jean Bethke Elshtain, a distinguished professor at the University of Chicago, wrote an editorial for the *Los Angeles Times*, in which she too considered Iraq in light of the just war tradition.[2] But she reached a different conclusion: she saw a "strong case" for the use of force against the Hussein regime. Her argument was buttressed by a number of factors, including the seventeen UN sanctions that Iraq had ignored and that the UN had failed to enforce, egregious human rights violations perpetrated by Iraq against its own people since the late 1970s, genocidal practices against the Kurds, Hussein's repeated threats of terrorism against American and European interests, and the destabilizing effect of his policies on the region. Elshtain ended by pointing out that the mere fact that "America's political and military leaders take seriously the question of just cause, and restrain themselves in their use of force, is a credit to the continuing relevance of the just war tradition in our violent world."

We juxtapose these clashing commentaries not to defend a particular view of American involvement in Iraq but rather to raise the more fundamental question of how to understand the just war tradition. Carter and Elshtain both regard this tradition as essential for American deliberation about war, and yet they employ it to arrive at starkly different conclusions about the justness of war in Iraq. How can this be? Has Carter or Elshtain (or have both) simply misunderstood or misapplied the tradition? Or is the tradition itself somehow incoherent? And if so, what is the point of invoking it? These are serious questions, and we return to them below. But there is something else to notice about the commentaries by Carter and Elshtain, which is their underlying, albeit submerged, agreement. Both maintain that the just war tradition is a venerable tradition, an expression of our ethical ideals and a measure of American greatness. Both suggest that American policies need to be justified *in terms of* this tradition; and both give the impression that if we forsake it, we shall forfeit our credibility in the world, no longer being the people we once were. The tradition is thus for both authors the framework in which American statesmen and citizens should be deliberating collectively about war.

But are Americans in general prepared to engage in such deliberation? The answer is undoubtedly *no*. According to a recent survey, only 19.3 percent of college seniors today (some of our most highly educated citizens) can distinguish a valid and long-standing criterion of a just war (legitimate authority) from a list of bogus criteria presented in a multiple-choice format. The seniors who were surveyed (more than seven thousand in all) included students from some of our nation's leading institutions—Harvard, Yale, and Princeton, among them.[3] This suggests that we are failing to impart to our own the most basic understanding of a just war. Accordingly, we are in real danger of losing our grip on a tradition that commentators as diverse as Carter and Elshtain regard as simply indispensable—indispensable if we wish to act ethically in a violent world, and also (we would add) for our practice of democratic citizenship. It is the job, no doubt, of military and political leaders to protect us. But it is the job of citizens to ensure they do so in a way that both represents who we are and embodies our ideals. If we lose sight of those ideals, we lose our ability to determine our own character. We become subjects rather than citizens. A reengagement of the just war tradition seems therefore vitally important.

This book is designed to respond to this problem by studying the just war tradition from its inception, observing its development over time, and reflecting on how the various voices within the tradition relate to each other and to different, rival ways of understanding war.[4] Yet the account that unfolds in the chapters ahead is complex, and for this reason some introductory remarks will be helpful. Here we begin by contrasting the just war tradition with three more or less closely related perspectives: realism, pacifism, and what is today called just war theory (as distinct from the just war tradition). Next, we offer a broad overview of the tradition itself—first in terms of seminal thinkers who represent in their respective era the heart of just war moral reasoning, then in terms of the philosophical terrain the tradition covers. Finally, we reflect on the value of the tradition for our time.

Realism and Pacifism

The most common way of misunderstanding the just war tradition is to suppose that its goals are identical to those of realism or pacifism and then to blame it for failing to achieve those goals as effectively as it could. Let us therefore distinguish it from realism and pacifism.

As an approach to international relations, realism stands out for what it deemphasizes as much as for what it emphasizes. It deemphasizes the expectation that the relationship among states is, or will be, determined to any significant degree by the moral constraints found in domestic affairs. What it emphasizes instead is a sober analysis of states' "interests" and how these can be secured and advanced vis-à-vis other states. As such, realism is as old as Greek antiquity, if not older. We find it expressed in the Melian Dialogue of Thucydides, in the early-modern political works of Machiavelli and Hobbes, and in a host of contemporary writers ranging from military strategists and statesmen to political theorists and theologians.[5] For most realists, the relationship among states appears as a perpetual "state of war," whether this takes the form of actual battle or of more subtle peacetime posturing. For this reason, statesmen must learn to use force as well as the threat of force without moral scruples, lest one's nation suffer in the balance.

Pacifism, by contrast, is the doctrine that war, in the words of the popular bumper sticker, is "not the answer." (One might suppose this depends on the question.) Pacifism, of course, comes in a number of varieties, religious and secular; and it can stem from pragmatic or deontological considerations. Pragmatic pacifists argue that war is wrong because its costs always outweigh its gains or because less-destructive options are always available. Deontological pacifists argue that war is wrong because it violates universal principles of right that define what is moral for individuals in any context. But however pacifism is construed, its position diverges from the just war position in its total or near-total rejection of war as a possible response to injustice and violence in the world. The just war tradition does not reject war as a possibility, although it does not relish it either.[6]

The temptation to adopt a realist or pacifist perspective is evidently very great. But whatever their merits, they leave something significant to be desired that the just war tradition supplies in abundance. They leave their adherents with virtually no language, no conceptual tools, no guiding principles, for evaluating the justice or injustice of particular wars or particular practices of war. The pacifist approach does not offer this, of course, because it rejects war in toto. What is the point of parsing details when war per se is unjust? And the realist paradigm does not offer this because its emphasis on strategic over moral considerations tends to make talk of morality seem naive. The just war tradition is the only framework that offers a rich, highly inflected language, a storehouse of categories, concepts, and commonplaces developed over centuries of reflection, in which the moral particulars of war can be examined. One thus observes that when pacifists or realists must address specific ethical questions of war, they necessarily fall back on the language of the just war tradition, whether they like it or not.

Beyond this, the relationship of the just war tradition to realism and pacifism is complex due to considerable areas of overlap. The just war tradition shares with realism a keen awareness that man is often incorrigibly violent and unjust and that war is sometimes necessary to secure peace and to promote justice. It shares with pacifism a profound sadness about war as well as an indefatigable love of peace as an animating motive. One is thus tempted to view the just war tradition as a blend or compromise. On a continuum running from morally unencumbered action at one end (extreme realism) to practical paralysis at the other (extreme pacifism), the tradition appears somewhere in between. But this is not, in fact, the best way to think of it. For the difference among approaches is not really one of degree but of kind—it is a principled difference about what justice requires, not a difference of how much justice to practice.

This can be clarified if we consider the basic premises underlying the just war approach in terms resembling a practical syllogism.

1. In order to maintain justice and peace among nations, wars are sometimes (tragically) necessary.

2. Humans are by definition moral creatures who wish (anomalies aside) to act in ways that are good. And therefore,

3. Wars should be fought—to the extent that they must be fought at all—in ways that are compatible with our moral sensibilities.

In this light, the just war tradition arises, again, as the attempt to respond to the challenges implied by man's desire for the good by articulating moral guidelines for war. It differs from pacifism in that pacifism rejects (or questions to the point of paralysis) the claim that war is sometimes "necessary." Because pacifists reject this claim, they fail to face the challenge of setting out moral guidelines for war. Realism, for its part, rejects (or severely curtails) the claim that humans are basically moral. Because they reject this or—what amounts to the same thing—

believe that moral aspirations have no hope of success in an anarchic international environment, realists likewise fail to face the challenge of setting out adequate moral guidelines. That the three approaches thus differ in kind, not merely in degree, is revealed by how they categorically differ on the basic parameters of the problem. Only the just war tradition focuses first and foremost on the problem of reconciling the desire to act morally with the necessity of war.

At this juncture, two ways of wrongly dismissing the just war tradition can be addressed. First, the purpose of the tradition is not—not essentially, at least—to prevent war. This is an important point to stress, since it has often been argued that the failure of the tradition to stop specific wars from occurring is a telltale sign of its irrelevance.[7] Against this claim one may remark that it is difficult, in fact, to determine how many wars of the past may have been abandoned in light of just war considerations. Wars that were not fought are difficult to count. However, the objection itself reflects a skewed view of the purpose of the tradition. The essential purpose of the just war tradition is not to prevent or abolish war (desirable as this may be) but to consider how wars might be waged justly. It does not attempt, first and foremost, to prevent wars, because it is committed not only to peace but also to justice, which sometimes requires force.

Nor, second, can the just war tradition be dismissed on the grounds that wars continue to be fought for unjust causes and by unjust means. Here it is not the bare fact of war that animates the criticism but rather its ethical character today. As the charge runs: if the just war tradition were credible, it would generate just wars; but if wars continue to be fought for unjust reasons or by unjust means, then the tradition is obviously ineffective.[8] The problem with this charge is twofold. In the first place, wars are too massively complex to be described simply as just or unjust in a single breath. As justice is pursued at one level, injustices occur at another: soldiers rarely deserve the hardship of war, nor do innocents deserve to have their lives turned upside down or to become the victims of violence. Thus, the tradition does not stand or fall by the mere presence of injustice. Moreover, the charge involves a basic confusion about the relationship of moral reflection to practice. Moral reflection may shed light on why certain actions are right or wrong in relation to more basic conceptions of the good. But the mere existence of a tradition of moral reflection does not guarantee that leaders will act consistently by its lights. Over this, the tradition has no control.[9]

Just War "Theory"

The just war tradition comes to light, then, as a collaborative meditation stretching back in time and continuing even today on questions at the intersection of ethics and war. The results of this meditation, outlined below in an introductory way, can be understood as something like a framework—a permanent structure in which various questions have been differentiated from one another, various ways of answering those questions explored, and various terms and concepts developed to facilitate analysis. What we want to stress in the following is that this framework is significantly larger and richer than is often assumed and that it is, contrary to popular belief, not a fixed theory or doctrine. Why have people become confused about this? Part of the reason relates to the substitution of the phrase "just war theory" for "just war tradition"—a semantic point, perhaps, but one with profound implications. The problem is that many just war writers today actually believe that the tradition can and should be abridged into a single (if complex) doctrine and, in extreme cases, that it should be presented in the form of a "checklist" of just war "criteria" that captures once and for all what is just and unjust in war.[10]

Of course, the desire to reduce the complexity of the moral life to a bare list of rules is understandable to an extent. Soldiers need clear guidelines, as do leaders and citizens in times of war. The pressure of events may deny us time to ponder the competing impulses of a whole tradition before deciding upon a course of action. Rules and checklists are therefore useful. But we are faced here with a pedagogical problem. Are citizens better served in the long run by reflecting on war through the lens of an entire tradition or by consulting the latest text of just war theory? Let us point out some advantages to approaching the just war tradition not as a theoretical argument or list of rules.

The first relates to the foundations of moral beliefs. Taken as a whole, early just war writers were frankly more thoughtful about the grounds they assumed for their reflections than just war theorists are today. Ethical theories do not exist in a vacuum. They emerge out of networks of assumptions about more basic questions of life: What are the possibilities and limits of human perfection? Is there a divine hand in human affairs? How should humans rank the various goods to which we are drawn? The classic writers of the tradition engaged these questions comprehensively as a backdrop to their reflections on war, and they unabashedly took stands. Thus, Augustine, for example, offers an account of the Fall and of human sin to explain why wars are necessary. But today, theorists are reluctant to disclose the grounds of their arguments. Because grounds can be contested and appear to evolve over time, they seem parochial, whereas theory ought to be universal. Today's theorists thus attempt to theorize without recourse to "grounds."[11] But this is neither possible nor desirable. It is not possible because every claim about what is right or wrong in war reaches back ultimately to *some* assumption about what is good and bad in general. The assumptions may be unspoken or undetected, but they cannot be willed away. Nor is it desirable, since theories whose grounds are obscured from view are ultimately unpersuasive.

Another advantage to studying the entire tradition is that one is unavoidably confronted by its striking diversity. Precisely because the ethical questions of war can be approached from markedly different operating assumptions, we find not a single theory but rather a host of theories within the tradition, each emerging from its own set of theological and metaphysical starting points. So, for example, the theologically oriented just war approach of Augustine is quite distinct from the more secularized approach of Locke. Such diversity cannot and should not be eschewed. It is a legitimate pluralism that results from the different ways we humans can account for the conditions in which we find ourselves. Moreover, pluralism within the tradition gives rise to a number of important questions that need to be explored if our understanding of justice in war is to be even remotely complete: What is the relationship among these various just war approaches—why and in what ways do they differ? To what extent are they potentially reconcilable? Or to what extent are they irreconcilable? And what are the possible ways of coping with diversity in cases where profound differences seem intractable? These are urgent questions and should be explored further, but the basic point is that such questions do not even arise unless and until the just war tradition is approached as a tradition rather than as a theory. Because theories, no matter how complex, are at bottom univocal claims, the effort to present the just war tradition as a theory necessarily obscures its diversity, along with the questions to which its diversity gives rise.

A final advantage to approaching the tradition in all its richness and diversity is that this facilitates better comprehension of the terms and arguments put forth in the tradition itself, avoiding what we might call degeneration of meaning. The danger here is a serious one that philosophers have long noted in other contexts: naked argument, it turns out, is never quite up to the task of expressing completely what is meant. A host of background material is always assumed and needs to be present in a listener's mind if arguments are to be understood and applied correctly.[12] But what happens when a novice approaches arguments of old lacking the experiences and the assumed background that went into them? The potential result, of course, is that literalism will supplant real meaning as essential qualifications and conditions are obscured.

This problem can be illustrated with the idea of "last resort," a widely acknowledged "criterion" of just war theory today. Former president Carter invoked this in his editorial mentioned above: "In order for war to be just, it must be a last resort." But what does this mean? Does it mean that as long as something remains to be tried, or tried once again—one more diplomatic exchange, one more set of sanctions, one more forbearance, ad infinitum—war is unjust? This is regrettably how the criterion has come to be understood, even by Carter. But this is a simple misunderstanding that stems from the overly parsimonious way in which the "criterion" has been expressed in our contemporary "checklists." The fuller thought expressed by those who first articulated this stipulation was that wars are unjust as long as some solution short of war, a solution with reasonable likelihood of success, remains to be tried. Reasonable likelihood of success was the essential qualification; without it, the thought becomes absurd. All wars, after all, can be postponed indefinitely, and villains can be allowed to harm innocent people unopposed. But at a certain point, when all reasonable alternatives have been tried, the failure to respond becomes itself incompatible with the just war tradition properly understood, a tradition which maintains that acts of aggression can and sometimes should be resisted by a judicious use of force.[13] The problem with just war *theory* is that its attempt to speak in the starkest possible terms—rules, checklists, and so on—often leads to confusion rather than clarity. The remedy for the problems just noted is as straightforward as it is daunting: it is to study the tradition in its more expansive expression as it emerges over time in the works and words of those who advanced it. *Ad fontes*, as the Renaissance humanists used to say—to the sources! Only by engaging the seminal texts of the tradition and endeavoring to understand them sympathetically shall we reap the rich harvests of insight that are available. But since our purpose in this chapter is merely to introduce the tradition, let us turn next to consider the broad contours of its historical development before asking how to make sense of its progress over time.

Paradigmatic Approaches

Though the just war tradition has roots reaching back to Roman and Hebrew antiquity, its origin as a tradition can be attributed to St. Augustine of Hippo (354–430).[14] Augustine's Rome was under severe military pressure from outside. In fact, Augustine was alive and writing at the time of the fall of Rome to the Visigoths in 410, an event so shocking and unprecedented that it led to probing questions about Rome's internal health. Could the rise of Christianity in the empire be somehow to blame for Rome's weakness? Did the orientation toward another world, in combination with the Christian disregard for the traditional Roman gods, subvert the civic virtues that had undergirded Rome's success? Responding to such fears, Augustine tried to explain to pagans and Christians alike just how vigorous Christians could be as citizens and soldiers. Yet at the same time, Augustine had to reckon with those passages of scripture that seemed to prohibit Christians from engaging in war: Love your enemies and pray for those who persecute you. Do not resist one who is evil. If someone strikes you on the right cheek, turn to him the other also. Blessed be the peacemakers.

Augustine's most important contribution to the just war tradition was to show that such Christian precepts of peace do not absolutely preclude the use of force against wrongdoers. His demonstration proceeded by taking into account the entirety of scripture, not just certain passages in isolation. His exegetical approach was also not strictly literal but allowed for the possibility of spiritual readings, much like his mentor, St. Ambrose. Augustine also had recourse to a basic philosophical distinction between external act and internal intent. In a nutshell, Augustine taught that it was possible for Christians to engage in war as long as they were acting under the authority of a legitimate ruler, their goal was peace, and their wills were animated by love for another. Like a parent who disciplines a recalcitrant child, it is possible to engage in war with the good of one's "enemy" in mind, to exercise a "benevolent harshness," as Augustine dubbed the loving use of force.[15]

Building on Augustine, Gratian and St. Thomas Aquinas stand out in the development of the just war tradition in the Middle Ages. Gratian wrote in the twelfth century and is known as the father of canon law. Recognizing that on many important ethical questions facing the church, a vexing diversity of opinion existed, Gratian attempted to organize the authoritative opinions he could find on any given subject and, when possible, to synthesize these into a coherent teaching. Where such a teaching was unattainable, Gratian simply allowed divergent opinions to stand side by side in evident disharmony. His work, entitled the *Concordantia Discordantium Canonum* (Concordance of Discordant Canons), treated the question of war (see Causa 23) in a way that revealed an obvious debt to Augustine. However, Gratian did not merely echo Augustine but also tackled new problems that were characteristic of his age, particularly whether church officials, like secular rulers, could declare war when the faith seemed threatened. Gratian's answer, a qualified yes, represents the medieval (but not the modern) view on the subject, and it served to validate the Crusades as well as the violent suppression of heresy within the church.

Thomas Aquinas (ca. 1225–1274) was similar to Gratian both in his debt to Augustine and in his dialogical approach of reasoning through opposing viewpoints. In Question 40 of the *Summa Theologica*, however, Aquinas offered a much clearer statement than any writer before him of the essential core of the just war concept. In Aquinas's laconic yet infinitely expandable formulation, for war to be just, three things are necessary: the authority of a sovereign by whose command the war is to be waged, a just cause, and right intention. Of course, this invites as many questions as it answers (for example: Who counts as a sovereign authority? What is a just cause? What constitutes right intention?), and Aquinas went on to explore these issues to the extent that space allowed. But the *Summa* was also structured in a way that facilitated readers' deep reflection. By strategically placing Question 40, "On War," within his broader treatment of human virtues and vices in general, and his treatment of *caritas* (charity) in particular, Aquinas was able to illuminate the ethical possibilities and perils of war in a new and powerful way.

During the Reformation period, the two most prominent reformers, Luther (1483–1546) and Calvin (1509–1564), both endorsed the just war position, though they adapted it in different ways to their own religious and political concerns. Luther's well-known preoccupation with personal salvation and individual conscience, for example, led him to reconsider and rework the question of soldiers' responsibility. If a soldier is commanded to fight in an unjust war, should he disobey the command? Or was Augustine's thought correct that the command of a superior absolves soldiers from responsibility? Luther's answer was that each soldier should endeavor to learn for himself whether the cause he is fighting for is just, and he should not participate in causes known to be wrong.[16] Luther is also noteworthy for his handling of the question whether force could be justly used in the name of religion, either to stamp out heretical beliefs or to protect the church from infidels. He is indeed the first major figure in the tradition to denounce rather than endorse religiously inspired warfare. Interestingly, on this point Calvin arrived at the opposite view, in part because of his distinctive understanding of government. Calvin believed that true government is not a strictly secular government but one that is religiously infused, listing fostering worship, guarding against false doctrine, and preventing sacrilege among government's primary tasks.[17]

From the Middle Ages through the Reformation, the just war tradition comes to light as a primarily Christian theological tradition.[18] Arguments were grounded in scripture and intended for Christians anxious about salvation. However, this began to change gradually with the early-modern writers Francisco de Vitoria (1492–1546), Francisco Suárez (1548–1617), and Hugo Grotius (1583–1645). Though all three were theologians (as well as legal scholars) and continued to cite classic Christian texts and arguments, each attempted at the same time to present just war principles as grounded in natural law. In other words, they appealed to a universal human nature, knowable by reason and regulated by a natural sense of justice. This resulted in arguments that were at once more comprehensive and compelling. The just war tradition could now be applied to an audience larger than the Christian West. Vitoria and Suárez, for example, applied it to the native inhabitants of the New World, defending their rights against Spanish conquerors, whereas Grotius applied it to all peoples, regardless of location or custom.

The work of John Locke (1632–1704) was particularly significant for the early-modern development of the just war tradition. Locke also viewed the question of war through the prism of natural law. "The state of nature," wrote Locke, "has a law of nature to govern it, which obliges every one: And reason, which is that law, teaches all mankind, who will but consult it, that being all equal and independent, no one ought to harm another in his life, health, liberty or possessions."[19] Those who violated this precept of natural law were "aggressors" in Locke's view and could justly be subjected to force. Locke departed from earlier writers in the tradition, however, in the degree to which he muted scriptural texts and wrote instead with an eye toward a distinctly secular set of goods: political liberty, the right to property, and the hope of material progress. Gone now was the anxiety about salvation that had animated the tradition from the start, or the requirement stressed by Augustine and those following him that for war to be just it must be motivated by love. Locke, in effect, adapted the tradition to an early-modern climate in which church and state—or as Locke would put it, "care of the soul" and "care of the body"—were viewed as necessarily distinct.

Through Vitoria, Suárez, Grotius, and Locke, the just war tradition merged with the development of international law. We do not always think of the international laws of war such as the Hague and Geneva Conventions, the Kellogg-Briand Pact, and the Nuremberg Principles as concrete expressions of the just war tradition, but that is precisely what they are. Consider some of the principal stipulations of the Hague and Geneva Conventions: attempt to settle disputes peacefully; fight only enemy combatants; do not harm enemies who surrender; do not kill or torture prisoners; destroy no more than the mission requires; respect private property and possessions; treat all civilians humanely. All these stipulations derive from the just war tradition, even if they are developed in greater detail as they are written into treaties. The first Hague

Convention took place in 1899. From then to the last decades of the twentieth century, it is fair to say that the primary locus of development of the just war tradition was in the law. Law had now taken the place of theology and philosophy as the idiom in which questions of justice in war were to be considered.

However, the fields of law, morality, and theology are not perfectly coterminous, and while benefits accrued from incorporating the tradition into law, certain costs soon appeared as well. Law is a blunter instrument than morality and theology. Many things may be legal that are not necessarily moral. Nor do we look to the law to save our souls. Therefore, the need for ethical and theological analysis of war did not evaporate with the codification of the tradition—or large swaths of it—into law. On the contrary, it has seemed necessary to many just war scholars from the late twentieth century to the present to rejuvenate the ethical and theological modes of reflection in order to supplement and reform international law. Writers like John Courtney Murray, Paul Ramsey, and Oliver O'Donovan have approached this task from the theological side; Michael Walzer has developed the ethical (strictly philosophical) approach; while several writers, from William V. O'Brien to James Turner Johnson and Jean Bethke Elshtain, have endeavored to blend theology and philosophy in mutually illuminating ways.[20] What is interesting to consider now is the degree to which this tradition has shifted in character over time and what such shifts might represent.

Linear Motion or Permanent Possibilities?

How should one understand the tradition's historical development? In other words, does it exhibit progress over time? If so, wherein lies the advance? The most common answer to this question is to view the movement from early writers like Augustine to later writers like Locke as a gradual process of secularization.[21] There are, however, several problems with this commonly held view.

It can be shown in two ways that the tradition's development is more complex than the secularization thesis suggests. In the first place, the thesis fails to explain how and why the tradition evolved from Augustine in the fifth century to Calvin in the sixteenth. Was Calvin more "secular" than Augustine? Was he more secular than his immediate predecessor, Luther? Surely not. And yet the tradition did develop during the twelve centuries from Augustine to Calvin—in fact, this period constitutes the bulk of its development. If our only thesis about historical development is secularization, then we have no tools to understand most of the major shifts that occurred in the tradition. What, then, explains the changes during this time?

A second problem with the secularization thesis is its inability to explain why so many just war writers approach their subject from an expressly Christian vantage point even today. One may venture to say that most (though certainly not all) just war writers take an avowedly religious perspective. But this would be unintelligible if the tradition were moving inexorably toward secularism. Certainly by the twenty-first century, long after the initial secularizing impulses of Locke, a more sweepingly secular approach should have been achieved.

The question is one not merely of history but also of the philosophy of history: what sorts of processes are at work in intellectual history? We moderns have a hard time resisting the pervasive image of "perpetual progress toward secular enlightenment," even where that image is not apt. In the just war tradition, the shifts of emphasis from one author to the next are quite clearly not explained by an inexorable move toward secularism. So what sort of progression is occurring, if any?[22]

Some clarity can be gained on this question by understanding that the history of ethics in general—of which the history of just war thinking is a part—exhibits a plurality of possible basic approaches along with an apparently infinite number of inflections or combinations of these approaches. So, for example, writers may shed light on problems of ethics by proceeding in terms of natural law, consequentialism, utilitarian calculation, deontology, scripture, and so on. Moreover—and this is the key consideration—such approaches are not related to each other such that the momentary ascendance of one simply removes the others from the field. Rather, each approach captures something distinct and illuminating about what it means to think and act ethically, even if it does not capture everything or exhaust all that can be said. In fact, what one observes over time is not the gradual yielding of one ethical school to another but rather the gradual if intermittent development of many different approaches, each with its own pioneers and subsequent adherents.

Applied to the just war tradition, what this suggests is that different writers have contributed chronologically to exploring a number of distinct approaches and that whereas their mutual efforts may involve some tensions or even contradictions when set side by side, they may also be complementary in some respects. But again, the key consideration is that the momentary prevalence of one approach does not permanently remove the others from the field. Certainly, one still finds contemporary just war writers who identify explicitly with various "past" phases of the tradition: Augustinians, Thomists, Lutherans, Calvinists, Scholastic natural lawyers, Lockeans, international lawyers, and so on. All these approaches have attracted adherents and continue to do so because they offer something permanently illuminating in the way they respond to the puzzles and tensions of ethical life.[23]

The implications of this for how and why we study the just war tradition are profound. To study the tradition historically is not simply to study the dead past or to feed our idle curiosity about how we came to our present state of "enlightenment"; rather, it is to engage dialectically with a network of voices, each contributing something unique to the collaborative exploration of a rich and complex terrain.[24] Although we shall certainly have to negotiate various tensions and contradictions as we engage this network of voices, we shall also undoubtedly gain insights into aspects of the ethics of war that might not have been visible through the monocular lens of one approach.

Cumulative Wisdom

Given the inadequacy of the secularism thesis to explain how the tradition evolves, does the tradition not advance in any substantive way? Is it doomed merely to flit from perspective to perspective without ever gaining ground? Not at all. The progress of the just war tradition occurs on several planes. First, the gradual increase of approaches, each with its distinct preoccupations and emphases, cannot help but expose weaknesses or omissions in other approaches. Second, progress can be observed within the various approaches as each works out problems initially sensed only vaguely or not at all. An example is the Lutheran development of a doctrine of armed resistance to political authority, a development that came about only gradually under the pressure of events but that certainly constituted progress because it removed an incoherence in the overall Lutheran approach.[25]

Finally, progress occurs on the plane of "ethical differentiation," as we shall call it. In our view, this is the most important kind of progress.[26] Ethical differentiation is the process by which one gradually becomes conscious of natural subdivisions within an ethical problem, subdivisions that, as one eventually realizes, must be treated on their own terms if ambiguity is to be avoided. Ethical differentiation is the most important kind of progress because (a) its gains are permanent, (b) it informs all the approaches once the gains are made (in other words, there is no pluralism of ethical differentiation; new differentiations are absorbed by all), and (c) it supplies the very language by which individuals engaged in radically different ethical approaches can nevertheless converse in a concrete way.

In the just war tradition, the process of ethical differentiation has revealed a highly complex set of invaluable distinctions. Starting from the basic and rudimentary question of justice and war—"Is this a just war?"—the terrain has come to be divided into three broad subquestions distinguished by the Latin terms *jus ad bellum*, *jus in bello*, and *jus post bellum*. In other words, what does justice require when deciding whether to go to war (*ad bellum*)? What does it require of conduct in war (*in bello*)? And what does it require of a victor after war (*post bellum*)? Simply to recognize that these are separate questions under the broad heading of justice is to remove a host of ambiguities. How often does one hear commentators declare that a war is just or unjust without specifying precisely in what respect? A war may be just *ad bellum* but not *in bello*, in the way it is actually fought. Or it may be just *in bello* but not *post bellum*, in the way the defeated nation is treated. Distinguishing among these categories is certainly essential for precise ethical thought, speech, and action.

But this is not all. Under each of the broad headings—*ad bellum*, *in bello*, and *post bellum*—there are a host of subquestions, too many to trace here. Yet the size and complexity of the terrain can be indicated by simply following the *ad bellum* trajectory through a few more divisions. Under the question of *jus ad bellum*, the tradition has come to differentiate five subquestions that demand consideration. These are questions of (1) legitimate authority, (2) just cause, (3) right intention,

(4) likelihood of success and of doing more good than harm, and (5) last resort. Other issues may be identified as well, but these five are among the most frequently considered. Moreover, under each of these headings, one finds further subquestions. So, for instance, under the heading of just cause, the tradition distinguishes several kinds of causes that may potentially lead to a just war. The most obvious of these is when a nation attempts to repel an unprovoked attack. But other causes have been deemed potentially just as well: to assist a third party or ally who has been unjustly attacked; to recover stolen goods or to bring international criminals to justice; to prevent a nation from inflicting unconscionable harm on its own people (humanitarian intervention); to stop an attack that has not yet occurred but that is imminent and threatens grave harm (preemption).

So far, we have merely traced one path of the just war terrain part of the way—not all the way—down from general to particular questions. That the total terrain consists not merely of *jus ad bellum* (our starting point) but also *jus in bello* and *jus post bellum* should supply some indication of its vastness. Yet as vast as the philosophical terrain is, every bit is essential to thinking clearly about the justice of war. It is not as if the issues become less salient the further down one goes. Rather, the more particular questions seem to be the ones that matter most.

Recall that in 2003 the United States engaged in a debate about whether war with Iraq would be just. The debate at that point was one of *jus ad bellum*, and although it was relatively unfocused at first, it gradually settled into the classic subquestions: Was there a just cause? Was the president of the United States the proper authority to wage the war? Was the intention of the United States one of ultimate peace and goodwill, or were ulterior motives at work? What was the likelihood of success? Under the heading of just cause in particular, the debate was only as fruitful as various specific causes were identified and carefully discussed. Eventually, the Bush administration presented Americans with four possibly just causes. These were (1) self-defense, (2) preemption, (3) humanitarian intervention on behalf of the people of Iraq, and (4) the need to enforce the terms of the 1991 peace—the treaty that ended the first Gulf War on conditions of disarmament.[27] None of these justifications was free from problems, but the point is that citizens who failed to consider the question of just cause in these specific terms failed to reflect on the matter with appropriate precision. Unfortunately, this seems to have characterized the responses of most Americans—a fact that is supported by the survey results mentioned earlier (see note 3), if not by recollection of the debate itself. That debate seemed at every turn to be marred by knee-jerk reactions of pacifism, realism, and unbounded political cynicism. Commentators like Carter and Elshtain who invoked the tradition explicitly were the exception rather than the rule.

Why the Tradition Still Matters

We do not think it an exaggeration to assert that anyone who wishes to achieve an advanced level of understanding in some complex subject does well to engage the tradition in that subject. By tapping into a tradition, one inherits a rich storehouse of terms and distinctions that have been hard won over years of engagement with the material at hand. Indeed, it would be foolhardy to suppose one could singlehandedly and in a single lifetime obtain all the insights that a long-standing tradition of engagement hands down. ("Handing down" is the literal meaning of the Latin *traditio.*) The cumulative differentiating work of generations is necessarily greater than what any individual can accomplish. This is not to say that individuals cannot contribute to a tradition or revise its errors on the level of doctrine. But it is to say that the best way to begin to achieve an advanced level of understanding in any field is to engage the tradition while one also engages the material.

The just war tradition is also important in the political sense. Political decisions are for the most part moral decisions, and many of them are extremely complex. In these situations, the tradition supplies a map of the complexities as well as a history of paradigmatic attempts to think through these complexities. This twofold gift of tradition has immediate political benefits. First, the firmer the grasp of the ethical terrain surrounding questions of justice and war that citizens have, the more effectively they can participate in shaping policy, and the more our national debates will be inclusive as well as informed. We would even suggest that a regime in which citizens possess the knowledge to participate more effectively and to understand public deliberations better is a more legitimate regime.

A second benefit is less obvious but just as important. Because the just war tradition conveys not only a map of the terrain but also a number of distinct paradigmatic voices, citizens who study it become more familiar with ways of thinking different from their own. Citizens come to see that ethical questions can be illuminated in unexpected ways when viewed from different starting points, and everyone becomes more practiced at thinking in the manner of others. This seems all to the good. Put simply, our debates would be potentially more fruitful if we were more familiar with the recurring patterns of thought of our fellow citizens. To illustrate this point, let us return to the editorials by Carter and Elshtain.

At the beginning of this chapter, we described these two commentaries as "clashing," and in a certain sense they are. However, a closer look through a more differentiated lens reveals that although they admittedly reach different verdicts on the likelihood of a just war in Iraq, they do so on the basis of categorically different considerations. Elshtain concentrates almost exclusively on the question of just cause (i.e., what has the Hussein regime done wrong?). Carter, on the other hand, voices concerns about legitimate authority, last resort, proportionality, likelihood of success, and noncombatant immunity. Since Carter nowhere denies what Elshtain claims about just cause, and Elshtain nowhere denies what Carter maintains on the topics he considers, the commentaries never really intersect.

Still, while these commentaries do not directly clash, they nevertheless differ in a way that is instructive to consider. Carter's understanding of the just war tradition is unmistakably informed by the "international law" approach, as is evident from the criteria he considers, the legalistic tone of his reasoning, and the degree of authority he bestows upon international organizations such as the UN Security Council. Elshtain, by contrast, takes a religio-ethical approach harking back to Augustine. One characteristic of this approach, especially as it has been practiced in the twenty-first century, is that it facilitates passing judgment upon international law and international organizations when these fail to live up to our ideals. Thus, the commentaries by Carter and Elshtain demonstrate the very plurality of approaches we discussed above.

When one first compares these two commentaries, one may be moved to despair. How can the same tradition produce such opposing viewpoints? What is the use of the just war tradition if it cannot speak univocally? Yet if we think about this tradition in a more pluralist way—as we must if we are to do justice to the individual voices that constitute it—then we have grounds for hope rather than despair. Indeed, the commentaries by Carter and Elshtain exemplify the kind of exchange that becomes possible among interlocutors familiar with traditional resources. And yet this exchange was only a beginning. Each author raised questions that needed to be further discussed. Their nonconnecting commentaries needed to be made to connect so that a more holistic deliberation could occur.

That, however, depended and still depends upon American citizens becoming more familiar with the just war tradition in all its diversity than we currently are. And that is the purpose of this book. To the extent that American citizens are aware of this tradition, they are all too apt to view it in narrow terms as a theory, as an outmoded vestige of our Christian past, or as something rendered obsolete by international law. What is needed therefore is an account of the tradition's diversity over time. Moreover, because the proper way to study a tradition is not to memorize a list of facts but rather to learn to see the world through the eyes of past observers, the engagement cannot be superficial. Our goal as authors must be to present the important figures of the tradition as they understood themselves.

Finally, because American citizens are so often barraged with misinformation about the just war tradition, we have found it necessary to correct some characteristic mistakes and to return with some frequency to the question of the just war tradition's defining features. It is with this in mind, for instance, that we devote sections of the book to such figures and movements as the early church fathers, historic Anabaptism, Immanuel Kant, and various strands of contemporary realism and pacifism.

2

Early Christian Attitudes Toward Soldiering and War[1]

In his influential book *Christian Attitudes toward War and Peace*, Roland Bainton asserts:

> The three Christian positions with regard to war . . . matured in chronological sequence, moving from pacifism to the just war to the Crusade. The age of persecution down to the time of Constantine was the age of pacifism to the degree that during this period no Christian author to our knowledge approved of Christian participation in battle.[2]

And because, according to Bainton, "the history of the [early] Church is viewed by many as a progressive fall from a state of primitive purity," the conclusion would seem unavoidable that "if the early Church was pacifist then pacifism is the Christian position."[3] Bainton's position would seem to take on a prescriptive and not merely historical cast; a proper theological understanding of the earliest Christian history *requires* a pacifist reading of the fathers.

In the writings of the enormously influential Anabaptist theologian John Howard Yoder, one finds fundamental agreement with this viewpoint: the early church was pacifist, and this precommitment is rooted in Jesus' teaching on nonviolent love. Proof of this model is the fact that

Jesus offers himself as a sacrificial lamb rather than resisting the powers. Yoder reasons:

> If it is granted that nonresistant love is the way of the disciple . . . , can the Christian be the policeman? In the past, every party to this discussion has rapidly concluded that the answer is negative. . . . That such a conclusion is the most normal one can hardly be contested. . . . The answer of the pre-Constantinian church was negative; the Christian as an agent of God for reconciliation has other things to do than to be in police service. . . . Christians saw their task as one of patient suffering, not taking over themselves the work of the police. . . . The post-Constantinian church obviously accepted government service by Christians, but for reasons which cannot be deemed adequate.[4]

As with Bainton's, Yoder's position, clarified and reinforced in sundry writings,[5] is meant to be prescriptive: the early church was pacifist, an orientation embodied once more by Anabaptists of the "radical Reformation," who, in contrast to the church of the previous ten centuries, properly discerned the radical demands of obedience to Christ that are incumbent upon all. Yoder is adamant that Christians of any era, following the normative pacifism of the pre-Constantinian church, are not to participate in the affairs of the state. For to do so is to collaborate with evil, to be "co-opted" by the powers, and thereby to "compromise" the church's witness.

In his magisterial work on New Testament ethics published in 1996, *The Moral Vision of the New Testament*, Richard Hays observes that "Christian theology, at least since the time of Augustine's *City of God*, has usually countenanced the participation of believers in police forces and armies deemed necessary for the preservation of order and a relative approximation of justice."[6] The straightforward implication for Hays is that before the early fifth century, Christians would *not* have countenanced—much less participated in—social structures "deemed necessary for the preservation of order and a relative approximation of justice." Later in his assessment of early Christian attitudes, Hays states explicitly what had been implicit in previous commentary: "Although the tradition of the first three centuries was decidedly pacifist in orientation, Christian tradition from the time of Constantine to the present has predominantly endorsed war."[7] Throughout his exegetical and theological commentary, Hays's position assumes a prescriptive cast. In posing the question "Is it ever God's will for Christians to employ violence in defense of justice?" he instructs us: "The New Testament contains important texts that seem to suggest that this question must be answered in the negative."[8]

More recently, in an essay titled "The Christian Church and Peace through the Centuries," historian Robert Clouse, a founder of the Conference on Faith and History, argues that "during the early fourth century, the church fell away from its teaching with regard to warfare."[9] This "falling away," according to Clouse, stood in diametric opposition to "the quality of love found in the life and ministry of Christ"—a quality that "was not lost on the early church."[10] "The early church," observes Clouse, "saw an incompatibility between love and killing. Consequently, the early Christians would not serve in the Roman army. There is no evidence of a single Christian soldier after New Testament times until about A.D. 170."[11] In accounting for the relative silence among the church fathers up to 170, Clouse writes: "Thoughtful Christians were not pleased with the blurring of distinctions between the church and the world. These people condemned participation in warfare and urged believers to wage a spiritual conflict rather than a carnal one."[12]

Bainton, Yoder, Hays, and Clouse are by no means the only scholars to weigh in on the patristic evidence of early Christian attitudes toward soldiering and war. Rather, they are merely representative of what has become—and what remains—the standard interpretation of earliest Christian history. All share the common historical assumption that Constantine ushered in a new era. In the pre-Constantinian period, the church is thought to mirror universally and uniformly the pacifist conviction and a commitment to absolute nonviolence. From Constantine onward, the proximity of the church to the state resulted in the church's compromise and loss of moral purity as she accommodated herself to the secular needs of the empire. On this standard reading of the early patristic era, history tends to be pressed into the service of Christian social ethics: the portrait of the early church as pacifistic by conviction is meant to be prescriptive. Thus, for example, Clouse can write: "The same scruples that kept Christians out of the army led them to decline to serve in other governmental positions."[13]

The standard account of the early church's attitudes toward soldiering and war is grounded in and molded by several commonly shared presuppositions—among these:

- that the Sermon on the Mount—at least, a particular reading thereof—undergirds Christian attitudes toward military service and war;
- that military service and warfare were condemned from the beginning because of early Christians' aversion to violence and bloodshed;
- that the silence of patristic voices on the subject until the mid-to-late-second century is evidence that Christians were not participating in the military;
- that the fathers in general—and the two principal pacifist fathers, Tertullian and Origen, in particular—offer us uniformly *negative* testimony of Christian participation in the military and attitudes toward war; and
- that by the late fourth century, the church's progressive decline in moral purity was advanced to the point at which we may speak of her "fall" or her being "co-opted" by the empire; hence, the requisite language of a "radical critique of Constantinianism."

Although some details of this account vary, the wider story remains consistent, informed by the aforementioned assumptions.[14] So pervasive has been the force of these assumptions that even nonpacifists, who in principle would acknowledge the necessity of morally guided force to help order a fallen world (as well as Christian participation therein), accept the viewpoint that just war principles are only first a product of the age of Constantine, with a purported merger of church and state interests, and not the cumulative wisdom of Judeo-Christian and natural law ethical reflection.

Let us for the moment return to Robert Clouse's commentary on pre-Constantianian Christian attitudes toward war and soldiering. Summarizing early Christian thinking, he writes:

> Justin Martyr, Irenaeus, Clement of Alexandria, Tertullian, Cyprian, and Lactantius all caution their fellow Christians to remember their spiritual calling and that they owe their allegiance to a spiritual kingdom. . . . They refused to take part in the civil state because of the participation in sacrifices, oath taking, and torture that Rome demanded of civil servants. Just as there is no evidence for the presence of Christians in the Roman army before the end of the second century, so there is no record of believers in positions of authority under the Roman government until about A.D. 250. The early followers of Christ also thought of themselves as a new community . . . that replaced the old imperial ties.[15]

In his commentary, Clouse does hint that Christians indeed began appearing in the Roman army in the late second century, but this development is neither salutary nor imitable for other Christians. In Clouse's estimation it is, rather, evidence of the church's spiritual compromise and decline:

> Despite the arguments of the church fathers such as Origen, there was increasing pressure on Christians to serve in the government and the army. When Emperor Constantine made Christianity the official religion during the early fourth century, *the church fell away from its teaching with regard to warfare.* About half a century later, Augustine wrote as a product of the merger between church and state.[16]

As a historian, Clouse helpfully frames the questions that require further probing. Was there "increasing pressure" for Christians to engage in both civil and military service? If this observation is accurate, what factors accounted for such "pressure"? Can we speak of the church "falling away," a position requiring a reading of the New Testament that expressly forbids Christians from serving as magistrates or soldiers? And is it accurate to view the post-Constantinian church as having "fallen away from its teaching with regard to warfare"?[17] Such positions presume that the church in fact did have an authoritative teaching on warfare. But what precisely *was* its teaching? To what authoritative source might we look? Can we accept Clouse's contention that "thoughtful Christians" were confined essentially to the first century and a half and then extrapolate that thereafter the church was characterized by unthinking and spiritually dull Christians, for whom compromise and conflation was the necessary order of the day? These are claims and assumptions that will need adjudication. For our present purposes, they are claims that require the univocal support of patristic evidence.

Much of the standard inquiry into early Christian attitudes toward the military has been motivated, if not dominated, by theological and ethical rather than historical concerns. For this reason, what follows is a reexamination of pre-Constantinian patristic sources—with a particular focus on Tertullian and Origen, given their place as key patristic witnesses for what is thought to be normative ideological pacifism in the early church—as well as New Testament teaching that bears on the Christian's orientation toward soldiering and war. We will probe those assumptions that have contributed to the dominant portrait of the early church as universally and uniformly pacifist.

As a rule, past scholarly treatments of early Christian attitudes toward war and military service have tended to reflect the interpreter's own confessional viewpoint.[18] This is as we might expect. However, upon reexamining the relevant biblical and patristic evidence, a much more diverse portrait of the church of the first three centuries begins to emerge. And although this adjusted portrait is intended to be descriptive, it should inform the thinking of theologians, philosophers, Christian ethicists, and historians all, given that the standard reading of early Christian history seems to function prescriptively—and inevitably so—for virtually all who adduce it.

Reassessing Patristic Attitudes toward War, Soldiering, and the Use of Force

What is conspicuous about early patristic literature is how little the subject of Christians and military service surfaces. The earliest sources contain no allusions per se to Christian participation in the army. Characteristically, they reinforce what one might expect: Christians as a social subset are known for their peaceable, contented, and conciliatory nature.

Thus, for example, Justin Martyr notes, "We who formerly murdered one another now refrain from making war even upon our enemies, but for the sake of not telling lies or deceiving those examining us we gladly die confessing Christ."[19] Tatian wishes to emphasize that the Christian life is one of simplicity: "I do not wish to be a king. I am not anxious to be rich. I decline military command. . . . I am free from a mad thirst for fame."[20] Athenagoras mirrors Jesus' teaching on nonretaliation: "We have learned not to return blow for blow, nor to go to law with those who plunder and rob us, but to those who smite us on one side of the face, to offer the other side also, and to those who take away our coat to give likewise our cloak."[21] And Irenaeus stresses the same: "Therefore . . . we have no need of the law as pedagogue. . . . Nor an eye for an eye and a tooth for a tooth, to him who counts no man his enemy, but all his neighbours, and therefore cannot even put forth his hand to revenge."[22]

What unites the early fathers in their writings is their depiction of a distinctly Christian lifestyle—a lifestyle that mirrors a clear and unmistakable bias toward peaceableness as well as a vigilance heightened by the fear of idolatry. This orientation, however, as we shall observe, is not to be equated with a broad-based or universal rejection of soldiering or war per se. For example, at about the end of the first century one finds in the first letter of Clement supplications that would seem to fall short of pacifism in the narrowest ideological sense.

> Thou, Lord and Master, hast given them the power of sovereignty through Thine excellent and unspeakable might, that we knowing the glory and honor which Thou hast given them may submit ourselves unto them, in nothing resisting Thy will. Grant unto them therefore, O Lord, health, peace, concord, stability, that they may administer the government which Thou hast given them without failure. . . . For Thou, O heavenly Master, King of the ages, givest to the sons of men glory and honor and power over all things that are upon the earth. Do Thou, Lord, direct their counsel according to that which is good and well pleasing in

> Thy sight, that, administering in peace and gentleness with Godliness the power which Thou hast given them, they may obtain Thy favor.[23]

In addition, Clement notes that the state has been entrusted by God with sovereignty, power, and honor and that for this reason Christians should be subject to it.[24] Such petitions for civil rulers are commonplace in the second and third centuries,[25] even to be found in Tertullian, who arguably demonstrates the greatest reserve toward the state among the early fathers.

Tertullian

In Tertullian's early writings, we find no explicit prohibitions against Christians serving in the military; rather, he prays for emperors to have a "long life," a "secure rule," a "safe home," and "brave armies."[26] Fifteen years later, however, a shift occurred in Tertullian's thinking—a shift that most plausibly was due to social developments and not a pre-commitment to ideological pacifism. Because standard accounts of the early fathers proceed on the assumption that Tertullian and Origen, the chief pacifist fathers, are representative of the pre-Constantinian church, our reassessment of this period must begin with them.

With the passage of time, Tertullian seems to display an increasing hostility toward the powers of the state. In the *Apology*, for example, Tertullian acknowledged the necessity of war and claimed that Christians even contributed by praying for brave armies, for a faithful Senate, for the peace of the world, and for peace within the empire, acknowledging the need to defend territorial borders against invading barbarians.[27] Furthermore, he emphasized in his earlier writings that Christians participate responsibly in society. He can write unabashedly that like normal people throughout the empire, they frequent the marketplace, the inns and the public baths; they eat the same food, wear the same attire, and have the same customs.[28] What's more, "We sail with you and fight [in the military] with you and till the ground with you, [and] we conduct business with you. We blend our skills with yours, [and] our efforts are at your service."[29] In the *Apology*, Tertullian attempts to refute the late-second-century accusation of Christians' social detachment. Thus, he offers a list of assorted activities and vocations in which Christians can be found and gladly participate.

While Tertullian concedes the presence of Christians in the Roman legions, he nevertheless wishes to underscore the peaceful character that governs Christian believers' relationships to others:

> For the wont of the old law was to avenge itself by the vengeance of the glaive, and to pluck out "eye for eye," and to inflict retaliatory revenge for injury. But the new law's wont was to point to clemency....[30]

In Tertullian's later writing, however, warfare and military service are inappropriate for the Christian, despite the fact that he (a) acknowledges the presence in the Roman army of Christians and (b) is aware that John the Baptist and Jesus did not call believers away from military service.[31] But it is less bloodshed and violence than the possibility of idolatry that Tertullian fears. He writes in *De Corona* (*On the [Military] Crown*):

> I think we must first inquire whether warfare is proper at all for Christians. What sense is there in discussing the merely accidental, when that on which it rests is to be condemned? Do we believe it is lawful for a human oath to be superadded to one [that is] divine, for a man to come under promise [i.e., to be pledged to another master] after Christ [has become his Master] . . . ?[32]

Here we observe the conflict in Tertullian's mind over idolatry. The arguments that he proffers against Christian participation in the army concern military observances and ceremonies that are religious or quasi-religious in nature. "Is the laurel of the triumph made of leaves, or of corpses?" he asks. "Is it adorned with ribbons, or with tombs? Is it bedewed with ointments, or with the tears of wives and mothers? It may be made of some Christians too."[33]

Elsewhere, Tertullian reflects on Christian participation in military service and concludes that the meting out of punishment, tainted even further by "sacrifices" to another authority outside of Christ, disqualifies the Christian. "There is no agreement between the divine and the human sacrament," he insists while invoking Exodus 23:13, "[between] the standard of Christ and the standard of the devil, the camp of light and the camp of darkness. One cannot be due to two masters—God and Caesar."[34]

For Tertullian, the fear of idolatry was not due to the cult of Mithraism, popular among the soldiers, but specifically due to rituals of the Roman army that bore religious significance under the rubric of abstract deities such as Honor (*Honos*), Courage (*Virtus*), and Reverence (*Pietas*). Two quasi-sacred aspects of military life are particularly problematic for Tertullian, as evidenced in *De Corona*: the *sacramentum* (the military oath) and the military standards. The oath was taken upon enlistment and renewed twice each year by each soldier, by which he was bound unconditionally to the emperor as commander in chief.[35] Further, soldiers venerated and swore by the standards, at the center of which cult the eagle, symbolizing Jupiter, stood. The standards were typically enshrined at the center of the military encampment and possessed religious overtones because of the belief that they transmitted divine enablement from the gods to the emperor and the army.[36] We also know from military history that higher ranks in the Roman legions sacrificed to the emperor and wore badges that bore the emperor's effigy.[37] Adopting a literal application of Jesus' words, Tertullian insists, as we already noted, that one soul cannot swear absolute allegiance to two masters—Christ and Caesar.[38]

In all of early Christian literature, the only work devoted specifically and exclusively to the subject of the military is Tertullian's *De Corona*. The inspiration for this work derives from the martyrdom of a Christian soldier who refused during celebration to wear the military crown, bestowed upon soldiers for combat. Because of the danger of idolatry, Tertullian reasons, one should eschew military service, since one's ultimate loyalties will inevitably be divided.

But, as Tertullian sees it, the danger of idolatry is ubiquitous; one cannot be too careful. In *On Idolatry*, his list of forbidden occupations includes civil service to the state, not simply military service, because both, he believed, entailed a form of pagan sacrifice. The danger of idolatry, however, is not limited to the state. It extends far and wide and should also prevent Christians from becoming teachers and students, for both require studying the classics of Greek and Roman literature. In addition, trades such as gold- and silversmithing as well as woodcarving are to be avoided by Christians, since these vocations so frequently entail making idols for clients. Even the signing of contracts is condemned, given the potential for idolatrous associations. And not only vocations but our lifestyles as well are potentially idolatrous. So, for example, fancy hairstyles, certain attire and outer adornments are to be eschewed.[39] And because of the widespread superstition that pervades society around us, even house entrances, lamps, and doorposts become potential pitfalls to the believer. Tertullian cautions:

> There are among the Romans even gods of entrances . . . [such as] Cardea (Hinge-goddess), called after hinges, and Forculus (Door-god) after doors, and Limentinus (Threshold-god) after the threshold, and Janus himself (Gate-god) after the gates. . . . Among the Greeks likewise we read of Apollo Thyraeus, i.e., of the door, and the Antelii . . . or demons, as presiders over entrances.[40]

Because this world is filled with demons, and because idolatry lurks at every corner, Tertullian calls the believer to watchfulness, in the conviction that Christians all too often—and all too unwittingly—accept friendship with the world.

Bearing on our discussion is a noteworthy event reported by both Roman[41] and Christian[42] sources and mentioned twice by Tertullian—in his *Apology* and in his letter *To Scapula*—that occurred in the early 170s.[43] It concerns the famed "Thundering Legion" (*Legio Fulminata*) of the Roman army during the reign of Marcus Aurelius, the "most grave of emperors," according to Tertullian.[44] The incident occurred along the Danube in the Balkans, where the noted Twelfth Legion was defending against the invasion of Germanic hordes.[45] Placed under the personal command of Marcus Aurelius, the Twelfth Legion was fighting in conditions that severely depleted their water supplies owing to a drought in the region. According to the account of Eusebius, upon seeing the enemy approaching, soldiers knelt on the ground in prayer. Their supplication was followed by a thunderbolt from heaven that both put to flight enemy troops and sent rain to refresh the parched Twelfth Legion. Tertullian, writing two decades later, says that Marcus Aurelius himself gave the

Christians credit for this miracle,[46] as does Eusebius,[47] although pagan accounts attribute it variously. What is of interest in this story, regardless of its embellishments and varied accounts, is that Christians were already serving in the army as well as the fact that Tertullian mentions this incident on two separate occasions without a hint of suggestion that these believers were wrong in joining the Roman legion.[48]

In the end, how is Tertullian to be interpreted? We have noted the willingness in his earlier writing to refute the accusation that Christians were indifferent to—or enemies of—the state. His response is that "we fight alongside you and serve in your army." In his later response, he is increasingly resistant to the idea of Christians serving in the Roman army: there exists a fundamental incompatibility between the two "masters" of Christ and military service. As one historian notes, "It is difficult to believe that the man who wrote the *Apology* is the same man who wrote *On the Military Crown* about fourteen years later, though the later document is a product of his Montanist [and thus, extremely sectarian] point of view."[49] We might reasonably conclude that his later argument against soldiering and warfare is set forth precisely because not all Christians agreed with him.[50] And indeed, this response is understandable, because by this time baptized Christians were joining the army. Tertullian's increasingly rigorist stance, however, is neither a necessary outcome of the position of the apostolic church nor a reflection of the New Testament's ethical teaching.[51] And because of his wholesale condemnation of civil service (including serving as a ruler), literature, art, forms of dress, and signing of contracts, his opposition to military service is properly understood as part of the logic of apostasy.

Origen

Despite the sheer number of his writings, Origen says very little about war or military service, and he does not address the ethics of war per se. He does, like the other early fathers, emphasize the peaceable nature of Christians' relationships:

> And to those who inquire of us whence we come, or who is our founder, we reply that we are come agreeably to the counsels of Jesus, to "cut down our hostile and insolent 'wordy' swords into

> plowshares, and to convert into pruning-hooks the spears formerly employed in war." For we no longer take up "sword against nation," nor do we "learn war any more," having become children of peace, for the sake of Jesus, who is our leader.[52]

Accordingly, Origen believes that Christians differ very much from their Jewish ancestors, who "were permitted to take up arms in defense of the members of their families and to slay their enemies."[53] Indeed,

> if the Christians truly owed their origin to a rebellion [like their Zealot counterparts], they would not have adopted laws of so exceedingly mild a character. For their laws do not allow them on any occasion to resist their persecutors, even when it was their fate to be slain as sheep. . . . Christians were taught not to avenge themselves upon their enemies. . . . For they have obtained this reward from God. . . . On certain occasions, he has restrained those who rose up against them and desired to destroy them. . . . On special occasions, some have endured death for the sake of Christianity. . . . However, God has not permitted the whole nation [of Christians] to be exterminated.[54]

At the same time, he is not opposed to pointing out the fact of Christians' presence in the Roman army in response to the criticisms of the pagan philosopher Celsus. Celsus had pressed the argument that Christians who did not serve in the Roman legions would contribute to Rome's collapse at the hands of the barbarian hordes. Celsus, according to Origen, "urges us 'to help the king with all our might, and to labour with him in the maintenance of justice, to fight for him; and if he requires it, to fight under him, or lead an army along with him.' "[55] Origen's response is noteworthy:

> To this our answer is, that we do, when occasion requires, give help to kings, and that, so to say, a divine help, "putting on the whole armour of God." And this we do in obedience to the injunction of the apostle, "I exhort, therefore, that first of all, supplications, prayers, intercessions, and giving of thanks, be made for all men; for kings, and for all that are in authority";

> and the more anyone excels in piety, the more effective help does he render to kings, even more than is given by soldiers, who go forth to fight and slay as many of the enemy as they can. And to those enemies of our faith who require us to bear arms for the commonwealth, and to slay men, we can reply: "Do not those who are priests at certain shrines . . . keep their hands free from blood, that they may with hands unstained and free from human blood offer the appointed sacrifices to your gods; and even when war is upon you, you never enlist the priests in the army. If that, then, is a laudable custom, how much more so, that while others are engaged in battle, these too should engage as the priests and ministers of God, keeping their hands pure, and wrestling in prayers to God on behalf of those who are fighting in a righteous cause, and for the king who reigns righteously, that whatever is opposed to those who act righteously may be destroyed!" And as we by our prayers vanquish all demons who stir up war . . . and disturb the peace, we in this way are much more helpful to the kings than those who go into the field to fight for them.[56]

Origen believes that Christians have an appropriate place in war by serving a "priestly" function through their prayers. This service is far more effective than military service, but it is service to the empire and to the civil order nonetheless. In this way, Origen maintains, Christians fully support the work of justice without going into battle; they do this, however, on their knees. Lest he be mistaken as to Christians' involvement in public affairs, Origen reiterates:

> And we do take our part in public affairs when along with righteous prayers we join self-denying exercises and meditations. . . . And none fight better for the king than we do. We do not indeed fight under him, although he require it; but we fight on his behalf, forming a special army—an army of piety—by offering our prayers to God. And if Celsus would have us to lead armies in defence of our country, let him know that we do this too.[57]

What's more, insists Origen, "Christians are benefactors of their country more than others. For they train up citizens, and inculcate piety to the Supreme Being; and they promote those whose lives in the smallest cities have been good and worthy."[58]

What is noteworthy in Origen's argument is that Christians do participate responsibly in civil affairs, and they do support the governing authorities, since Scripture requires as much.[59] Thus, unlike contemporary pacifist interpretations of early Christian history, Origen not only does not deny that Christians are serving in the military (a matter Tertullian also concedes, even when both are opposed), but more important, he sees the need for Christians to support the authorities and contribute to a just and civil society even when he believes that Christians should not be soldiers. Thus, it should be noted that even when Tertullian and Origen, as the two chief pacifist fathers, prohibit Christians from bearing the sword, neither denied to government the moral duty of self-defense nor denied that Christians actually served in the military.[60]

Clement of Alexandria

Throughout his writings, Clement of Alexandria offers statements that might be interpreted in differing ways. In contrast to Tertullian and Origen, he does not proscribe military service from the standpoint of faith. Moreover, in an intriguing bit of commentary on the Beatitudes and peacemaking, he speaks of war and peace in the context of our battle against the carnal dispositions of the mind. "Peacemakers," Clement notes, are those who teach "faith and peace" and who "war against sin."[61] In his writings, Clement does not offer any commentary on the ethics of war or soldiering per se, but he does observe: "But for a man, bare feet are quite in keeping—except when he is on military service."[62] Hereby he intimates that military service is part of normal civic life and therefore a valid profession.

Clement's advice to soldiers who convert to Christ stands in notable contrast to that of Tertullian, even when both acknowledge that John the Baptist did not call soldiers away from their vocation. Whereas Tertullian admonishes soldiers who convert to leave the military, Clement exhorts Christians, regardless of their station, to manifest Christian witness in their vocation. So, for example, farmers are to acknowledge in the field the God who gives yield, while sailors who navigate call upon their heavenly Pilot and soldiers honor their Commander in performing justice.[63]

Hippolytus

A leading presbyter in the church at Rome at the beginning of the third century, Hippolytus was persecuted, exiled, and died a martyr. His *Apostolic Tradition* was written to enunciate requirements of church membership. In this context, it is said that a soldier who possesses authority must not execute people, and if commanded to do so he must disobey the order.[64] Whether Hippolytus is addressing prisoners of war or Christians being persecuted is unclear. Furthermore, according to Hippolytus no baptized believer can enter military service without denying God. Like Tertullian, Hippolytus understands certain lifestyles and types of work to negate automatically any membership in the church—for example, acting, prostitution, participating in the games, and teaching pagan classics.[65] Of Christians and military service, he writes:

> A soldier of the civil authority must be taught not to kill men and to refuse to do so if he is commanded, and to refuse to take an oath. If he is unwilling to comply, he must be rejected for baptism. A military commander or civic magistrate who wears the purple must resign or be rejected. If an applicant or a believer seeks to become a soldier, he must be rejected, for he has despised God.[66]

Cyprian

A pagan rhetorician at the time of his conversion in A.D. 246, Cyprian became bishop of Carthage. He fled and worked underground during the Diocletian persecution in the mid-third century and was martyred in 258. Cyprian writes of his own day that "roads are blocked by robbers, the seas are beset with pirates," and that wars are

> scattered all over the earth with the bloody horror of camps. The whole world is wet with mutual blood, and murder, which is admitted to be a crime in the case of an individual, is called a virtue when it is committed wholesale. Impunity is claimed for the wicked deeds, not on the plea that they are guiltless, but because the cruelty is perpetrated on a grand scale.[67]

Cyprian points to the restraint of Christian virtue: believers do not hate, they do not retaliate; they repay with kindness; they depart from rage, discord, and carnal contention because of Christ.[68] In contrast, he does not hesitate to criticize the excesses of military life. At the same time, despite his lament of the degree of savagery of his own day, he stops short of condemning Christian participation in the military and in fact acknowledges Christian acquaintances who are serving in the Roman army. In fact, he prays for the success of the emperor's armies, he views the decline of the military as a sign of divine judgment, and on occasion he employs military metaphors in a seemingly approving manner.[69]

Dionysius of Alexandria

Dionysius, a disciple of Origen who became bishop of Alexandria in A.D. 247, writes that the martyrs of his day include "men and women, both young men and old, both maidens and aged matrons, both soldiers and private citizens."[70] Moreover, he offers a noteworthy account of a certain group of soldiers. "These men," he notes, "had taken up their position in a mass in front of the [military] tribunal. A certain person was on trial as a Christian, and he was about to deny [the faith]." As a result, these soldiers "ran quickly up to the bench of judgment and declared themselves to be Christians" too.[71] Dionysius' account of this incident takes on a descriptive rather than prescriptive cast.

Lactantius

Though he does not specifically address Christians in the military, Lactantius is usually cited as an unremitting pacifist who opposes warfare on the grounds of bloodshed, which he believes to be wholly inconsistent with Christian virtue, and idolatry. "Why would the righteous person carry on war and mix himself with the passions of others when his mind is engaged in perpetual peace with others?" he asks. The Christian, by contrast, "considers it unlawful not only himself to commit slaughter, but to be present with those who do it."[72] In fact, Lactantius' pacifism is such that he believes "it makes no difference whether you put a man to death by word . . . or . . . by the sword."[73] Lactantius believes that if human passions are restrained, then no one will use violence militarily. Indeed, no one will lead an army to carry off and lay waste the property of others. For what does it say of the interests of any nation if it acts to the detriment of another state or nation? To extend one's borders violently, to increase the power of the state, to improve the revenues of one's nation—all these things, insists Lactantius, are not virtues but "the overthrowing of virtues."[74]

In the aftermath of the Diocletian persecution, Lactantius recounts the treatment of soldiers who refused to sacrifice to the emperor. Diocletian "ordered not only all who were assisting at the holy ceremonies, but also all who resided within the palace, to sacrifice. And further, by letters to the commanding officers, he ordered that all soldiers should be forced to the same impiety, under pain of being dismissed from the service."[75] According to Lactantius, Diocletian's simple wish was to exclude Christians from the imperial court and from the army.[76]

Given his very pointed opposition to soldiering and war in *Divine Institutes*, Lactantius seems to undergo a change of mind. Notwithstanding his opposition to violence, he acknowledges that killing might be of necessity if a man were compelled to go to war.[77] In addition, he issues a near-unqualified support for Constantine's battles, which he believed to be divinely inspired.[78]

Reassessing New Testament Teaching on War, Soldiering, and the Use of Force

Apostolic Teaching on the Magistrate's Authority

To struggle with the ethics of war and force is to reveal our assumptions about political power. While this does not mean that all Christians need to study political theory, it does mean that we must take seriously scriptural injunctions regarding authority. This task is not as easy as it might seem, for even within the Protestant camp differing views emerge. For example, mainstream reformers such as Luther, Calvin, Zwingli, and Bullinger held a relatively high view of political authorities, believing that all vocations—including the soldier and the magistrate—were honorable. Radical reformers such as the Swiss Brethren and Menno Simons, by contrast, viewed the powers with greater suspicion, and understandably so, since they were persecuted by both Catholics and Protestants; to this day, they tend to be radically separatist.[79]

But even beyond these divisions, approaching New Testament texts such as Romans 13 requires much qualification given the church's at times conflicted history. Anabaptists and other pacifists are keenly aware, with good reason, of ways in which this text has been misused. But the variegated interpretive history of Romans 13 is not our focus. The fact that the text can be "misinterpreted" says nothing about its meaning and its potential faithful application—*abusus non tollit usum*. What may be said, and what frequently goes unnoticed, is the contrast in Pauline thought between the personal sphere and political authority, i.e., between the context of Romans 12 and Romans 13. Following Pauline admonitions on Christians relating to Christians, Romans 12 ends with a list of exhortations aimed at Christian interaction with the world. A telling barometer of how believers relate to the world is how they handle persecution and personal abuse. In this vein, the apostle's exhortations are straightforward: avoid a retaliatory mode. As far as possible, strive for peace, seeking to do good to those who mistreat you. Believers are not to take justice into their own hands, for justice has a proper context in which it is displayed.

That proper context is illuminated in chapter 13. Whereas force and vengeance are prohibited in 12:17–21, they are both permitted and sanctioned in 13:1–10. Paul's argument is not that force and retribution, represented in chapter 13 by the *ius gladii*, are inherently immoral. In the realm of private relationships, justice is illegitimate and proscribed; in the hand of the governing magistrate, however, it is prescribed. And because the powers derive their authority from the Sovereign Lord, they are to be *respected*—a watchword in 1 Peter (cf. 2:13–17)—irrespective of whether the office is inhabited by honorable individuals. It is the clear and unambiguous teaching of the New Testament that the authorities exist for one purpose, and that is to preserve the moral-social order. The use of power—and by extension, force—is thus the essence of politics and governing. Governing is not governing without power. And because all authority inheres in and is on loan from the Sovereign Creator, the necessity of a moral and just application of force should be beyond controversy.[80]

In addition to Romans and 1 Peter, the Pastorals as well suggest a proper view of the powers. Observe the tenor of Paul's admonition to Timothy. Among the first duties of the Body of Christ when it is assembled is to intercede on behalf of "all those who are in authority" (1 Timothy 2:1–2). The purpose of this intercession is observed to be civil or domestic tranquility, which, by Paul's reasoning, helps to preserve human dignity and further the spread of the gospel (2:2–4). When we consider who may have been on the imperial throne, who presided in the Roman Senate, or who were the local political authorities at the time of Paul's writing, Paul's instructions are nothing short of scandalous.

That politics and government require power to operate, however, is not an assumption shared by all. The more separatist Tertullians among us, in every age, believe that because politics and governing do not save us, they are therefore unimportant at best and inherently evil at worst. Christians, hence, should invest themselves in pursuits that are spiritual, otherworldly, and radically Christ-centered. If we as Christians are convinced that politics and power are inherently corrupt, as separatists of any age tend to do, we will surely not involve ourselves in the political process or in social institutions that need our leavening influence.

In his important work *The Politics of Jesus*, published in 1972 and reissued in 1994, John Howard Yoder argued that Revelation 13, not Romans 13, represents the normative New Testament teaching on the state. For this reason, the Christian is not to cooperate with the powers, since they are inherently evil and intractably hostile toward God. Yoder's assumptions about the political powers are extended to the early church. The reason for Christians' acquiescence to the state in the fourth century and their increasing involvement in the affairs of the state from Constantine onward, including the military, is readily explained: the church was "co-opted" by the empire and with the end of formal persecution lost its prophetic witness. Subsequently, gone was the pristine beauty and purity that had characterized early generations of believers. This account of the first four centuries, as we noted at the outset, has been popularized by Roland Bainton and others and is broadly assumed by wider Christendom.

Additional New Testament information about the early church is not easily dispelled. The conversions of Cornelius (Acts 10) and the jail keeper in Philippi (Acts 16) raise questions, even when they elude neat answers. In both cases, there is no trace of condemnation of the military profession, which would be foundational to the claims of those who equate Christian faith and ideological pacifism.[81]

The Teaching of Jesus

Standard accounts of the early church's pacifism are not without biblical justification. They typically proceed on the assumption that the ethic of Jesus was one of "love" and nonviolence. Beginning with the admonition to be "peacemakers" (Matthew 5:9), this view anchors itself in a reading of the Sermon of the Mount that understands Jesus' call as one to nonretaliation and nonviolence. The resultant interpretation of Matthew 5:38–42 is that Jesus renders obsolete the *lex talionis* or "eye for an eye" principle set forth in the Old Testament and that he intends the imperatives "do not resist an evil person" and "turn the other cheek" as flat prohibitions of force.

The matter of retaliation certainly challenges Christian ethics. This exhortation is placed among six case illustrations by which Jesus is "reinterpreting the law." To begin, note what introduces this body of teaching. A common misperception about ethical living and the basis for ethics seems to persist. "Do not think that I have come," he warns the audience, "to abolish the law or the prophets; I have not come to abolish them but to fulfill them" (Matthew 5:17; cf. also 7:12). This warning is framed in a clearly ethical context: the disciples' "good deeds" are to be concrete and visible to others, not hidden, and in this way are to be glorifying to God (5:13–16). Furthermore, the righteousness of the disciples must exceed pharisaical measures (5:20). The six case illustrations (5:21–48) that follow, then, serve to drive home Jesus' teaching in a concrete manner. Significantly, each of the six is introduced with the rabbinic *kelal* or formulaic key "You have heard it said but I tell you . . . ," suggesting that certain popular misunderstandings need to be exposed and rectified.

As in each of the other case illustrations, Jesus' teaching on retaliation (5:38–43) does not set aside the ethical core of the commandment; rather, Jesus shows how the violation of the commandment begins in the heart with an improper attitude. Contrary to much existing commentary, the *lex talionis* as a measure of just retribution is not set aside by Jesus, because its intended purpose was to limit retribution based on proportionality. Justice demands that no more than what is proportionate to the offense be required. Moreover, private citizens could not extract retribution; rather, this was the responsibility of the judges (Deuteronomy 19:15–21; cf. Romans 12:17–21 and 13:1–10). By Jesus' day, as historians verify, rabbinic reinterpretation of "just rewards" for personal injury had become illegitimate, and thus a misuse of the *lex talionis* appears to lie behind Jesus' teaching, rather than a negation or abolition of the "law of the tooth."

Just as important is the framing of the commands that follow. Not resisting evil and turning the other cheek (5:39) are contextualized among several instances of personal "injury." Consider the nature of the other three: the loss of an article of clothing, being conscripted to walk a second mile (in all likelihood, applying to soldiers forcing civilians to carry their gear), and loaning to the person who wishes to borrow. These situations of daily life are personal and mirror issues of discipleship, not statecraft or policy. In terms of emphasis, then, Matthew 5–7 finds a parallel in the latter part of Romans 12, which addresses the Christian's relationship to the world and, specifically, handling personal injury or insult. To conflate the Sermon on the Mount and its parallel, Romans 12 (vv. 17–21 in particular), with Romans 13—that is, to fail to distinguish the context and the qualification of justice properly and improperly applied—is to confuse the personal and the political. Indeed, it is to do violence to the New Testament text and to Christian social ethics.[82]

Neither Christ's injunction to render to Caesar those things that are Caesar's (Matthew 22:15–22; Mark 12:13–17; Luke 20:20–26), nor his rebuke of Peter in using the sword (Matthew 26:50–54; Luke 22:47–53), nor his explicit teaching on Christian discipleship provides us with any resolute, universal, and apodictic acceptance or rejection of soldiering and warfare.

John the Baptist

In underscoring the nature of political authority, Calvin observes that it is the mandate of the ruler, and the nature of his office, "not only to restrain crimes of private individuals by judicial punishments, but also to defend territories committed to their charge by going to war against any hostile aggression."[83] Calvin anticipates the objection. He reasons that if we object that the New Testament contains nothing permitting Christian participation in soldiering or war, then John the Baptist presents an obstacle. If Christian participation in all warring is illegitimate, then the soldiers who sought out the Baptist (Luke 3:14), insists Calvin, would have been directed of necessity to throw away their arms and leave their profession. But they were admonished to do two things: act justly and be content with their wages. Military life was not at all prohibited.

Like Calvin, the seventeenth-century legal theorist Hugo Grotius reasons in much the same way. Grotius ponders as well why the soldiers coming to John the Baptist did not renounce their military calling as inconsistent with the will of God. Grotius is struck by the fact that right motives, rather, were enjoined by the greatest prophet who ever lived, whose unmistakable message was repentance and preparation for the kingdom of God.[84] What is significant about the Baptist's encounter with soldiers is that all the Synoptic accounts frame John's work and message in terms of repentance (Matthew 3:1–13; Mark 1:4–8; Luke 3:1–20). The demands of the Baptist are unflinchingly ethical: "Produce fruit in keeping with repentance!" When some soldiers ask, "And what should we do?" John replies, "Do not extort money and don't accuse people falsely—be content with your pay" (Luke 3:14).

Beyond John the Baptist, however, it is surely not insignificant that neither Jesus nor the apostles call soldiers away from their vocation as an expression of repentance and authentic faith. Even when Jesus forbids the sword as a means to advance the kingdom,[85] the New Testament cannot be said to teach absolute pacifism, nor does it forbid the Christian from "bearing the sword" in the service of society and the greater good of others, even when prohibition was the practice of some in the early church. In the end, no express teaching of the New Testament suggests that military service is incompatible with Christian faith.

Second Thoughts on the Pacifist Interpretation of the Early Church

Our reexamination of early Christian witnesses leads us in the direction of certain observations. One is the relatively scant attention the early fathers devoted to the subject of war and the military in their writings. Were the ethics of soldiering and war of considerable magnitude or clearly proscribed in the early church, one would certainly expect far greater attention. At the very least, soldiers qua soldiers would be excommunicated or denied the sacraments (which was not the case).

Possible explanations for this patristic inattention are multiple. Perhaps the issue was so vexing it defied neat categorization. Or perhaps it was so vexing even the fathers of the church themselves hesitated to speak definitively on the subject. Correlatively, perhaps the issue exposed the fact that the early Christians were less prone to ethical or theological reflection than later generations of Christians. On the other hand, it may be the case that soldiering and warfare were taken for granted as necessary functions of the state and, as such, required no extensive ethical-theological reflection other than the need to be good citizens. It is possible the issue may not have perplexed the ancients as it does us moderns. Or the issue may have been so crystal clear it warranted no commentary.

In all likelihood, the answer lies somewhere in the middle. Following their penetration into the surrounding culture, Christians took seriously—and engaged in—virtually every vocation and lifestyle, including military life, civil service to the state, and governing, each of which Tertullian and Origen flatly proscribe for believers. Where participation was diminished, this may have been due chiefly to the fear of idolatry inter alia. Such is the clear impression we get upon reading the early fathers collectively. This impression, it should be emphasized, accords with the general tenor of apostolic teaching, wherein idolatry and sexual immorality constitute the chief forms of unfaithfulness that exclude one from fellowship with God and with the Christian community.[86] While some in the early church were opposed to soldiering and war on the basis of ideological pacifism,[87] this was not universally the case. In fact, as James Turner Johnson has shown, attitudes toward soldiering differed greatly according to geography. Depending on where one was located in the empire, military service was of lesser or greater attraction to individuals professing Christian faith.[88]

Ultimately, a host of reasons for nonparticipation in the military on the part of many early Christians might be cited. These reasons, quite familiar to us, include—but are not limited to—the bias of the Christian gospel toward peace over violence; the expectation of an imminent Parousia; the spiritualizing of Old Testament accounts of warfare; aversion to killing and bloodshed; the emperor cult; Mithraism; the military culture with its attendant oaths, ceremonies, and festivals; social diversity among Christians; geographical location; and the fear of idolatry. Together these obstacles, notwithstanding the very real difficulties they presented for early believers, suggest both complexity and ambiguity regarding the issue of Christian faith and the military.

Even when some of the early fathers read particular sayings of Jesus—notably from the Sermon on the Mount—as prohibiting Christians from engaging in warfare or military service, mainstream patristic interpretation of the New Testament disallows the passages from being interpreted as universal prohibitions against the use of force or warfare that Christians are ethically bound to honor. For if flat prohibition of violence is the teaching of Christ, then everyone—and not merely the religiously inclined—has the same duty at all times and in all situations.[89] Although the New Testament indeed teaches charity and forbearance, nowhere does it prohibit the use of force as a means of advancing justice, retarding evil, and maintaining communal order. It is, rather, the vengeful spirit that is denounced. In fact, Ambrose, Augustine, Aquinas, and Luther join other mainstream voices in the Christian tradition to argue that moral application of force, even going to war, may be a legitimate expression of charity.[90]

A further difficulty with a purely pacifist interpretation of the early Christian centuries is hermeneutical. Such an interpretation logically requires the view that the Old Testament and New Testament have different moral standards. The problem of presupposed ethical discontinuity might well be illustrated in the *lex talionis* passage from Matthew 5:38–42, in which Jesus' supposed nonviolence is thought to be grounded.[91] If we presuppose that the *lex talionis*, explicated in Exodus 21:12ff. (cf. Deuteronomy 19:21), is an expression of illicit human revenge, then there does indeed exist ethical discontinuity. If, on the other hand, the "law of the tooth," as it is applied in the scriptures, serves both to permit and limit retributive justice, then it can be understood as part of natural moral law. Indeed, the measure of justice developed in the Old Testament is based on the principles of proportionality and restitution, which are hallmarks of justice in any age or culture and thus are abiding in nature. Jesus' intent in the Sermon on the Mount is to adjust contemporary application of the law, not to abrogate the law as an abiding ethical foundation.[92]

Yet an additional problem with the pacifist interpretation—a problem that might be viewed as a subset of the previous hermeneutical criticism—is the manner in which the early church's relationship to the state is construed. While an extended treatment of this relationship brings us too far afield of the present discussion, important questions press to the fore that are simultaneously historical and theological. John Howard Yoder has framed the issue perhaps most starkly, and helpfully, drawing attention to two erroneous though related ways in which Romans 13 has been interpreted as the basis for church-state relations.[93] One error is observed to be "positivistic," by which Yoder means that the Christian equates the will of the nation-state with the will of God. The Christian is thus understood to offer uncritical obedience to the political authorities. The second error identified by Yoder is "legitimistic," by which he means that the state is to be viewed as legitimate and worthy of obedience insofar as it is instituted by God. What troubles Yoder is that any form of "obedience" might be rendered to political authorities. Here he separates himself emphatically from the just war tradition. For this reason, Yoder prefers to view Revelation 13 and not Romans 13 as normative.[94]

But there is another perspective on church-state relations that requires our consideration. Kurt Aland has framed this oft-neglected perspective in a manner that sensitizes us to the all-too-frequent tendency to read our own contemporary concerns into the early church. Emphasizing the attitude of loyalty that would have characterized the early Christians, Aland writes:

> For the Christians of the early period, the Roman State is their State; that which damages the State . . . also damages them; that which is beneficial to the State . . . is beneficial to them also. . . . From the beginning, the Church turns toward the State. She is ready to give to the State, God's divine institution, all except one thing: that is the requested worship of the emperor as representative of the State's power. The Christians pray with all their hearts *for* the emperor, but not *to* him. . . . The totali-

> tarian claim of the State . . . exceeds the limits of the Church's loyalty, but does not destroy this loyalty. Conflicts occur again and again, because the State does not want to recognize the limit set by the Church. But the Church does not see the nature of the State as the cause of the conflict.[95]

Historian Louis Swift stands in fundamental agreement with this view of the early Christians, noting that the church draws the line at idolizing or deifying the state in any form. In drawing the line, however, the church does not refuse its loyalty or its fundamental respect, as apostolic teaching suggests.[96] In fact, contrary to contemporary scholarship, Swift argues that we should view the post-Constantinian period as "an outgrowth in many ways of an earlier thrust rather than a departure from the past."[97] Regardless of whether one accepts Swift's interpretation, the division between the pre-Constantinian and post-Constantinian fathers does not imply an ethical volte-face in the Christian community on the issue of war and military service after A.D. 313. Rather, it is more appropriate to speak of "a significant shift in emphases, a change in the dominant thrust of Christian thinking within the constant tension that exists between Christian ideals and the created world," an adjustment in Christians' assessment of the role of temporal power vis-à-vis the kingdom of God.[98]

In the present chapter, we have sought to argue that evidence from both patristic literature of the first three centuries and the New Testament—a period that is typically thought to be univocal in terms of Christian attitudes toward war and soldiering—indicates the presence of both pacifist and nonpacifist thinking in the early church. Failure to acknowledge the presence of divergent strands of thinking breeds a deficient, one-dimensional interpretation of early Christian history and Christian ethics. The fact that patristic literature up to the mid-to-late-second century is silent on the subject of Christians and soldiering does not require an interpretation that views it as evidence of universal or uniform convictions among Christians, as is broadly assumed. Historical and sociological considerations are sufficient to indicate that military service would not have been a pressing matter for the first four generations of Christians.[99] Moreover, the early silence does not explain why, by the late second century, things had already begun to change.[100]

Clearly, based on the opposition of the "later Tertullian" and Origen's response to Celsus, the situation was very different and in large measure provoked because of increasing numbers of Christians serving in the army.[101] From the mid-to-late-second century, then, we find evidence of a divergence in Christian opinion and practice. Furthermore, it is significant that patristic witnesses from the third century onward mirror strikingly diverse viewpoints.

An important implication of our findings is that the presumption of a "compromise" with the empire by the fourth- and fifth-century church—a view that has been broadly accepted by most of Christendom—needs a measure of adjustment. The notion that the empire, or the Roman army itself, was "Christianized" overnight or that the fathers of the church from the fourth century onward somehow became the unwitting and uncritical handmaiden of the empire is simplistic, predicated on both a highly selective, discolored reading of patristic sources and a failure to appreciate the vicissitudes characterizing relations between the church and the state through the first four centuries.[102] Additionally, the New Testament, from the standpoint of Christian ethics, neither proscribes nor devalues military service or the use of force, which lends support to our interpretation and therefore should inform our reading of the pre-Constantinian fathers.

Thus, we must urge a reevaluation of the conventional thinking about the early Christians that heretofore has governed our thinking. Rather than approach the early fathers with an ideological bias that mirrors contemporary theological and ethical concerns, we might acknowledge the full weight of patristic evidence, simultaneously considering patristic witnesses that are not as one-sided as we have been led to believe while also rereading the "pacifist" fathers with a view to appreciating the complexity and ambiguity that may be mirrored in their arguments. And because most contemporary accounts of the first three centuries attempt to make this period an example to—and thus proscriptive for—the present, scholarly and theological integrity requires an accurate accounting of the complexity and diversity of pre-Constantinian Christian attitudes toward the military. Surely, it is worth noting that dissenting attitudes toward Christian enlistment in the Roman army during this period are individual and not collective or ecclesial. No controversy involving the entire church or even between churches erupted concerning Christian participation in the military. And we are justified in asking whether those individuals who did dissent were in fact representative of the church at large.[103]

Indeed, we should not be overly surprised to find ambivalence or disagreement among early Christians on such controversial matters. In truth, diversity is more likely than uniformity to approximate the full range of Christian thinking—then and now—about soldiering and war.[104]

3

Origins of the Just War Tradition: Augustine

St. Augustine is often called the founder of the Christian just war tradition, and we stand in fundamental agreement, though a caveat is in order: Augustine was not, of course, the first theologian to claim that Christianity and war could be reconciled under certain conditions—that teaching belongs to Augustine's spiritual mentor, St. Ambrose, if not to others before him.[1] Augustine was, however, the founder of the just war tradition in a crucial sense: the unique way in which he reconciled Christianity with war became the standard point of departure for later writers. Gratian, Aquinas, Luther, Vitoria, Calvin, Suárez, and Grotius all owe an unmistakable debt to Augustine, echoing the manner in which he framed and resolved the question. To Ambrose and earlier Christian writers, by contrast, we find only occasional references.

What, then, was Augustine's unique approach? This cannot be answered simply by reference to a single text, since Augustine's reflections on war emerged sporadically over the course of his long career and appear in numerous dialogues, treatises, letters, and sermons. Nonetheless, it is possible to present an Augustinian understanding of the just war by cobbling together (as later medieval writers did) the various insights he offered.

Politics and Sin

The best place to begin is with Augustine's understanding of why wars occur. What explains the permanence of war as a feature of the human landscape? This question is not usually addressed by just war theorists today, even though it bears directly on the possibility of justice in war. If wars are completely beyond man's control, for example, then the space for questions of justice would be significantly diminished. If, however, wars are the product of human freedom and judgment, then the possibility of concern for justice is expanded. For Augustine—whose view would survive in whole or in part at least through the Reformation—wars occur because of the fallen nature of man, because of human sin. This is true in two related senses: On the one hand, most wars are rooted in such concrete sins as the implacable lust for power (*libido dominandi*) and for vengeance.[2] On the other hand, wars are sent by God as a punishment for human sin. Thus, God commanded Moses to make war on the iniquitous enemies of Israel in the Old Testament.[3] In this last instance, concern for justice seems to be principally God's concern, though man is expected to execute His judgment. Yet such God-commanded violence is rare in the history of warfare. Thus, we are left with considerable room for human freedom and choice.

Augustine's foundational emphasis on sin has led some commentators to label him a "realist."[4] Augustine believed that there is no perfect justice on earth. All regimes are flawed, all politics are full of sin, and conflict is simply inevitable. In a famous passage of the *City of God*, Augustine likens all earthly cities to bands of robbers:

> Justice removed, then, what are kingdoms but great bands of robbers? What are bands of robbers themselves but little kingdoms? The band itself is made up of men; it is governed by the authority of a ruler; it is bound together by a pact of association; and the loot is divided according to an agreed law. If, by the constant addition of desperate men, this scourge grows to such a size that it acquires territory, establishes a seat of government, occupies cities and subjugates peoples, it assumes the name of kingdom more openly. For this name is now manifestly conferred upon it not by the removal of greed, but by the addition of impunity.[5]

To the extent that passages such as this are considered, Augustine appears thoroughly pessimistic about the possibility of any connection between justice and politics, especially international politics.

Yet it would be wrong to conclude that Augustine viewed justice and politics as completely divorced. While Augustine was among the first great political writers to break from the ancient view that politics might somehow make man truly good or bring about a state of *eudaimonia* (happiness, blessedness), he was nevertheless convinced that politics was indispensable for creating a modicum of peace on earth (what he referred to as the *tranquillitas ordinis*), a space in which the chaotic violence of fallen man might be mitigated to a small degree so that individual Christians could more fruitfully pursue their hope of salvation.[6]

Moreover, Augustine must have thought that politics was not only necessary for peace but also a vehicle for justice, at least to some extent. How else could Christians be called to "be subject to the governing authorities . . . instituted by God . . . as an avenger who brings wrath on the one who practices evil" (Romans 13:1–7), or to "render to Caesar the things that are Caesar's and to God the things that are God's" (Matthew 22:21)? The gospel does not treat all political action as necessarily sinful, and Augustine was well aware of this.

But here was the problem that Augustine needed to solve. If everyone is to obey the secular authorities, then Christians might eventually (not to say inevitably) find themselves in the position of having to act not as citizens of the heavenly city but as inhabitants of the "city of man." Indeed, the governing authorities might call upon Christians to kill. Yet this seems hard to reconcile with the very prominent scriptural injunctions concerning peace. "Blessed are the peacemakers, for they will be called the sons of God" (Matthew 5:9). "Do not resist one who is evil, but if anyone strikes you on the right cheek, turn to him the other also" (Matthew 5:38). "Love your enemies and pray for those who persecute you" (Matthew 5:44).

Augustine's unique way of resolving this apparent contradiction constitutes the proper foundation of the Christian just war tradition. His solution involves both a certain hermeneutical approach and the application of a key set of philosophical distinctions.

Reconciling War with the Sermon on the Mount

Augustine's hermeneutical approach involved a willingness to look behind the literal meaning of scriptural passages to more figurative and spiritual meanings. Indeed, he was almost forced to do this by his awareness of the havoc that blind literalism would wreak on the coherence of scripture as a whole. So, for example, in considering the famous exhortation to "turn the other cheek" in Matthew 5:38, Augustine points out that Christ's words, taken literally, do not comport with Christ's own deeds, since Christ did not turn the other cheek when he was struck in the face by an officer (see John 18:23) but rather responded with a stern rebuke: "If I have spoken evil, give evidence of the evil; but if I have spoken well, why do you hit me?" Similarly, St. Paul, upon being struck at his trial, responded, "God shall strike you, you whitewashed wall!" (Acts 23:3–5). In the face of such complicating details, Augustine understandably sought an interpretation of Matthew 5:38 that might remain faithful to the essential core of the text while also remaining faithful to scripture as a whole. He concluded that one did not have to literally turn one's left cheek to an assailant after being struck on the right but rather that "one must above all else be careful so that patience, which is more valuable than everything an enemy can take from us, is not itself lost to the desire for vengeance."[7]

In effect, Augustine saw that the references to turning the other cheek were but images, pointing the way to an essential spiritual teaching. The problem was that images could take on a life of their own. Readers could mistake the image for its source, sign for referent. And this would be a disastrous mistake from Augustine's point of view, because one might then quite literally offer the other cheek while yet harboring resentment and a desire for vengeance in the heart. Augustine therefore tried to articulate the spiritual teaching behind the images, and in this sense his interpretation might be regarded as more literal, not less, than the scriptural passage itself.

The same hermeneutical approach is evident when Augustine interprets Matthew 5:9 ("Blessed be the peacemakers"). This apparently straightforward and unqualified teaching seems to rule out military occupations for all who hope to be saved. Yet Augustine points out that such an inference does not accord with the deeds of numerous scriptural figures.[8] David, for instance, served in the military. And though one may be tempted to dismiss his example as a relic of Old Testament times, consider that in Matthew 8:8–10 the centurion says to Christ, "Lord, I am not worthy . . . for I am a man under authority, with soldiers under me." Christ does not dismiss the centurion for his role in the military but responds: "Truly, I say to you, not even in Israel have I found such faith."[9] In the face of such considerations, Augustine was again led to qualify the common (mis)interpretation of the passage. "Blessed be the peacemakers," reads the beatitude. Augustine does not abandon the thought, but he interprets it so that it harmonizes: "Be a peacemaker, then, *even by fighting*. . . . For war is waged in order to attain peace; [and] through your victory you might bring those whom you defeat to the advantages of peace."[10]

Along with this sophisticated hermeneutical approach, Augustine routinely employed a set of philosophical distinctions that separated the external from the internal, body from mind, action from intent. These distinctions were essential for reconciling acts of physical coercion with the biblical precepts of patience and peace. Consider, for example, Christ's overturning of the money changers' tables in the Temple and his chasing the money changers out with a whip. With such physical acts in mind, Augustine writes: "These precepts of patience are always to be retained in readiness *in the heart*; and benevolence, which prohibits returning evil for evil, must always be abundant *in the will*. However, with respect to those who, contrary to their own will, need to be set straight, many things must be done with a certain benevolent harshness [*benigna asperitas*]."[11]

The concept of "benevolent harshness" may sound paradoxical, yet it is both facilitated and illuminated by Augustine's philosophical distinctions. "In correcting a son however severely," writes Augustine, "paternal love is surely never lost sight of." The love is internal, a matter of one's purpose or intent, while the acts of discipline are external and may appear harsh. And so too in war: a just war may be waged with benevolence if the welfare of the victims as well as the conquered becomes the principal concern.[12] In this way, the biblical precepts remain active internally even while the external deeds of war seem harsh and cruel.

Christians can thus participate in war, according to Augustine. And wars themselves can be deemed "just" if certain conditions are met. Here we arrive at the heart of Augustine's theory of the just war. What conditions, besides benevolent intent, must be met for wars to be just? Augustine identifies a number of fundamental considerations.

Just Cause and Prudence

The first condition for just war is a just cause. Augustine's account of just cause (*justa causa*) distinguishes sharply wars of necessity from wars of desire. He maintains that wars of desire are unjust: "To inflict war on one's neighbors and then to proceed to others and, out of the sole desire to rule, to conquer and subdue peoples by whom one has not been molested, what else should this be called but grand larceny?"[13] Wars of necessity, by contrast, arise in response to some wrong that has been committed—a wrong so grievous that neither the wrongdoers nor their victims would be well served by leniency. "It is the *iniquity* of the opposing side," writes Augustine, "that imposes upon the wise man the duty [a regrettable one] of waging wars."[14] It should be stressed that for Augustine, war is a matter of free choice, not of blind fate or necessity. The "necessity" to which Augustine refers in this passage is a moral, not a mechanical, one. Wars are thus waged either unjustly out of a desire for gain or justly out of a desire to correct a wrong, both of which involve human desire, deliberation, and will. Thus, the cause for which one is fighting determines, first and foremost, the justice of the war.

Just wars, therefore, are reactive rather than proactive. Moreover, they must be prudent. In other words, just wars must be deemed the "benevolent" remedy for *all* parties involved. While Augustine was willing to allow that war might be the best way to resist the iniquity of the opposing side, he held out great hope that patience and forbearance might be an even better strategy for reorienting the minds of wrongdoers toward higher goods than the temporal goods that generate violence. He writes:

> He who conquers evil with good patiently foregoes temporal conveniences in order to teach how such things, the excessive love of which made the evil man evil, are scorned for the sake of

> faith and justice. In this way the wrongdoer might learn from the very person whom he wronged.[15]

This relates closely to what modern just war theorists refer to as "last resort," though the idea is in no way legalistic for Augustine. Rather, it is governed entirely by considerations of effective instruction, not by a simple desire to avoid war. If patience and forbearance seem unlikely to succeed, they need not be attempted. This is a prudential decision for leaders to make.

It is noteworthy that Augustine does not distinguish as sharply as later writers between religious and secular wrongs. In a rather startling passage of his famous letter to Marcellinus, Augustine writes that anyone whose "license for wrongdoing is wrested away is usefully conquered, for nothing is less prosperous than the prosperity of sinners, which nourishes punishable impunity and strengthens the evil will, which is, as it were, an enemy within."[16] The passage can be interpreted as legitimating the use of force against sinners given that Augustine makes no distinction here between sin and crime.[17] But one must remember too that Augustine's basic posture was not as bellicose as this passage makes him sound. On the contrary, his comments on war are frequently tinged with a tone of lament, as in the *City of God*:

> If one remembers that he is a human being, one will be much readier to deplore the fact that he is under the necessity of waging even just wars. For if they were not just, he would not have to wage them, and so there would then be no wars at all. . . . Let everyone, therefore, who reflects with pain upon such great evils, upon such horror and cruelty, acknowledge that this is misery.[18]

Such passages have the effect of tempering, if not actually limiting, Augustine's otherwise expansive doctrine of just cause.

Proper Authority

Another condition for just war is that it be waged by someone with proper authority (*auctoritas*). This, according to Augustine, is no less than what the natural order of things requires. If every citizen or subject could declare war at will, wars would be much too frequent and arbitrary. And if every citizen or subject could enter into deliberations about war, the social peace would be too profoundly disturbed.[19]

While Augustine did not devote as much attention to the question of who is the proper authority as later writers, he clearly had in mind figures like generals, kings, and emperors, but he did not encourage many questions about legitimacy beyond simply establishing who was in office. The reason for this is not hard to see, although Augustine's teaching on this point seems far from satisfactory. All authority, he reasoned, hailed from God (cf. John 19:11 and Romans 13:1), for God must either place certain authorities in their various offices or at least permit them to so serve. It followed for Augustine that any wars waged by authorities in office were waged (directly or indirectly) by God.

This, of course, comes close to converting an "is" (the status quo) into an "ought" (a divinely willed act). It suggests that everything a ruler does has, in some sense, a divine purpose or mandate. And this in turn has the effect of compelling complete obedience from soldiers in the ranks.

> If a just man should happen to serve as a soldier under a human king who is sacrilegious, he could rightly wage war at the king's command, maintaining the order of civic peace. For what he is commanded to do is not contrary to the sure precepts of God, or else it is not sure whether it is or not. In this latter case, perhaps the iniquity of giving the orders will make the king guilty while the rank of servant in the civil order will show the soldier to be innocent.[20]

This is Augustine's doctrine of absolute obedience, flowing as it does from the supposed divine sanction of the powers that be. Augustine did not think that everything done by an established authority must be blameless from a moral point of view but rather that God must have some reason for allowing all successful deeds to have succeeded. God often uses such means, according to Augustine, to punish sinners or put saints to the test.[21]

Augustine's teaching that all just wars must be waged by a proper authority thus seems both salutary and potentially dangerous. It is salutary insofar as it requires war to be a public act. There can be no legitimate wars that, like terrorism, are private in nature. This in turn stands to limit the number of actual wars. But the teaching is hazardous because it fails to distinguish adequately between legitimate and illegitimate exercises of public authority, and consequently between praiseworthy and blameworthy acts of obedience on the part of soldiers. Augustine's refusal to invite such distinctions was certainly not accidental. Once subjects are invited to judge their superiors, the problem of sovereignty becomes suddenly more complex, and the possibility of civil war is then added to that of international war. The question of proper authority thus opens up a host of subordinate questions and problems that would fall to later theorists in the tradition to address. Eventually, the Augustinian framework of an all-controlling God, one who wills or permits office holders to do whatever they do, would give way to a framework in which office holders are judged by the extent to which their deeds conform to the dictates of scripture, natural law, and /or human legal convention.

Serve Peace and Show Mercy

Another condition for just war concerns the kinds of acts that are permissible in battle—what later theorists would call *jus in bello* restrictions. Augustine's reflections on this topic are sparse but seminal. It is essential, he maintains, that "in executing military commands, soldiers serve *peace* and the *common well-being*."[22] This catch-all requirement places serious constraints on the kinds of things soldiers and their leaders can do, because any act that cannot be reconciled with some view of peace and common well-being (a well-being that includes that of the opposing side) is here deemed illicit. One can see, moreover, how this requirement could grow naturally out of Augustine's reflections on right intention *in bello*. To Boniface, the Roman governor of Africa, Augustine wrote specifically about the intention of belligerents:

> When you are arming for battle, think first that even your bodily strength is a gift of God. In this way you will not think of using the gift of God against God. . . . The will should be concerned

> with peace and necessity with war, so that God might liberate us from necessity and preserve us in peace. Peace is not sought in order to provoke war, but war is waged in order to attain peace.[23]

As later theorists would perceive, this basic Augustinian position has many implications for the conduct of war. For example, no peace treaty (as Immanuel Kant would later observe) can be legitimate that has the foundations of a future conflict built into it. Furthermore, Augustine echoed Cicero in maintaining that all promises must be kept when they are made, even to an enemy in war.[24] War, therefore, was not an occasion for the abandonment of all moral constraints. It was not an all-or-nothing affair but rather an area of human action where moral responsibility still applied.

The final condition for a just war, according to Augustine, pertains to the sorts of actions that might occur after a war is over. Here Augustine was brief. Though he did not—as contemporary theorists do—mark a formal distinction between *jus in bello* and *jus post bellum*, he was nevertheless concerned about what happens after a war's end, and his stipulation was simply that mercy be shown to the losing side: "As violence is returned to one who rebels and resists, so should mercy be shown to one who has been conquered or captured, especially when there is no fear of disturbance of peace."[25]

The Augustinian Perspective

Thus far, we have sought to describe the main contours of Augustine's just war doctrine, paying particular attention to the areas in which he had the most profound influence on later tradition. His way of reconciling just war with the admonitions of the Sermon on the Mount—his emphasis on just cause, right intention, proper authority, and moral constraints in battle—paved the way for later Christian theorizing. In this sense, Augustine's work supplies a perfect illustration of what we described in the introduction to this volume as a "compact" (rather than fully differentiated) account. The divisions among *jus ad bellum*, *jus in bello*, and *jus post bellum* are implicitly present in Augustine, even though he does not draw the lines explicitly, as later writers would. And on any number of specific topics—for example, proper authority—Augustine begins to treat problems that would in time receive more sustained attention and result in more sophisticated articulation. Augustine thus sets the just war tradition in motion by offering an expandable, though not fully expanded, framework within which the issues of justice in war could be fruitfully addressed. This sets his achievement apart from that of his predecessors, even though earlier writers such as Cicero and Ambrose (among others) contributed significantly to his approach.

Before turning to those thinkers who followed Augustine in the tradition, we will highlight two aspects of his perspective that do not find their way unaltered into later just war theorizing. In other words, what makes Augustine's perspective unique among other just war voices? We maintain that the just war tradition confronts readers with a number of diverse approaches or "permanent possibilities" that cannot be simply conflated into one approach.

One distinct aspect of Augustine's approach is his relative (and in some ways shocking) lack of concern for death, including the death of innocents and even Christians. This stands in stark contrast to later just war writers who regard the protection of innocent life as perhaps *the* essential just war consideration. Augustine writes in *Against Faustus the Manichean*:

> What is it about war that is to be blamed? Is it that those who will die someday are killed so that those who will conquer might dominate in peace? This is the complaint of the timid, not of the religious. The desire for harming, the cruelty of revenge, the restless and implacable mind, the savageness of revolting, the lust for dominating, and similar things—these are what are justly blamed in wars.[26]

And again, concerning the wars of the Roman Empire, Augustine writes:

> Many Christians were killed, and many were destroyed in hideous ways. If this is difficult to bear, it is nevertheless common to all who have been born into this life. This I know: no one has died who would not have died eventually. . . . Hence, how they are to die ought not be a concern to those who necessarily will

> die, but rather to what place they will be compelled to go when they die.[27]

This is not an accidental excess in Augustine's writing, but a fixture of his perspective. Nor is it unintelligible if one considers his metaphysical and theological prior commitments. The fundamental distinctions Augustine drew between internal and external, soul and body, act and intent, surface again to suggest that the salvation of the soul, not the preservation of the body, is the chief Christian concern. In other words, just as bare life is not the *summum bonum* for Augustine, so death is not the *summum malum*. Rather, sin poses the greatest threat to human beings, and sin is more a matter of our internal dispositions than our external conditions.

This perspective poses a challenge to Christian just war theorists today who seem to have abandoned the spiritual orientation in war in favor of a distinctly modern emphasis on physical life and its material conditions. The problem is not that physical life and its conditions are irrelevant from a Christian point of view but rather that their degree of importance should be limited by their relationship to higher goods. Nor are we arguing that all Christians today should adopt Augustine's view uncritically. Rather, we are claiming that meditation on Augustine's texts prompts us to account for our own thoughts about war in unexpected and provocative ways. We need not adopt Augustine's view if it fails to hold up to critical scrutiny in the end, but we should at least try to account for why we disregard it, if and when we do.

A second unique aspect of Augustine's approach is his highly nuanced and almost paradoxical account of the overall moral status of war. Despite all that Augustine wrote about the possibility of just wars, he nevertheless maintained the view that war was a horrible evil. One has "lost all human feeling" who can think of war "without anguish of soul."[28] Augustine refers to wars repeatedly as a "necessary evil," but if war is evil, then how can it be just? Here is the difficult question, and Augustine never completely removes the mystery. War is evil because, in Augustine's view, it is the product of human sin—of pride, self-assertion, greed, and lust. War is (or can be) just, however, because it can arise from a benevolent concern for others who are being afflicted by injustice, or it can even arise out of concern for the unjust themselves.

Yet Augustine never allows his readers to take satisfaction in victory over the unjust, no matter how spotless the war (though, of course, war can never be spotless). Again, this is because war is evil from the start, and to celebrate the victory of good over evil is to fail to regret the evil that gave rise to the necessity for war in the first place. There is indeed a certain paradox in this view, but there is also profound truth; and it stands as an important corrective to the predominant modern tendency of viewing wars dichotomously as good or bad, right or wrong, as well as the tendency to regard victory with smug satisfaction. Such tendencies may be natural, but they are not, Augustine insists, properly Christian.

4

Just War in the Middle Ages

Although Augustine supplied a theological and ethical framework for later writers in the just war tradition, his reflections were far from systematic or complete. The twelfth-century thinker Gratian, however, is quite different. Gratian's explicit purpose was to systematize. Indeed, his goal was to bring together as many diverse pronouncements (or canons) as possible on various controversial subjects in order to harmonize them into coherent teachings. Where, despite his best efforts, coherence seemed impossible, he nevertheless supplied an invaluable service in presenting relevant canons side by side, thus revealing their disharmony.

The canons Gratian compiled ranged widely from passages of scripture to quotations from the church fathers to papal letters and pronouncements, along with the rulings of various ecclesiastical councils. Because of the thoroughness of his method, his text quickly became authoritative and his influence was significant. Indeed, it is fair to say that no single writer has done more to shape the European code of war than Gratian. St. Thomas Aquinas for his part relied heavily on him, as did other medieval writers, and Gratian's influence can also be felt in Reformation writers like Melanchthon and Calvin.[1] In the twentieth century, Gratian was one of the chief sources used by popes who wanted to codify Roman Catholic canon law.[2]

GRATIAN'S *DECRETUM*: CAUSA 23

Gratian's text, the *Concordia Discordantium Canonum* (*Concordance of Discordant Canons*), often referred to simply as the *Decretum*, was composed around 1140 and consists of three major sections: *Distinctiones, Causae*, and *Tractatus de Consecratione*.[3] Gratian's most sustained treatment of war occurs in a lengthy portion of the second section, called Causa 23. The Causa is divided into eight questions, under which Gratian has arranged some 163 canons along with his own dicta.[4]

Gratian begins Causa 23 by setting forth a hypothetical scenario in which certain bishops are engaged in heresy and are leading their followers into heresy. The pope responds by commanding "regalian bishops" (bishops whose powers include secular authority under the emperor in addition to their episcopal authority) in the region to take measures against the heretics. And they do indeed take action, assembling an army and making war upon the heretics. By the end of the affair, many heretics are killed, others are despoiled of their property, and still others are imprisoned. No doubt this scenario owes something to its historical context. Gratian was writing in the wake of the Investiture Controversy (1078–1122) and the First Crusade (1095–1101), a time when difficult questions were being raised about the church's proper jurisdiction in worldly affairs and the extent of its authority to command the use of force: Could the church use force against its foes? Could it command secular rulers to use force? What were the limits, if any, of the church's role in military affairs? These questions and others were neatly encapsulated in Gratian's hypothetical scenario, and it was clearly his purpose to set out a systematic teaching on the Christian ethics of war.

Gratian's doctrine on war, however, is more difficult to determine than one might suppose owing to the method he employed. Gratian did not always comment on the canons he compiled, preferring at times to let them speak for themselves. Yet to allow a canon to speak for itself is not the same thing as to endorse it. Scholars have occasionally been too quick to assign positions to Gratian that the magister may not have actually held, and some rather hazardous inferences have been drawn from extremely indirect evidence. Here we try to steer clear of speculation and merely attempt to set out the main contours of Gratian's analysis, taking care to specify when we are quoting from Gratian himself and when we are quoting from the underlying canons.[5]

Gratian begins with a question (Quaestio 1) that is preliminary to just war theory proper but that must be addressed before any theory calling itself Christian can get off the ground. The question concerns the legitimacy of violence per se: Is it ever right to use force, or is soldiering (*militare*) always and everywhere a sin? As we have seen, this matter was of great concern to Augustine, and Gratian's response follows directly along Augustinian lines. First, he admits that soldiering appears sinful on its face because numerous passages of scripture counsel the avoidance of violence and the exercise of patience.[6] But Gratian then offers his own dictum that the precepts of patience apply less to one's outward acts than to one's inward disposition, and he bolsters this view with passages from Augustine. Love sometimes requires one to use force against sinners in order to separate the sinner from the sin. Here Gratian adopts without qualification Augustine's distinctive way of reconciling the biblical precepts of patience with the practical necessities of war. In doing so, Gratian likely did more than any other medieval writer to institutionalize the Augustinian perspective, since so many subsequent canonists and theologians would take their bearings from Gratian.[7]

In Quaestio 2, Gratian sets out the basic characteristics of a just war, but does so without drawing the kinds of sharp distinctions that would later become standard. Themes of right intention, legitimate authority, and just cause appear somewhat blurred together as Gratian presents three authoritative canons. The first comes from Isidore of Seville (c. 560–636), who defined a just war as one waged by a formal declaration (*ex edicto*) in order to recover stolen goods (including immobile goods such as land) or to repel an enemy attack. This definition is significant because it requires an edict, something that was not part of Augustine's formula.[8] It is also significant for its emphasis on goods or property. According to Roland Bainton, the structure of medieval society was much more agrarian than that of the Roman Empire. Life depended more on land and produce than on trade and commerce, and this led medieval writers to articulate a new justification for war: not only for the defense of city and subject but also for the recovery of property.[9] Bainton's account is unfortunately flawed, as one can trace Isidore's doctrine back to its classical roots in Cicero, who also defined just wars in terms of the recovery of property.[10] But there is yet something true in Bainton's account, which is that the recovery of property is indeed a different kind of cause than is the repulsion of an enemy attack, and the medieval writers certainly recognized this.

Gratian's second canon comes directly from Augustine—namely, just wars are those that avenge injuries, as for instance when a country must be attacked for refusing to punish its own subjects who have committed crimes against others, or when a country must be attacked for refusing to return stolen goods. By combining the canons from Isidore and Augustine, Gratian arrives at three legitimate causes: the repulsion of an attack, the recovery of property, and the avenging of prior injuries committed either by another country or its subjects. And in a dictum immediately following the second canon, Gratian offers the following catch-all formula: "A just war is one waged by an authoritative edict to avenge injuries."

A third canon in Quaestio 2 suggests another possible route (or routes) to war. Gratian quotes a passage from Augustine describing a war between the Israelites and the Amorites. The Amorites, according to Augustine, had refused the Israelites right of passage across their lands, and the Israelites responded with force to defend the right of free passage that human custom guaranteed. According to Augustine, this war was just. Gratian does not comment. Yet if the inclusion of this canon in Quaestio 2 is significant, it suggests, in the first place, that just wars might be waged to defend a legal right or custom, a right stemming not from the divine law but from the *ius gentium*. Second, and perhaps more significantly, it raises the possibility of a war waged by a religious as opposed to a secular authority. The tribe of Israel was of course a nation, but it was also a religious community. Thus, the categories of "religious" and "secular" here are intertwined, and this in turn led to the sorts of questions Gratian wanted to explore: To what extent, if at all, is it just for a *religious* authority to employ force? Are there certain causes or injuries that fall more under the domain of the church than under secular authority? If so, what should be the precise role of secular and religious authorities in addressing them?

Gratian's exploration of these topics begins with Quaestio 3. He argues that the church can command the use of force at least in cases of heresy. But since this claim is far from obvious, Gratian starts his argument on less controversial ground. Citing a passage from Ambrose for support, Gratian argues that individuals have a right and even a duty to protect their associates (*socii*) from harm. Indeed, those who fail to protect associates when it is within their power to do so are as guilty as the actual offenders.[11] In this context, *socii* refers not to "allies" in the international sense but to family members, friends, and neighbors. Gratian does not articulate a doctrine of third-party intervention but rather the principle that those with legitimate authority can and ought to protect from injury those under their care. Next, Gratian expands this basic principle to include the right of the church to protect itself and its members from harm, for the members of the church also constitute a community, a group of *socii*; and since the leaders of this community are charged with guiding its members toward salvation, they have the right and even the duty to protect those members from harm. Indeed, if the secular community has the authority to protect its members from physical harm, how much more should the church, whose task is so much more vital than that of the secular order, have the authority to protect her members from harm? But of course, the threats to a spiritual community are spiritual harms. Thus, the church has the duty of protecting her members from false and destructive doctrines, which is to say, heresy. And if heretical teachers will not cease their activities, then the church may be compelled to use force against them.

There is an obvious objection to this line of reasoning, and Gratian pauses to consider it in Quaestio 4. Should the church not be patient and tolerant toward heretics and other deviants? Should it not minister to them spiritually rather than punishing them physically? Indeed, should not the judgment and punishment of sinners be reserved to God alone? Such is the teaching of a number of canons Gratian presents. Yet he does not ultimately accede to these canons but rather lays down a number of distinctions that open the door for the church to punish wrongdoers in general and heretics in particular. First, Gratian admits that in some cases punishment must necessarily be reserved to God: if the wrongdoers are not within the jurisdiction of the church or if their wrongs cannot be proven. Moreover, punishment is sometimes imprudent, as when wrongdoers are so numerous that to punish them would be to disturb the peace of the church. Still, Gratian insists that sometimes the church is right to punish threats and injuries to its community.

St. Paul's first letter to the Corinthians states, "For what have I to do to judge them that are without? . . . For them that are without, God will be judge (1 Corinthians 5:12–13). The implication for Gratian is that those within the church can be judged by the church. Moreover, Gratian cites Christ's "persecution" of those he expelled from the Temple as an example of the legitimate use of force against religious deviants.[12]

But Quaestio 4 leaves several important questions unanswered. First, if false doctrine is indeed a just cause for war or at least for corporal punishment (Gratian tends to conflate the two), how far might this extend? Could the church respond militarily to threats from outside the faith as well as from within? In other words, could the church declare war against infidels, or is the right to use force limited to the prosecution of heretics? This question was highly relevant in Gratian's age because the Christian church had already called crusades into existence, with Pope Urban II promising rewards in heaven for those who died in battle against the infidel.[13] Second, were there any limits to the levels of force that could be used or were all available means of violence permitted? And third, what would be the various roles of the church and secular authorities in resorting to force? Who would command military force and who would execute it?

In just war thinking after Gratian, these questions would eventually be separated out. The first is a matter of *jus ad bellum* and particularly of just cause. The second concerns *jus in bello.* The third is a matter of "legitimate authority," which, along with just cause, would be analyzed under *jus ad bellum.* But in Gratian's work, these strands are intertwined, and one senses the extreme difficulty involved in attempting to sort them out. In any event, Gratian does respond to each of these questions in his own way over the course of Quaestiones 5–8, a highly nuanced and vexingly obscure section of Causa 23. Here we merely summarize his basic teachings.

On the matter of infidels, Gratian maintained that threats posed to the church by other religions could at times be serious enough to constitute a legitimate cause of war. Canon 46 of Quaestio 5 is a sanguinary exhortation by Leo IV to the Frankish army, promising rewards in heaven if they were to die in battle, from which Gratian draws the principle that "those who die in battle against infidels merit the kingdom of heaven." Moreover, in Gratian's final dictum of the entire Causa (the dictum after canon 28 of Quaestio 8), he reaffirms this point: the example of Leo IV establishes that it is licit for prelates to exhort anyone and everyone "to defend themselves against the adversaries of the faith" and to keep the force of the infidels at a distance. Based on these and a number of other canons (cf. Q. 5, canons 8, 18, 23, 32, 40–41, and 43–44), F. H. Russell has concluded that for Gratian, "anyone seen as a threat to the Church on earth merited physical punishment even by war, [and] the waging of these wars was a positive moral duty."[14]

Did Gratian recognize any limits on the ways and means of war? In other words, did he have a nascent doctrine of *jus in bello*? A widely held view is that the first intimations of *jus in bello* doctrine appear only with the *Summa Theologica* of Thomas Aquinas, roughly a century after Gratian.[15] However, this view overlooks important evidence from the *Decretum*. In the first place, Gratian's sustained emphasis on right intention in Quaestiones 1–4 functions at least in part as a *jus in bello* doctrine. If war is not waged with a benevolent spirit, and with the aim of bringing about a just peace, then war is not waged legitimately. Later in the tradition, right intention would be grouped under the headings of *jus ad bellum* and *jus in bello*—a right intention is a precondition for a just war as well as a guiding light in waging it. That right intention is an *in bello* consideration for Gratian is nowhere more evident than in Quaestio 4, where he offers a penetrating discussion of vengeance (*vindicta*). Vengeance may be rightly or wrongly administered, he says. It is administered properly when the will of the agent is focused on love of justice but not when it is focused on love of inflicting punishment.[16] This surely applies to *jus ad bellum* as well as to *jus in bello*, and thus we should credit Gratian with an awareness of such constraints upon the waging of war.[17]

Gratian discusses other stipulations that fall properly under *jus in bello*, though these are scattered rather randomly across his text and are never fully developed. For example, in Causa 24, Gratian makes clear that he regards pilgrims, women, clerics, and the unarmed poor as exempt from violence, thus anticipating something like the idea of noncombatant immunity, as it is termed today. Gratian's point in this section is that these categories of individuals should be exempt from having to fight, not that they are exempt from being attacked, though the latter would seem to follow naturally from the former.[18] Gratian also cites Augustine's teaching that faith (in the sense of keeping one's promises) must be maintained even to an enemy in war.[19] And he devotes considerable space to the question of whether battles can be fought during Lent. This too is a matter of *jus in bello*, even though Gratian's actual position was to allow Lenten fighting, reasoning that if Christians refuse to fight during Lent, God might assume they were failing to do everything they could to prevail in their just cause.[20]

However, one does not find in Gratian any reference to specific actions or weapons or strategies that were illicit for Christians to use in war. This omission has attracted the attention of Russell, who points out that there was during Gratian's time a powerful ecclesiastical movement to condemn certain weapons thought to be too deadly to be used against Christians. In fact, this movement had its view enshrined in the Second Lateran Council of 1139, a council whose canons on other topics Gratian did cite but not on the matter of weapons.[21] Russell speculates that Gratian's omission of the contemporary ban on weapons was intentional and that Gratian in fact disagreed with the ban on principle. "If a war was necessary and just," writes Russell, "then all possible means to victory must be employed including the use of more effective weapons. And if the war was unnecessary, then it should not take place at all, much less during Lent or with deadly weapons."[22] Whether Gratian intended the omission or not is difficult to say, but that he offered nothing by way of restrictions on weapons is certainly worth noting.

In general, then, one can say that Gratian had a sense of the type of issues that would eventually fall under the heading of *jus in bello*, but his views on the subject were not nearly as systematic or developed as his views on other aspects of war. In fact, where he did consider *jus in bello* in detail, he tended either to be derivative—merely presenting canons from earlier writers such as Augustine—or to take positions that were permissive rather than restrictive.

Finally, we come to the topic of legitimate authority, which was Gratian's most pressing concern in Quaestio 8, the final section of Causa 23. In particular, could the church act as a legitimate authority in war, or must this be exclusively the business of the secular powers? Gratian here faced the unenviable challenge of having to reconcile seemingly irreconcilable canons. On the one hand were canons that prohibited priests from participating in any matters involving bloodshed. Those who took up arms should be degraded and retired to a monastery, says one canon, for they cannot serve God and the secular powers concomitantly.[23] Similarly, a canon from Nicholas I prohibits bishops from playing even minor roles in military affairs (e.g., keeping watch for pirates) lest they become too involved in secular affairs.[24] On the other hand, Gratian had to confront more recent canons from the Carolingian period that seemed to involve the church directly in war. Leo IV had called an army to defend Rome against Saracen pirates, and Adrian I had exhorted Charlemagne to wage war against the Lombards.[25] How could such clashing canons be unified?

The answer involves Gratian drawing some rather painfully fine distinctions, which must seem to us highly artificial, not to say contrived. First was the distinction between actually declaring war and merely exhorting others to do so. Priests, according to Gratian, had the power to exhort secular authorities to declare war, and they could order laymen to "take up arms in defense of the church," but they could not mention the actual shedding of blood. Second, Gratian distinguished between bishops with regalia and those without. Regalian bishops, who possessed some secular power in addition to their episcopal sees, were of course obligated to fulfill the tasks associated with their positions. Thus, if their tasks required them to assemble troops and declare war, then they could. But Gratian required that these bishops proceed with the express permission of the pope and that they avoid the actual shedding of blood.[26] In effect, Gratian was declaring that the church did indeed have legitimate authority in matters of war, even if that authority had limits. The church could initiate wars by exhorting secular authorities to do so, or it could rely on its regalian bishops to declare war, or it could command the faithful to take up arms. And the church had one final power in its arsenal: it could refuse Holy Communion to anyone who failed to heed the call.[27] Thus did Gratian reconcile the long-standing prohibitions on the shedding of blood by priests with the more contemporary customs and practices whereby the church was becoming an ever more active participant in secular affairs.

In sum, Gratian's doctrine on war addressed many of the issues that would in time become standard in the just war tradition: the various types of just cause, the proper intention or spirit with which belligerents must fight, and the legitimate forms of authority. In addition, he considered various aspects of proper conduct in war, such questions as whether certain types of individuals should be exempt from violence or whether certain days of the year should be off-limits for combat. Certainly, Gratian's expansive doctrine of holy war and his consideration of the extent to which the church could serve as a legitimate authority are most noteworthy. These aspects of his teaching may seem archaic to us now, since from the early-modern era onward, just war theorists have consistently eschewed the notion of "holy war," wars waged on behalf of the faith. However, this was a prominent part of the just war tradition at its inception. And as we shall see, the concept of holy war would receive significant attention—both positive and negative—during the years of the Reformation. If there was a structural weakness in Gratian's analysis, it was his tendency to conflate the use of force in domestic affairs with the use of force in international affairs. In other words, Gratian viewed the police powers of the city and of the church as equivalent to the international power of war. Of course, these diverse powers were to a certain extent analogous, and fruitful comparisons could be drawn; but to treat them as identical, as Gratian evidently did, fostered the awkward situation of having multiple legitimate authorities, all with the power to wage war. This was, of course, precisely the problem Gratian faced and tried to resolve through the subtle distinctions of Quaestio 8. His solutions, however, were not consistent with the needs of a state to operate under only one legitimate authority. They would thus prove inadequate over time, however useful they may have been to an age of crusades and controversies between *regnum* and *sacerdotium*.

Thomas Aquinas on War

Although Gratian was more systematic than Augustine, he was (it is fair to say) far from concise. In fact, one is hard-pressed at times to determine Gratian's own position, as we have shown. This problem would be remedied by the monumental efforts of the thirteenth-century theologian Thomas Aquinas (c. 1225–1274), whose *Summa Theologica* employed a much more refined method of synthesizing and harmonizing divergent texts than the one devised by Gratian. In the prologue to the *Summa*, Aquinas complains of the loquacity of his predecessors. His own work thus took brevity as a goal. Aquinas wanted to refine to the barest essentials the method of medieval *disputatio* practiced in the schools. His technique was to begin with a clear but controversial question, one that could be answered either affirmatively or negatively. He then presented the most persuasive arguments for one side of the question, announcing these with the phrase *videtur quod* ("it would seem that"). Then came a *sed contra* ("but on the contrary"), where Aquinas presented one or more points on the opposite side. And only then did he offer his *respondeo* ("I respond that"). Here readers could be sure they were hearing Aquinas's own position. And yet his work was hardly finished simply because his view had been offered. For, as Aristotle had earlier recognized, any person in possession of truth, especially a truth arrived at dialectically, should be able to explain exactly how and why the opposing views are wrong. Thus, Aquinas often ended his consideration of any given question with a series of "replies" to the views surveyed in the opening section. Although this method sounds elaborate (and it is), in Aquinas's hands it was also extremely economical. Indeed, the challenge of reading him is almost always one of unpacking the dense material he has presented in extremely compact form.

Aquinas's *Summa* treats the question of war most directly in Question 40 of the *secunda secundae partis* (i.e., the second part of the second part).[28] This analysis is frequently taken out of context, and yet the context is crucial for a proper understanding of Aquinas's view. Question 40 occurs in a section of the *Summa* dealing with the human virtues, specifically within the discussion of charity.[29] Here we already see the mark of Augustine's reflections on war, as we do in so much of Aquinas's analysis. The principal act of charity, which is to love, is reflected in a number of virtues, including joy, peace, and mercy. Each of these virtues, however, is opposed by a corresponding vice; and war, according to the structure of the *Summa*, is best understood as a vice opposed to peace. Since war is presented so clearly as a vice, it is quite natural to wonder whether it must always be such. And this is precisely the question with which Aquinas begins: whether some kind of war is lawful (*utrum aliquod bellum sit licitum*).

The objections in the *videtur quod* suggest that war is indeed always sinful. According to Matthew 26:52, "All who take the sword shall perish by the sword." Thus, the Lord threatens to punish those who make war, and punishment is never inflicted except when someone has sinned.

Consequently, it must be a sin to make war. And again, whatever is contrary to a divine precept must be a sin, and war is contrary to the precept expressed in Matthew 5:39: "Do not resist one who is evil." Thus, war is a sin. Finally (and most significantly, given the structural position of Aquinas's discussion of war in the *Summa*), everything contrary to an act of virtue is a sin, and war is contrary to peace; therefore, war is a sin.

The *sed contra* is supplied by Augustine. Aquinas cites Letter 138, "To Marcellinus," where Augustine points out that the soldiers who sought advice from John the Baptist were not turned away but merely counseled to terrorize no one and be content with their pay. Yet if the Christian religion forbade all war, then the soldiers should have been advised otherwise.

Aquinas reconciles the opposing views on whether war is sinful in his famous *respondeo* of Question 40, which maintains that "in order for war to be just, three things are necessary." The first is the authority of a sovereign (*auctoritas principis*), which is necessary, Aquinas suggests, because war is a public act, requiring that people be summoned together and made to act collectively in the interest of the commonweal. When war is waged without recourse to sovereign authority (as in the case of civil war or contemporary terrorism) the results are chaotic. Domestic turmoil and violence may be added to the injustices already committed. Thus, Aquinas cites Augustine's view from the treatise *Against Faustus the Manichean*: The natural order conducive to peace (*ordo naturalis mortalium paci accommodatus*) demands that war be waged only by a sovereign authority. No other arrangement will work.[30] This, moreover, sheds light on the error contained in the first objection: "All who take up the sword shall perish by the sword." Yes, says Aquinas, but to "take up the sword" means to have recourse to arms without the permission of the sovereign authority. In contrast, when one has such permission, one does not "take up the sword" but merely uses it as commissioned by another.

The second requirement for just war, according to Aquinas, is a just cause. No one should be attacked who does not deserve it due to some kind of fault. War should be declared only in response to wrongdoing; otherwise, it becomes a wrongful act itself. This commonsense requirement reveals something of the complexity of war vis-à-vis the virtues and vices Aquinas is treating. On the one hand, war emerges as a vice opposed to charity and particularly to the charitable virtue of peace. This is the case when war is waged for no legitimate reason. But war can also be understood (and undertaken) as an act of justice, which is also a virtue. This is the case when war is used to punish a wrong that cannot be effectively punished in any other way. In such instances, war can be described cautiously as a virtue—the virtue of justice in action. But it is a virtue that runs a high risk of being transformed into vice. That is to say, it is an act of justice that risks violating the requirements of charity. From this perspective, we can see exactly what Aquinas must do to show that not all war is a sin. He must show how wars can be just and also true to the requirements of charity.

This is precisely what he accomplishes in the third requirement. In order for war not to be a sin, the intention of the belligerents must be to act with the advancement of the good in mind or the avoidance of evil.[31] They must concentrate on securing peace, uplifting the good, and punishing evildoers but not motivated by such selfish motives as the thirst for vengeance or the desire to inflict harm. It may actually happen, according to Aquinas, that a war is waged for a just cause and with the authority of a legitimate sovereign but is still a sin. So crucial is right intention that if the belligerents' intentions are not right, then their every act will be sinful. The danger is that in executing justice the belligerents will oppose peace. But this can be avoided if the belligerents keep charity foremost in mind. Charity—the good of the belligerents as well as those whom they are attacking—is the only means of reconciling justice and peace, according to Aquinas.

With all this in mind, Aquinas responds handily to the objection that war must be a sin because it is opposed to a virtue—namely peace. The matter is more complicated, as Aquinas says in his reply to objection 3: "Those who wage war justly aim at peace, and so they are not opposed to peace, except to the evil peace." Nor is war necessarily a violation of the divine precept, "Do not resist one who is evil," Aquinas argues in reply to objection 2, since such precepts will always be "borne in readiness of mind." As Augustine maintained, the internal disposition is as important as the external act. It is sometimes necessary for an individual to act harshly, but when his internal disposition is focused on the good of his combatant, then harshness becomes "benevolent harshness," as when a parent punishes a child.

Aquinas's debt to Augustine is evident throughout the first article of Question 40, but he also accomplishes something that neither Augustine nor Gratian achieved. Aquinas places the problem of war within a coherent framework of virtues and vices in order to illuminate its proper and improper manifestations more clearly. Moreover, he incorporates previous Christian teaching into his system of objections and replies while making his own position perfectly clear. This is also the case in the second article of Question 40, where Aquinas turns to the issue that so preoccupied Gratian: whether it is lawful for clerics and bishops to fight. It was particularly unclear after Gratian's treatment of this question how bishops and clerics could be authorized to induce others to fight but not to participate in actual fighting. If fighting was not a sin, then it should be allowed for priests and laymen alike. If, on the other hand, it was a sin, then priests should not encourage others to participate in it.[32]

Aquinas brought a great deal of clarity to this issue, and like Gratian he maintained that bishops and clerics could exhort people to war but not participate in actual bloodshed themselves. Aquinas's reasons, though, made the matter more coherent. The reason had nothing to do with war being by nature sinful. As we have just seen, war may or may not be sinful depending upon the conditions under which it is fought. The reason for clerical abstention was that "certain occupations are so inconsistent with one another that they cannot be fittingly exercised at the same time."[33] Military activity is full of unrest and thus it disturbs the mind from the contemplation of divine things, the praise of God, and the prayers that are the general duties of the cleric. Moreover, military activity is incompatible with the clerical life because the cleric's unique task is to present the Passion of Christ on the altar by enacting it sacramentally. Since this deed is one of self-sacrifice, it is especially unfitting for them to shed the blood of others. Again, this has nothing to do with the sinfulness (or lack thereof) of war, but rather it has to do with the unique role that churchmen perform and the incompatibility of that role with bloodshed. Yet it is perfectly reasonable (as Aquinas explains in replying to one of the objections) for churchmen to exhort people to war; for just wars have as their end the very "divine, spiritual good" to which they themselves are deputed. Yet since clerics cannot themselves fight, even in just wars, they should counsel other men to fight wars on behalf of justice and peace.[34]

The final article of Question 40 is devoted to the issue of whether it is licit to lay ambushes in war. The question is controversial because ambushes involve deception, and deception would seem to be unjust. Moreover, writers from Cicero to Augustine had counseled against breaking faith with one's enemies in war, and ambushes would seem to entail the breaking of faith. But Aquinas was not convinced, and he marshaled substantial evidence to show that ambushes were not necessarily a sin. First, he quoted from a passage of Augustine: "Provided the war be just, it is no concern of justice whether it be carried on openly or by ambushes."[35] This was corroborated by the fact that God commanded Joshua (in Joshua 8:2) to lay ambushes for the city of Hai. Next, Aquinas drew a crucial distinction between two types of deception. To lie to someone—that is, to say something simply untrue or to fail to keep a promise—is indeed a sin. In matters of war, such conduct was independently banned by the "rights of war and covenants" observed in Aquinas's own day.[36] But it was something different and in no way sinful, according to Aquinas, to conceal one's purposes or meaning. As he pointed out, sacred doctrine itself often conceals its meaning,[37] and thus concealment is licit in war. But again, such concealment is bound by the conditions that always obtain in war: the concern must be for the ultimate good, not the ill, of those involved.

One of the most important advances that Aquinas would make in discussing the just use of force concerned the matter of obedience. As we saw, Augustine maintained a rather austere doctrine of political obedience, effectively condoning all actions commanded by an established authority. Aquinas was not so austere, although his break with Augustine was approached with a degree of circumspection, not to say circumlocution. According to Aquinas, obedience is indeed a virtue, and God's will is for Christians to obey the secular authorities.[38] However, Aquinas breaks with Augustine in recognizing certain limits to obedience and offering criteria by which one might judge whether a particular command is legitimate or not. Thus, obedience is not required when a command runs contrary to the command of a higher authority. If, for example, a commissioner issues an order that runs contrary to the bidding of a proconsul, then the order is not binding. By the same token, if a secular ruler orders something that runs contrary to the will of God, then the ruler should not be obeyed.[39] Thus, Aquinas writes, "if a prince's authority is not just but usurped, or if he commands what is unjust, his subjects are *not* bound to obey him, except perhaps accidentally, in order to avoid scandal or danger."[40]

This idea of limits on obedience raised the possibility of a justified disobedience, and it would prove highly influential as time went on. Indeed, its echoes can still be heard in modern political writings, such as Martin Luther King's "Letter from a Birmingham Jail." However, Aquinas's doctrine also led to a new difficulty, one Augustine had more or less avoided. How were subjects to know whether any particular law or command was unjust? And how were they to know whether disobedience was required at the moment or whether a more patient and forbearing policy was called for? These questions received their first systematic treatment in the *Summa*, even if Aquinas's remarks there would leave considerable work for subsequent theorists. According to Aquinas, a law or command could be viewed under three aspects—its end, author, and form—each of which suggest a criterion for evaluating legitimacy. The proper end of a law or command is the common good (*ad bonum commune*). The proper author is one whose power is legitimately acquired and exercised within its proper jurisdiction. And for the form to be proper, it needs to place fair burdens upon its recipients—burdens that are equal or proportionate.[41]

These are some of the guiding principles that Aquinas introduced. They would have the effect of changing in significant ways the matrix of justifiable force. Suddenly, there were grounds for disobeying a command—whether it was going to war or performing some wartime act. And the possibility was now open for subjects to consider using force against a ruler, to remove an unjust ruler from power.[42]

Just War Trajectory in the Middle Ages

Reflecting on the trajectory of just war thinking in the Middle Ages, we find that several developments stand out. One is the increasing embrace of Augustine's notion of benevolent harshness: fighting not out of hate but out of love. Augustine, for his part, saw that the scriptural ideals of love and peace had to be reconciled in one way or another with the ideal of justice and that the duty to love one's neighbors sometimes requires that force be used to protect those neighbors from harm. Without the theoretical work of Augustine, there would be no Christian just war tradition. Thus, we find Gratian and Aquinas both harking back to Augustine's notion. It is no exaggeration to say that Augustine's concept of benevolent harshness constitutes the cornerstone of the Christian just war tradition, for it fuses justice and charity.[43]

A second movement to observe is the gradual systemization of the just war framework. In Augustine's writings on war, this framework is present but never systematically presented. In Gratian, it is set out in one major place, Causa 23, but it still appears disorganized because of Gratian's method of citing competing canons side by side. In Aquinas, though, the just war framework is presented for the first time in the form of a coherent teaching—a set of interrelated ideas and arguments that aim at establishing the just use of force under specific conditions, and at refuting counterarguments that suggest that force is never justifiable. This movement toward systemization is a major development in the just war tradition. It makes the entire just war framework easier to grasp, discuss, and refine. But systemization also comes at a price, which we are well prepared to notice because of what we observed in Augustine's reflections on war. Augustine was sensitive to a certain paradox about the so-called just war. There was mystery there that he was unwilling to set aside or to reduce through comforting rationalizations. For him, a war might be just and yet evil. Indeed all wars are evil, even wars where the justice of one side over the other was absolutely clear. However, as the trend toward systemization moves forward, this note of unease and regret begins to fade. And we must view this as a loss, for without Augustine's equivocal tones, it becomes possible to view war as a positive good and to approach it with a degree of self-righteousness dangerous not only to the human soul but also to the prospects for peaceful reconciliation after the fighting is done.

As the idea of the just war is carried through the Christian Middle Ages, there is a fascinating movement away from notions of absolute authority and political obedience toward notions of competing authority and political resistance. Another way to say this is that as the Middle Ages proceed, the state gradually loses its monopoly on force. In Gratian, the challenge comes in the form of the Christian church, which is viewed as a legitimate authority all its own and whose interests may or may not align with those of the state. In Thomas Aquinas, the challenge comes in the form of the rights of individuals and collectives to resist tyrannical rule. In both cases, the state is viewed as bounded by certain types of interests and certain moral limits; and this in turn makes room for the church or the citizenry to exercise its own authority, even to the point of force. What we witness at this stage of history is no doubt a pendulum swing in the direction of religious, as opposed to political, authority. This is, of course, a pendulum that will soon swing back the other way. By the dawn of the modern era, just war thinking will appear more secular in nature. But what is fascinating to observe at this point in the narrative is the way basic notions of political competition and even legitimate resistance against one's own government emerge out of the religious context of medieval just war thinking. These are ideas that are quite central to political theory in the modern era, and we are all too apt to forget their religious heritage.

5

Martin Luther and the Tradition

Historians of the just war tradition frequently cite Martin Luther (1483–1546) as a proponent of the just war in the sixteenth century and assimilate his views to those of earlier writers such as St. Augustine and St. Thomas Aquinas.[1] Whatever the differences between Luther and the Catholic tradition from which he broke, these differences did not affect his basic approach to war—or so historians have suggested. But in fact, Luther's relationship to the just war tradition was considerably more complex. In some key areas, Luther abandoned ideas that had become standard among earlier just war writers, and his departures rendered his own approach less nuanced. This is especially true of Luther's writings during the 1520s, the period in which he composed his best-known political texts. On the other hand, Luther also improved the tradition in significant ways, for example in his cogent rejection of the concept of holy war and in his evolving reflections on resistance to corrupt political authority. In this chapter, we examine Luther's writings on war in greater detail than has been customary in recent studies. By drawing upon a range of diverse writings—letters, sermons, and pamphlets—we pinpoint Luther's position (particularly as it appeared in the 1520s) and relate it point by point to the tradition of just war thinking that preceded him.[2]

Prior to his excommunication, in 1521, Martin Luther had been an Augustinian monk and a highly influential priest in Wittenberg. As such, he had had little occasion to concern himself deeply with questions of war. Upon his break from Rome, however, and with the wholesale reforms that were soon underway, Luther found himself in the difficult position of having to rethink virtually every topic of traditional Christian doctrine, including the church's teachings on war. Yet the dangers of rethinking a tradition from scratch are legion, and Luther did not entirely avoid these dangers. On the other hand, every rethinking of a tradition offers the possibility of improvement, as a particular people living at a particular time tries to sort out the relevance of the past to the present. Luther's most influential writings on war appeared in 1520–1530 and are in some ways the product of their times. A few historical points are thus worth recalling.

First, by the 1520s the Ottoman Turks had consolidated their power up to the Danube River and posed a significant threat to central Europe. The year 1520 saw the capture of Belgrade; and when in 1526 King Louis II of Hungary was defeated in the battle of Mohacs, a wave of fear swept across the European continent. In the face of a probable war against the Turk, many of Luther's friends and admirers plied him with difficult questions about Christian conscience and war.

Could Christians resist the Turk by force, or must they resign themselves to suffer whatever came their way? Questions of this kind were classic in nature, and yet needed to be considered afresh. Moreover, they were especially pertinent, as Luther himself had not long ago maintained (in his *Explanations of the Ninety-Five Theses*, written in 1518) that "to fight against the Turk [was] the same as resisting God, who visits our sin upon us with this rod." Was this still to be Luther's position? Or what would he recommend?

Second, the 1520s was a decade of intense rivalry between Lutheran reformers and various secular rulers opposed to reform. In 1522, Duke George of Saxony went as far as to issue an edict requiring subjects to hand over their copies of the German New Testament, which Luther had taken such pains to translate. And a constant threat was posed also by the Holy Roman Emperor, Charles V (an ardent defender of the Catholic faith), who needed to consolidate his power in order to combat the Turk on the one hand and France on the other. At the Diet of Worms in 1521, Charles V announced his intention to force the reformers in his territory back into unity with the Catholic Church.[3] Thus, the ethical question of whether reformers might take up the sword in self-defense was raised in connection with defending the Reformation from Charles V.

Finally, we must mention the Peasants' Revolt of 1524, which was likely sparked in part by Luther's writings on the freedom of the Christian. Influenced by Luther's writing and all too ready to apply his idea of Christian freedom to economic and social areas of life (where Luther himself had not applied it), many peasants in central Europe demanded the immediate abolition of serfdom and eventually took up arms against their lords and princes. Small-scale rebellions of this sort had taken place before, but this was by far the largest and bloodiest Europe had seen. And while Luther was at first sympathetic to the peasants' demands, he was adamantly opposed to their use of force against rulers. Thus, his pamphlet of 1525, *Against the Robbing and Murdering Hordes of Peasants*, called on German princes to "stab, smite and slay" the insurgents and to regard them as "a member of the devil," "an eternal firebrand of hell."[4]

These and other events certainly shaped Luther's views on war and the use of force in general. And yet his writings were not intended to speak only to the times. His was a tone of certainty. He spoke for all time, and did so with an impressive array of scriptural evidence and traditional sources of authority at his fingertips. Among the traditional sources on the topic of war with which Luther was familiar were the writings of Augustine, Gratian, and Thomas Aquinas. Although he did not always acknowledge or follow these authorities, he did frame his discussions of war in the traditional manner—namely with a discussion of the ambiguous place of temporal authority in Christian life. Let us turn then to Luther's understanding of temporal authority as a preface to his distinctive theory of just wars.

Luther on Temporal Authority

Although Luther's thoughts on this subject were rapidly evolving during the years 1521–1522,[5] they crystallized in a treatise of 1523 entitled *Von Weltlicher Obrigkeit* (*On Temporal Authority*). What is the ground of temporal authority from a Christian point of view? asked Luther. Much turns on this question. For if one finds no ground for earthly political authority divorced from heavenly authority, then one may be led, as some Anabaptists were led, to break off from secular life altogether and attempt to form a heavenly city on earth.[6] If, on the other hand, one grants too absolute a ground to temporal government, then one may lack adequate resources to resist it when it poses a threat to religious life and practice. This was the situation faced by reformers from the 1520s onward, when certain secular rulers were bent on turning back the reforms.

The difficulty in offering an adequate theory of temporal authority lay in the ambivalent nature of scripture on the topic. Reformers acknowledged, on the one hand, certain passages that enjoined unquestioning obedience to the powers that be. Perhaps the most frequently cited of these was Romans 13:1–2:

> Let every soul be subject to power and superiority. For there is no power but from God and the power that exists everywhere is ordained by God. And whoever resists the power resists God's ordinance. But whosoever resists God's ordinance shall receive condemnation on himself.

Luther alluded to this passage in 1518 when he denounced all resistance against the Ottoman invaders.

On the other hand, passages could be adduced to oppose Christian involvement in political life. For example, in the Gospel of Matthew (5:43–45), Christ teaches: "You have heard it said, 'You shall love your neighbor and hate your enemy,' But I say to you, Love your enemies and pray for those who persecute you." How can a Christian engage fully in political life—including, for example, waging war against neighboring countries and prosecuting local criminals in the courts—when Christ's words in Matthew so clearly command love of enemies? Similar passages were frequently cited by reformers as seemingly insurmountable obstacles to a range of political activities, from participation in the judicial system, to serving as a soldier, to mounting political resistance of any kind. The question, then, was how to reconcile the two sets of passages.

Luther's response to this classic conundrum turned on his famous distinction between two powers or kingdoms, the "kingdom of God" and the "kingdom of the world."[7] Here Luther seems to echo the Augustinian distinction between the city of God and the city of man, but he also transformed that Augustinian framework in striking ways. While both kingdoms were ordained by God, according to Luther, they were designed for different people. Thus, all mankind was divided, according to Luther, into those who were true Christians and just, and those who were un-Christian and unjust. Citing 1 Timothy 1:9, Luther argued that while true Christians require no law, no sword, and indeed no authority, since they are moved by the Holy Spirit to do all that they should, the un-Christian majority of men do require law, since they are in constant need of teaching and of force if they are to refrain at least outwardly from wicked deeds. The crucial part of the theory comes in Luther's next proposition, that in order for the law and the sword to function as they should, Christians must set an example by obeying the secular authority, even though they do not require it. The law and the sword must be obeyed as a service to the un-Christian.[8]

Luther's two-kingdoms theory, as articulated in *On Temporal Authority*, had the virtue of reconciling divergent passages of scripture in a most interesting way. With respect to a Christian's outward acts, precedence was given to those passages commanding obedience, and this on the ground that all authorities were established by God. But the spirit in which Christians were to obey secular authorities was at once different from that of the un-Christian and clearly inspired by those passages of Matthew that seemed initially to pose an obstacle. As Luther put it:

> Because a true Christian, while he is on the earth, lives for and serves his neighbor and not himself, he does things that are of no benefit to himself, but of which his neighbor stands in need. Such is the nature of the Christian's spirit. Now the Sword is indispensable for the whole world, to preserve peace, punish sin, and restrain the wicked. And therefore Christians readily submit themselves to be governed by the Sword. . . . All this even though Christians do not need it for themselves, but they attend to what others need.[9]

In other words, at those very moments when Christians may be called upon by secular authorities to commit some deed seemingly sinful (e.g., kill an enemy in war), it is not the Christian qua Christian who is called upon but the Christian qua obedient subject of the temporal powers. And as such, the Christian can fulfill his duty to serve not himself but his neighbor and at the same time obey the scriptural injunction to "be subject to power and authority."[10]

Such was Luther's solution, and it was bolstered by a stark and memorable description of what human life would look like were secular authority to vanish altogether. With no secular authority to keep the un-Christian in check, according to Luther, "people would devour each other and no one would be able to support his wife and children, feed himself and serve God." The whole world "would become a desert." Moreover, "to try to rule a whole country or the world by means of the gospel [alone] is like herding together wolves, lions, eagles and sheep in the same pen, letting them mix freely, and saying to them: 'feed, and be just and peaceable; the stable isn't locked, there's plenty of pasture, and you have no dogs or cudgels to be afraid of.' " What would happen? "The sheep would certainly keep the peace and let themselves be governed and pastured peaceably, *but they would not live long*." And because this is true, Luther insists, "care must be taken to keep these two governments distinct, and both must be allowed to continue [their work]."[11]

In fact, Luther went one step further than counseling mere obedience. He encouraged Christians to participate in government. "If you see that there is a lack of hangmen, court officials, judges, lords or princes," he writes, "and you find that you have the necessary skills, then you should offer your services and seek office." Otherwise, the authority that is "so greatly needed" might perish, and yet "the world cannot get by without it."[12]

But this raised another problem that Luther had to confront: volunteering for office could be viewed as more deliberate and self-willed than merely obeying the commands of a prince. If one *seeks* an office, one's acts seem to be truly one's own. Thus, again: how could such deliberate acts be reconciled with Christ's words in Matthew 5:39 ("Do not resist one who is evil") or Paul's words in Romans 12:19 ("Beloved, never avenge yourselves")? Politics—no matter what one's position or function—seems to demand a degree of resistance and self-defense. And if one undertakes such acts on one's own volition, then the risk of violating scriptural injunctions seems very high.

Can Christians Act in Self-Defense?

Luther's answer to the question of whether Christians can act in self-defense depended not only on his two-kingdoms theory but also on his understanding of a *vocatio* or calling. To wield the sword in public office was not necessarily self-defense if this was done with the right intention. Since government and the sword serve God, it followed for Luther that everything government requires for its effective operation equally serves God. And since there had to be *someone* "to catch the wicked, to accuse them, and execute them, and to protect, acquit, defend and save the good," Christians could and should engage in such acts of service as their talents allowed. In fact, Christians would make the *best* public servants, Luther thought, because their whole orientation was by definition directed toward the good of others. And this was the crucial point: Christians could hold public office while avoiding the sin of "self-defense" if, and only if, in discharging their duties, they oriented their wills outwardly and employed their talents on behalf of the community. "Love of neighbor has no regard for self," writes Luther, "neither does it consider whether what is to be done is important or trivial, so long as it is for the good of one's neighbor or the community."[13]

Luther's position on self-defense is especially interesting in light of the tradition running from Augustine through Aquinas. In 398, Augustine wrote to a North African landowner that it is certainly wrong to kill another in self-defense, unless one happens to be a soldier or some other agent of the state for whom the use of force is a public service.[14] Augustine's position had become slightly more nuanced. And by the years 413–414, it softened even more. Writing to Macedonius, the imperial vicar of Africa, he maintained that "it makes a great difference when one man is killed by another, whether it happened through a desire of injuring him, . . . or whether it happened in the course of inflicting punishment or carrying out an order, as by a judge, an executioner; or through self-defense or the rescue of another, as a thief is killed by a traveler or an enemy by a soldier."[15] The inclusion of self-defense among the extenuating circumstances for killing is a marked departure from Augustine's earlier statements on this subject and may well have reflected the lessons of political experience. In any event, the more mature Augustine did not refer to an absolute proscription against self-defense, and his letter to Macedonius seems rather to anticipate the later position of Thomas Aquinas, who argued that Christians could indeed kill in self-defense as long as the intended "effect" was not the slaying of the attacker but the protection of their own being. Leaning thus on a doctrine of "double effect,"[16] Aquinas had little difficulty exculpating acts of violent self-defense, taking for granted that self-defense in general was legitimate.[17] Against this historical backdrop, where did Luther come down? The answer is that Luther did not embrace Aquinas's position, anticipated by the late Augustine, but rather hewed to the position Augustine had taken in his earlier letter to the landowner. Self-defense was wrong per se, the only exception being for acts of public service. We may thus venture an observation about the general tendency of Luther's reforms as they emerged in the 1520s on matters relating to self-defense in particular and the use of force in general. Luther was not only inclined to reject the neat philosophical distinctions of Scholasticism, and hence the doctrine of "double effect," which turned on the distinction between "essence" and "accident"; he was also reluctant to allow (as Augustine eventually did) insights from political experience to modify the positions he initially thought to be sound.[18] Such philosophical and exegetical tendencies as these would make it difficult for Luther to accommodate the highly nuanced tradition of just war thinking that had developed prior to his time. This is not to say that Luther opted for a different tradition—one of pacifism, for instance. It is rather to say that Luther's just war doctrines were in significant ways divergent from (i.e., less nuanced than) the doctrines of writers before him.

Having thus discussed the ground for temporal authority as well as the problem of self-defense, Luther turned in the remainder of *On Temporal Authority* and elsewhere to consider some of the central tenets of just war thinking. Among these, the most relevant for our purposes are his treatments of just cause, right intention, last resort, and obedience to political authority.

A Limited Doctrine of Just Cause

When can rulers legitimately wage war? Luther always hesitated to speak too concretely on matters of law and policy. He was not a student of politics in detail, but he was willing to offer a few foundational principles. In *On Temporal Authority*, his first point about war concerns the importance of "prudence and wisdom": it is extremely difficult if not impossible, he points out, to wage war against the wicked without harming the innocent at the same time. Unintentional consequences abound in war. Therefore, Luther instructs that "where an injustice cannot be punished without a greater injustice, [a ruler] should not insist on his rights, however just his cause."[19]

The flip side of this principle also obtained for Luther. In considering the justice of any particular war, one must not merely consider the plague it creates, but also the plague it prevents.[20] That the Sword (along with all the violence of a just war) was instituted by God was sufficiently proved, as far as Luther was concerned, by Romans 13:1–4 and 1 Peter 2:13–14. Moreover, Luther maintained that even the worst horrors of legitimate wars could be understood in terms of love, even though they may not appear as love at first. In order to make this point clearer, Luther offered an analogy from medicine.

> A good doctor sometimes finds so serious and terrible a sickness that he must amputate or destroy a hand, foot, ear, or eye, to save the body. Looking at it from the point of view of the organ that he amputates, he appears to be a cruel and merciless man; but looking at it from the point of view of the body, which the doctor wants to save, he is a fine and true man and does a good and Christian work, as far as the work itself is concerned.[21]

So too must rulers often cause suffering as they go about their godly work of preserving peace for their people. The basic idea Luther wanted to convey here was that the toils and troubles of *just* wars are "only a very brief lack of peace that prevents an everlasting and immeasurable lack of peace—a small misfortune that prevents a greater misfortune."

What, then, should count as a just war? On this topic, Luther spoke decisively. No war is just "unless one has such a good reason for fighting and such a good conscience that he can say, 'My neighbor compels and forces me to fight, though I would rather avoid it.'" And in that case, says Luther, it can be called not only war but basic self-defense.[22] Luther then goes on to distinguish sharply between wars begun prior to an attack and those begun afterward. Only the latter, he insists, count as wars of necessity, whereas the former hail from the devil.[23] And in this way, Luther reached his conclusion that the only legitimate cause for war is an actual attack from the opposing side. Moreover, even this may not count as a sufficient cause—for one may yet try to settle through law or arbitration[24]—but it was a necessary cause; and thus no war could be justly waged without it. One exception to this conclusion was the case of God's commanding a ruler to wage war, as He did with the Israelites. In this case, neither a prior attack nor even an injustice committed by the other side was necessary. God's command was sufficient.[25]

In effect, Luther established his distinctive account of "just cause," or the legitimate reasons for going to war. A comparison with traditional accounts of just cause may therefore be illuminating. Augustine for his part enumerated several different causes for war. Like Luther, he required either that God command a war or that some wrong be committed by the opposing side. Yet his discussion of possible "wrongs" was significantly more expansive than Luther's. According to Augustine, war might be waged to punish some crime committed by a citizen or group from another region if that region refused to make amends; when some neighboring nation suffered an attack and needed help repelling the aggressors; or when a country's beliefs or practices were inimical to Christian religion. All these constituted legitimate reasons for war, according to Augustine, and there is no evidence to suggest he was attempting to be exhaustive.[26] After Augustine, Gratian expands these considerations, enumerating four legitimate causes for war: the repulsion of an attack, the recovery of property, the avenging of prior injuries committed either by another country or some of its subjects, and the protection of the faith.[27] Thus, a highly differentiated and nuanced tradition of "just cause" had been established prior to Luther's day that allowed for wars not only of a defensive nature (including the defense of a third party, such as an ally) but also of a restitutive nature, a retributive nature, and a religious nature.

Luther's abandonment of this tradition—whether intentional or not—had important theological and political implications. It was now necessary to explain why "love of neighbor"—which was the theological basis for wars of defense—should not extend also to wars wherein one nation assisted another to repel an attack, or wherein the church employed force to protect the faithful, or wherein either the church or the state sought compensation for a past wrong. The classical doctrine of just cause, grounded in neighbor love, allowed for all such cases to be interpreted in the same manner; they were all of a piece. Luther, by contrast, needed (but did not supply) some account of why neighborly love should stop at national borders and why only a military attack should count as a threat. From a political point of view, Luther's doctrine also seemed too strict, for it failed to account for the use of force in areas where political life often required it. The ability to form meaningful alliances between and among nations would certainly be weakened if one nation could not promise to help another when it came under attack.[28]

On the positive side, however, Luther was among the first major writers in the just war tradition to condemn wars fought in the name of "Christendom" or for the sake of stamping out false belief. Here his views from the 1520s remain quite compelling. A good place to observe this is in his treatise of 1529, *On War against the Turk*, where Luther explains that a war led under the authority of Emperor Charles V in response to a Turkish attack could be legitimate but not if it were fought (as in the past) under a Christian banner. For this would run contrary to Christ's own name, not only because Christ called upon Christians to suffer and not to resist, but also because—as Luther says—"there are scarcely five Christians in [our] army, and perhaps there are worse people in [our] army than are with the Turks." For Luther, Christians qua Christians were called upon to fight against the devil with prayer, not with the sword. They were of course obliged to fight against the Turk if the emperor commanded it, but this would be to fight under a temporal banner, not a Christian one. "If I were a soldier and saw a priest's banner in the field, or a banner of the cross," writes Luther, "I should run as though the devil were chasing me."[29]

Here Luther broke decisively and no doubt deliberately from the tradition of holy war that had become virtually institutionalized by Gratian's *Decretum*, which taught that the church did indeed have powers relating to war if it deemed that the faith was under threat (including threats stemming from heretical beliefs). It could thus initiate wars either by exhorting secular authorities to act on its behalf or simply by commanding the faithful to take up arms in return for rewards in the life to come.[30] Gratian's position was accepted by the Catholic Church in

Luther's day, and it helped to supply the theoretical foundation for the church's attempt to suppress the Reformation by force. Thus, it should come as no surprise that in 1520, leading up to his break from Rome, Luther publicly denounced and burned Gratian's *Decretum*.[31]

Right Intention and Last Resort

In addition to reflecting on just cause, Luther frequently articulated his views on another traditional topic of just war thinking: the proper intention with which belligerents ought to fight. Luther admonished rulers to orient their minds properly toward God before taking up the sword, meaning to act with fear of God in mind. Rulers needed to confess to God "that we have deserved these things" and remember that God himself may have brought the war upon them. They needed to pray humbly for "help against the devil."[32] And finally, they needed to attend assiduously to strategic matters, for God may well approve a cause and yet allow one's enemy to prevail if one is not "careful, diligent and cautious, even in the very smallest details—in so small a thing as a whistle."[33] Fear of God thus had implications for strategy and even for one's strength. As Luther, rather shockingly, writes in *On Temporal Authority*: "God helps the strongest"![34]

After orienting his mind properly toward God, a ruler's next responsibility was to offer the enemy a final chance to settle through law, arbitration, or some kind of agreement. The point of this gesture was not to compromise or otherwise forsake the cause of justice but merely to go beyond one's duty in extending an offer to an enemy who, as Luther says, was "not worthy of it." Once this offer had been made, rulers were free to "take to the Sword" swiftly and in good conscience. Indeed, failure to take action at this critical juncture might well be a sin all its own. For, according to Luther, God gives the sword to rulers in order that the wicked may be punished and the good protected. Thus, to permit "rascals to go about their wicked business" when it is within one's power to prevent it is in effect to take on the guilt of the crimes the wicked freely commit. When it comes to the sword, Luther insisted, "there is no place for patience or mercy."[35]

Yet before rulers could commit their troops to battle, there was one final step pertaining to "intention." Rulers needed to be sure their minds were rightly disposed toward their subjects. They needed to act always with love in mind, thinking not of their own advantage but that of others—to assist their subjects, "protect them, listen to them, and defend them." And here, according to Luther, the best model was Christ himself, who was not only the greatest of princes but also a humble servant to his people.[36] Once a ruler's will was properly disposed toward God and his subjects, his conscience could be clear.

Any reference to the traditional admonition to "love one's enemy," however, was missing from Luther's treatment of right intention. Yet this concept was central to just war thinking as it was originally conceived. Not only in Augustine and Gratian but also in Thomas Aquinas, the basic notion is that "it is necessary sometimes for a man to act otherwise [than gently] for the common good, *or for the good of those with whom he is fighting*."[37] Such was the traditional way of reconciling enemy love (not merely neighbor love) with war. With such a weighty and univocal tradition behind him, why did Luther not have recourse to this teaching?

It is difficult to answer this question with any degree of certainty. Luther did write a great deal in other contexts about the Christian duty to love one's enemies, but in the context of war, he was silent. Luther tended to demonize his enemies, whether they be political or theological foes, rather than to treat them with benevolence. And he sometimes encouraged his readers to do the same.[38] Whatever the causes, the effects of Luther's failure to incorporate the doctrine of enemy love explicitly into his treatment of war were significant, and they appeared especially in Luther's treatment of *jus in bello*.[39] For if enemies were demonized and thus dehumanized, there was little reason to approach them with even a degree of charity. We accordingly find some rather startling passages in Luther about the way wars could be waged. Soldiers were "to kill enemies without scruple, to rob and to burn, and to do whatever damages the enemy, according to the usages of war, until he is defeated." Luther even cites with approval the way Moses described the conduct of war in Deuteronomy 20, which entailed the massacre of males and enslavement of women and children.[40]

In these passages, Luther was speaking not only to rulers but also to subjects—loosing the hands of all whose job it was to fight. His general approach to questions of *jus in bello* is well illustrated by his description of the way "real soldiers" fight in *Whether Soldiers Too Can Be Saved* (1526). Real soldiers are "not playing games," Luther asserts with apparent admiration. "They are not quick to *draw* their sword; they are not contentious; they have no desire to fight. But when someone forces them to fight, watch out!"[41] In other words, Luther commended extreme patience and restraint when discussing *jus ad bellum*; but once the threshold was crossed and war began, virtually all was permitted. As Luther puts it: the sword is "not a foxtail with which to tickle people," rather it is "the wrath of God" against his enemies.[42] One finds scant mention in Luther's work of any restrictions *in bello*. He says only that one should "beware of sins and of violating women and maidens," and that once the enemy is completely defeated (and not before), one should extend mercy to those who surrender and submit.[43]

Soldiers' Obedience and Its Limits

Concerning the conditions of subjects taking up the sword, Luther had a great deal to say in his treatise *Whether Soldiers Too Can Be Saved*. And here more than anywhere one may observe the effects of the Peasants' Revolt on his thought. In the first place, Luther argues that subjects are never justified in using force against their political superiors, no matter how incompetent or unjust they may be. Subjects could register pleas and complaints, and in extreme cases they could simply move to another region where life might be better lived. But they could never act on their own volition to depose or otherwise molest a tyrannical prince. God places tyrants over men for a reason, Luther insists. To depose them is to resist God himself (Titus 3:1, Romans 13:1).

Here again Luther treats a traditional topic of debate without availing himself of traditional intellectual resources, dispensing with Scholastic subtleties and distinctions. The basic position of Aquinas on rebellion had been that rulers who were tyrants were guilty of sedition (*tyrannus seditiosus est*).[44] And on this basis, Aquinas articulated an opening (if only a narrow and highly conditional one) for the overthrow of tyrants. For Luther, no such opening existed. Indeed, the only exception to Luther's otherwise austere doctrine of obedience in the 1520s concerned the case of insanity: rulers who were not in control of their faculties were in effect not "rulers" at all, because they could not even govern themselves, much less their subjects. Patently insane rulers could thus be deposed without sin. But Luther insisted this did not extend to everyday tyrants, for while tyrants were frequently wicked, they were rarely insane.[45] Therefore, the reign of even the fiercest tyrant could not be challenged on this ground.

After the gruesome events of the Peasants' Revolt, Luther may indeed have regarded the matter of political rebellion as too explosive an issue to treat with Scholastic subtlety. What was needed was plain talk. And this is certainly what Luther supplied. Moreover, his reasons for proscribing rebellion remain quite cogent even today. First, he argued that there was a world of difference between changing a government and improving it. The rule of a single tyrant was often preferable to the "rule of many tyrants" which anarchy approached.[46] This is certainly an insight history has confirmed.[47] Second, Luther argued that it was not possible for subjects to exist in a condition of "obedience" and "resistance" at the same time. The two conditions were diametrically opposed, and Luther was convinced that there could be no stable government where rulers were not respected and where the ruled attempted to be subjects and judges at once.[48] It was on these grounds that Luther in the 1520s rejected the traditional (Thomistic) position on rebellion and repaired to his virtually unconditional doctrine of obedience.[49] Luther did not worry that this doctrine might give rulers a free hand to become tyrants as they wished, for he was aware that not every subject was a Christian, and therefore not every subject would exercise restraint. Indeed, God has many means of deposing tyrants when He wishes to do so.

This doctrine led to a final problem Luther had to confront. What were subjects to do if they knew, or at least suspected, that the war they were fighting was unjust? Should they obey the temporal authorities in such a case, even to the point of shedding innocent blood? This question was distinct from the question of whether a ruler could be deposed. Here Luther was concerned only with obedience to a particular command—the command to fight an unjust war—that might harm the souls of those who obeyed. The issue must have struck Luther as extremely significant, given his lifelong preoccupation with conscience. And here Luther advanced well beyond traditional just war teaching. Like other writers before him, Luther began with the scriptural argument that it is sometimes necessary to "obey God rather than men" (Acts 5:29). However,

Luther must have seen that this common saying was unhelpful unless it was accompanied by some account of when it was appropriate to obey God rather than men. Luther thus proceeded to differentiate three kinds of cases, as follows: (1) "If you know for *sure* that [your ruler] is wrong, then you should fear God rather than men, and you should neither fight nor serve, for you cannot have a good conscience before God." However, certain knowledge is hard to come by. And thus in cases where (2) you do not know and (3) you cannot find out whether your ruler is wrong, "you ought not to weaken certain obedience for the sake of an uncertain justice." In short, you should simply obey.[50]

In effect, what Luther articulated here was a multipronged, epistemologically sensitive account of how to reconcile political obedience with an active political conscience. And as we would expect, given the general thrust of the tract in which it occurs, Luther's emphasis falls heavily on the side of obedience: all cases of doubt redound to secular authority. But in cases where one's awareness of wrongdoing rises to the level of certainty—that is to say, where one possesses not only pangs of conscience but also full-blown political knowledge—one must refrain from acting.[51] This moment in Luther's thought constitutes, in our view, a most serious consideration of what is now called "selective conscientious objection." It is serious because it maintains neither that all war is wrong, nor that all obedience is safe, but rather acknowledges the genuinely competing goods of a clean conscience on the one hand and political order on the other. Moreover, Luther strongly suggests in this passage that it is the responsibility of individual subjects to inquire into the justice or injustice of the causes for which they fight.[52] This can be viewed as a great improvement over the position of Augustine, where the mere command of a ruler guaranteed that a soldier's participation in battle was just.[53]

Luther's Position in the Tradition

Now that we have examined Luther's writings on war in some detail, we can return to the question with which we began: To what extent were Luther's views as they emerged in the 1520s in harmony with the tradition of just war thinking that preceded him? In general, Luther tended to dispense with traditional subtleties and distinctions, sometimes rendering his account of war less nuanced and coherent than the accounts of earlier writers.[54] For example, Luther rejects Aquinas's allowance for the use of force in self-defense as well as Aquinas's highly conditional allowance for political resistance against tyranny, although Luther later acknowledged a right of armed resistance against the emperor. It may be argued, of course, that Luther did not reject tradition per se but Thomistic tradition in particular. However, this thesis is not supported by the evidence, for Luther also rejected (or at least failed to emphasize) significant Augustinian teachings as well. And the break would come at a price. Luther's writings on war seem less successful than earlier just war sources in reconciling war with the biblical injunctions to love one's neighbor and even one's enemy. Because Luther's doctrine of just cause was so thin, it could not account for the full range of situations in which force could (and often should) be used to help others in need.[55] And because his doctrine of *jus in bello* was so permissive, he was unable to show how "love of enemies" might extend even to soldiers fighting on the opposing side.

Still, while Luther's analysis of war neglected tradition at a price, there were some areas in which his neglect (or deliberate rejection) of tradition led to positions that would eventually become standard just war teachings. One such area concerned holy war. Luther's adamant condemnation of holy war as patently un-Christian was at once daring and persuasive. And though it would not be adopted as a general stance by Protestant writers until after the Reformation was politically secure,[56] it would eventually become *the* teaching of the just war tradition in the modern era.[57] Luther was thus a crucial figure in adapting the just war tradition for modern times. A second area in which he improved upon the tradition concerned conscience. As we saw, just war writers prior to Luther were inclined to absolve soldiers who fought in an unjust cause, so long as they fought under the authority of a legitimate sovereign. Luther too inclined toward this view, because obedience was both a theological and a political virtue. However, he carved out an important area of exception in cases where soldiers were epistemologically confident that they were fighting in an unjust cause. For such cases, Luther offered a doctrine of justified disobedience that anticipated our contemporary doctrine of selective conscientious objection. In this respect, too, Luther contributed to the modernization and liberalization of the just war tradition.

6

Calvin and Other Reformers

John Calvin (1509–1564) brought an impressive knowledge of law and a formidable classical education to bear on the Reformation debate about war. He was a trained lawyer, having studied with some of the most innovative legal minds of Renaissance France; and he was a student of humanist techniques of textual analysis, which included philology and exegesis upon texts in original languages. In terms of just war doctrine, Calvin's contribution was a fascinating blend of innovative and traditional elements.

Like Luther, Calvin leaned heavily upon his own interpretations of scripture and was interested in articulating a doctrine that was congenial to reformed theology. But unlike Luther, he found many Catholic resources, including writings by Augustine, Gratian, and Aquinas, to be largely correct in their dissection of the issues. The result of this blend of Christian tradition and reform was a distinct just war doctrine. Its principle elements included (1) a surprising return to "holy war" as a viable use of force; (2) a return to something approximating the Thomistic teaching on deposing tyrannical authorities, though Calvin modified that teaching in various ways to accommodate reformation ideas; (3) a return (though, again, with some modification) to the classical emphasis on right intention in war—i.e., "love your enemies"; and finally, (4) an unprecedentedly strong emphasis on "last resort" as a precondition of just war. To see how Calvin arrived at these positions and what undergirded them we must look to chapter 20, book 4 of Calvin's *Institutio Christianae Religionis* (hereafter, *Institutes*), supplementing where necessary from his biblical commentaries, sermons, and letters.

The Two Kingdoms

Like Luther, Calvin approached the topic of the sword only after distinguishing carefully between two kingdoms, the spiritual and the political.[1] However, Calvin's understanding of the relationship between the two kingdoms departed significantly from Luther's in allowing for a degree of overlap that Luther had rejected on principle.[2] And this difference would have implications for Calvin's doctrine of war. The overlap between the two kingdoms is not obvious in Calvin's initial description of their character. Like Luther, he described them as "two worlds, over which different kings and different laws have authority."[3] However, as Calvin proceeded to describe the role or end of secular government, his break with Luther became clear. Government existed, according to Calvin,

> to foster and protect the external worship of God, defend pure doctrine and the good condition of the Church, accommodate the way we live to human society, mould our conduct to civil justice, reconcile us one to another, and uphold and defend the common peace and tranquility.[4]

Foster the worship of God? Defend pure doctrine? These were precisely the sorts of encroachments that Luther's *On Secular Authority* was written to prevent, and thus it is significant that Calvin allowed for them.[5]

Moreover, Calvin clearly sensed that such blending of spheres might trouble his readers: it might "worry" some, he wrote "that I am now allotting to the human polity that care for the right order of religion, I seem earlier to have placed outside [merely] human determination." Calvin tried to assure his followers that this was neither inconsistent with his earlier statements nor wrong in principle. But his reassurances only made the break with Lutheran doctrine more perspicuous.

> I approve a political order that makes it its business to prevent true religion, which is contained in the law of God, from being besmirched and violated with impunity by public and manifest sacrilege. But in doing so, I no more allow men to make laws about religion and the worship of God according to their fancy than I did before.

In other words, the secular government would not create fresh laws about religious worship but only enforce those long-standing norms essential to the faith. Thus, secular government might have among its duties the prevention of "idolatries, sacrileges against the name of God, blasphemies against his truth, and other scandals to religion from emerging into the light of day and spreading among the people."[6] In fact, for Calvin this was not merely a role of government but its primary role, if by primary we understand "prior" in importance. Calvin emphasized this point in his comments on the "duties of the magistrate," where he insisted not only that magistrates attend to both tables of the Decalogue (man's duty to both God and neighbor) but also that they do so in the proper order. He writes, "No polity can be well constituted unless it makes duties to God its *first* concern," and "for laws to attend only to the well-being of men, while disregarding what is owed to God, is an absurdity."[7] Symbolic of Calvin's tendency to blend the two kingdoms together was his frequent use of the phrase "Christian polity" (*Christiana politia*) to designate the civil order. This was a phrase (and a concept) Luther had rejected categorically, as would John Locke later on. But it is one that aptly captured the kind of polity Calvin envisaged.[8]

Christianity and Citizenship

With the polity and the church to some degree intermingled, it became possible to reconceive the concept of citizenship along more religious lines. Citizens could be viewed not merely as secular agents but also as "agents of God." In general, the political realm was understood as an order established by God—this much Calvin had in common with Luther. But beyond this, Calvin emphasized that "civil authority is . . . by far *the most* sacred and honorable of all human vocations" in the sight of God.[9] This was an endorsement of civil authority that far outstripped Luther's view. "Our Lord has not only declared that civil authority is acceptable," writes Calvin, he has "particularly commended its dignity to us by adorning it with titles of the highest honor." Magistrates are "called Gods." They have a "commission from God." They are "endowed with divine authority," and they "in fact represent his person, acting in a certain sense in his place."[10]

Calvin's view of citizenship was in part the product of rhetorical necessity. Calvin hoped to discredit two alternative conceptions of citizenship that were difficult to discredit at once, because they were virtually opposed to one another. One was the view of certain Anabaptists who thought that Christian "freedom" should entail also a freedom from secular-political life in toto. "They think nothing will go well," wrote Calvin, "unless the whole world is given a new face, without courts or laws or magistrates." They wanted, in other words, to transform civil government into a purely spiritual kingdom for regenerate man.[11] Calvin was at pains to discredit the Anabaptist tendency to flee from political life, and he did so by insisting that the fruit reaped from grace was a spiritual fruit that in no way negated the need for bodily restraint or political rule.[12]

The second conception of citizenship Calvin opposed was that of Machiavelli and his like, whom Calvin described as "flatterers of princes, who vaunt the might of princes without [acknowledging] any bounds to it and do not hesitate to oppose it to the overlordship of God himself." This error required an opposite remedy: a restatement of the divine origins of political rule and of the strict limits Christian belief placed upon it.[13] Since Calvin wanted to steer clear of both Anabaptist and Machiavellian extremes in his text, he found himself defending a partially religious conception of earthly citizenship. In doing so, however, he effectively broke from the Lutheran conception of citizenship, which had insisted upon a stricter degree of separation between church and polity. This was the break that would become most significant from the perspective of the just war tradition in the sixteenth century, for it meant that politics (and with it, the sword) could become a tool for the protection of religious goods and the achievement of religious ends.

Besides being religiously infused, citizenship as Calvin conceived it had a marked republican or "democratic" quality.[14] In several prominent places—the *Sermons on Job* (1554), the *Sermons on Deuteronomy* (1554–1555), and the *Lectures on Daniel* (1561)—Calvin railed against the abuses of kings: "If we could uncover the hearts of kings," he wrote, "we would find hardly one in a hundred who does not likewise despise everything divine."[15]

Moreover, he went so far as to express a clear preference in the *Institutes* for an alternative type of regime. Because the defects of human nature were so great, he thought, power should be held jointly by several people who might assist, instruct, and admonish one another in order to prevent abuses of power.[16] Calvin therefore favored some form of institutional checks and balances. He in fact thought there was a "best regime," at least in theory, which was an "aristocracy," either in its pure form or mixed with "polity" so as to increase its representation. By aristocracy, Calvin meant the regime Plato and Aristotle had described—the rule of the best, most learned men. And by polity, he meant the regime that allowed the rich and the poor alike to participate in government. Such a regime, Calvin thought, would blend a degree of liberty with a degree of restraint and thus produce an ordered liberty. He thought that the inhabitants of such a regime would be so fortunate that they should acknowledge certain duties in return: for example, they should do their utmost to preserve their liberty. Indeed, any officeholders who failed in this regard owing to sloth or apathy should be regarded as "traitors to their office and their county."[17]

Despite his preference for a mixed regime, however, Calvin did not suggest that governments should be changed at will, nor did he think average citizens should spend their days weighing the pros and cons of various political forms. His so-called democratic spirit, therefore, had clear limits. "It would be utterly pointless," he writes in the *Institutes*, "for private men, who have no right to decide how any commonwealth whatever is to be ordered, to debate what would be the best state of the commonwealth in the place where they live." Calvin's reluctance to allow such freedom of thought and action stemmed from two closely related considerations. One was his belief that all governments in power must have received their power from God. In other words, God establishes good regimes and bad regimes alike for reasons that often transcend our ability to understand. Our task as Christians is not to question rulers but to obey them.[18] Further, Calvin was aware of the crucial role played by "circumstances" in the diversity of regimes. One needed to consider not only the abstract question of the best regime but also the question of the particular people, the various types of inequality that existed among them, and their relationship to neighboring regions. Reflecting on such complex factors as these, Calvin concluded that it was perhaps "not without a good purpose that divine providence so disposed that different regions are governed by different sorts of regime."[19]

While Calvin's conception of citizenship had democratic elements, its primary qualities were derived from scriptural exegesis and from long traditions of political theorizing. Citizenship was to be limited in its revolutionary zeal by the fact that God, not man, granted rulers their power. At the same time, it was to be energized by the fact that government was at once a secular *and* a religious affair. The polity that made the purity of religion its primary concern was a good polity in God's eyes. What all this would imply for the development of Calvin's just war teaching can be seen if we now turn to his understanding of "the sword," of "just cause," and of the various limits that should be observed in war.

Christians and the Sword

On the classic problem of whether Christians could shed blood, Calvin shared the basic approach of others in the just war tradition. He agreed that under certain circumstances, Christians could (and should) make war, but Calvin's tendency was, once again, to weaken the distinction between church and polity or between religious and secular motivations in war. In other words, Christians could act as Christians in shedding blood, not merely as agents of temporal power. Calvin demonstrates this by considering the matter first from the side of the magistrate and then from the side of the subject or citizen.

Magistrates for their part could shed blood not merely, as Luther had argued, because the un-Christian world required it but because their function was the "execution of God's judgments." They should thus have no scruples about killing. The law of God, of course, prohibits killing in one sense, yet "in order that murderers shall not go unpunished, the Lawgiver [God] himself puts the sword into the hands of his ministers." Calvin thus cites with approval Psalm 101, which presents "destroying the wicked of the earth" as a royal virtue. In this way, Calvin thought, "all who work iniquity might be eliminated from the City of God."[20]

As for citizens and subjects, they too can shed blood, as long as they act at the behest of their rulers to carry out "public vengeance." Should anyone object that the New Testament supplies no warrant for this claim, Calvin offers a multipronged response. First, the underlying causes of war, which obtained in Old Testament times, still obtain, so war is still necessary. Second, the New Testament is not the place to look for explicit instruction about war. Its purposes are spiritual, not political in nature. And finally, the New Testament offers evidence en passant that Christ changed nothing with respect to war. Here Calvin repeats the classic arguments from Augustine and others that if soldiering were a sin, then John the Baptist could not have baptized the soldier in Luke 3:14 ("Be content with your pay").

Calvin thus justified war and soldiering on scriptural grounds, but he also justified these endeavors on natural law grounds. According to Calvin, natural justice (*naturalis aequitas*) and the Holy Spirit here stand in perfect agreement: wars were a necessary fact of human life.

> If kings and peoples have conferred on them the power to preserve the tranquility of their territories, to repress the seditious upheavals fomented by rebellious men, to help those oppressed by violence and to take measures against the wicked, what better occasion can there be for employing that power, than in order to quell the fury of someone who disturbs the peace and quiet not only of private individuals but of entire communities? Someone who foments sedition and perpetrates violence and oppression and other outrages? If it is duty to act as guardians and champions of the laws, they must also make every effort to frustrate the enterprises of those whose crimes undermine the discipline of laws.[21]

It makes no difference, according to Calvin, whether the evildoer is a domestic criminal or a foreign foe, whether he is a single individual or an entire kingdom. The legitimate role of government and obedient subjects is to resist such elements.

According to Calvin, failing to take up the sword when it is needed constitutes a crime in itself. Here the Genevan lawyer echoes, knowingly or not, the dictum of Gratian that those who have the power to protect their associates (*socii*) but fail to do so are guilty of a crime.[22] In Calvin's own words, "If rulers sheath their sword and keep their hands unsullied by blood, while the wicked roam about massacring and slaughtering, then so far from reaping praise for their goodness and justice, they make themselves guilty of the greatest possible injustice." Those who committed this crime of neglect abdicated their duty and risked allowing innocent citizens to suffer harms that could otherwise have been avoided. It is certainly bad to live under a tyrannical king, Calvin writes, but it is much worse to live "under one who permits everything."

Just Cause

To simply say, however, that leaders must take up the sword when it is right elicits the question: When is it right to do so? Calvin's discussion of this topic is fascinating, especially against the backdrop of Luther's treatment. Calvin differed from Luther in significant ways. He de-emphasized the need for a prior attack and reasserted certain doctrines of just cause that dated back to Thomas Aquinas, Gratian, and even to Augustine. In other words, Calvin rejected Luther's strict limitation of just cause to wars of self-defense.[23] Moreover, Calvin allowed that wars could be waged in the name of religion, a notion Luther emphatically rejected.

Among the traditional doctrines Calvin restored was the idea that war could be waged in response to a crime, even if that crime fell far below the threshold of a military attack. War might be waged, for example, to recover stolen property or stolen goods, and it could be waged even if the perpetrator were but a single man.[24] In Calvin's words, "It is of no consequence . . . whether it is a king or the lowest of the mob who invades a foreign region where he has no jurisdiction, to murder and pillage. All of them are equally to be regarded as criminals and punished accordingly." And they are to be punished "by means of war" if this is what it takes.[25] Here Calvin's discussion parallels the discussion of just cause in Thomas Aquinas, where individual criminals are likewise acknowledged as a potential cause of war. Further, Calvin's approach has an Augustinian flavor. Like Augustine, Calvin held that war may be necessary whenever someone has committed "some wrong," some wicked and unjust deed, not necessarily a military attack.

Calvin also restored a traditional doctrine in allowing that wars might be fought to defend an ally. Technically speaking, this would not be a war of self-defense, and yet for Calvin it is perfectly legitimate for countries to make alliances (*foedera*) with "neighboring princes for mutual assistance against disturbances in their territories and in order to join forces for the suppression of the common enemies of the human race." Thus, when an ally has been attacked, or needs assistance tracking down some criminal who has committed wrongs in the region, it might call upon its neighbors to ensure that justice be done. Again, Calvin is able to foresee scenarios neglected by Luther in which a country might wage war—justly—without having been attacked.[26]

By far, the most significant departure from Lutheran teaching, however, concerns wars of religion. Because the function of government included the protection of true religion in Calvin's view, wars could of course be waged for this purpose. Proof that Calvin held this view can be found in the *Institutes*, where he cites a passage from Exodus 32 as an example of justified violence. In this passage, Moses has descended from Mount Sinai only to find his people worshipping a golden calf. Witnessing their idolatry, Moses' "anger grew hot," and he commanded the sons of Levi as follows: "Thus says the Lord, the God of Israel, 'Put your sword on your side, each of you! Go back and forth from gate to gate throughout this camp, and each of you kill your brother, your friend, and your neighbor.'" This is exactly what they did, slaughtering about three thousand of their fellow people. For this, Moses praised them: "Today you have ordained yourselves for the service of the Lord, each one at the cost of a son or a brother, and so have brought a blessing on yourselves this day."[27]

Calvin's reference to this passage is brief but unequivocal: rulers do not bear the sword in vain, Calvin writes, for they are God's ministers. And "if princes and other superiors know that there is nothing more acceptable to the lord than their obedience, let them spare no effort in exercising this ministry, if indeed they have any desire to please God by their piety, obedience and justice." This was precisely what Moses did, for how else could he, who was normally "gentle and peaceable," reach such a "pitch of cruelty as to run through the camp eager for further slaughter, when he was already bespattered and dripping with the blood of his brothers?" Calvin's answer is that he was carrying out God's vengeance. And thus Moses actually "sanctified those hands which [he] would have sullied by mercy."[28]

Calvin's view, and he stated it more than once, was that wars waged in the name of true religion—wars against idolatry, heresy, and other irreligious acts—were legitimate and just in the eyes of God.[29] Thus, Calvin rejected Luther's principled stand against religious warfare in favor of the older view defended by Catholic writers from Augustine to Gratian. But was this not a problematic position for any Protestant writer to take—to deem religious persecution a just cause? This was the very principle by which Catholics had persecuted Protestants, and the problem did not escape the notice of subsequent commentators. Hence John Locke, for example, writing in 1689 objected to Calvin's position emphatically: "What power can be given to the magistrate for the suppression of an idolatrous church, which may not, in time and place, be made use of to the ruin of an orthodox one?" If "at Geneva" the magistrate may "extirpate by violence and blood the religion which is there reputed idolatrous, [then] by the same rule another magistrate in some neighboring country may oppress the reformed religion."[30] Significantly, it would be the Lutheran and not the Calvinist position that would live on in Locke's doctrine of "toleration" and in modern just war theorizing.

Caveats and Cautions

So far, we have focused on the permissive aspects of Calvin's teaching. But Calvin also insisted upon a number of important restrictions that reined in his teaching. One such restriction was his insistence that magistrates exercise prudence in entering into war. They must take care not to damage more than they mend. Nor should they allow themselves to become too harsh: "Work zealously to avoid savage harshness."[31] Augustine's notion of "benevolent harshness" (*benigna asperitas*) seems to be in the back of Calvin's mind here as a limiting ideal.

Moreover, magistrates should not jump at every opportunity for war, even when a just cause arises and victory seems virtually certain. Other methods of resolving the conflict should be pursued first. Here Calvin clearly articulates a doctrine of "last resort" and seems to go beyond earlier writers in his insistence upon it. He does not merely maintain that "war must be necessary." Writers from Augustine to Luther had made that claim, but Calvin went beyond the classic doctrine of necessity in requiring that "everything else ought to be tried first before the recourse to arms." War should be "compelled by a necessity which permits no escape."[32]

Yet another restriction Calvin expressed with unprecedented clarity concerns "military interventions," the use of force against a foreign ruler who commits crimes against his own citizens or allows his citizens to commit crimes against each other. Calvin did not use the term "intervention," which is of modern coinage, but he plainly envisioned the scenario that term now designates and, surprisingly, rejected it outright. That he did so does not come to light in the *Institutes*. If the people or the prince of a foreign region were determined to be heretics, idolaters, or doers of base deeds, why should a war not be waged to put a stop to their wickedness? It would seem that it could. But in his *Commentaries upon the Prophet Daniel*, Calvin addressed the question directly. "We know that the kings of the East . . . did exercise cruel and barbarous dominion or rather tyranny toward their subjects." But "there is no cause why any man should contend much about this question," since all rulers are put in place by God. As Michael Walzer notes, Calvin turns out to be "too preoccupied with order to set about overthrowing, even in theory, states and kingdoms that God had established." Morally repugnant as another region's practices may be, they should not be remedied by force.[33] This was indeed a remarkable limit Calvin placed upon his otherwise expansive doctrine of holy war. The purity of the faith could be used to justify internal wars and persecutions, and to defend against external threats, but not, evidently, to meddle in the domestic affairs of other states.

Right Intention: *Ad Bellum* and *In Bello*

When it comes to the disposition of the will, Calvin is noteworthy for stating expressly and repeatedly what Luther, for his part, had failed to make clear, that force can never be justified unless the will of the person employing it be animated by love of one's own people and of one's enemy. This doctrine originated with Augustine but was necessary for Calvin to rearticulate, and he did so in a number of different contexts. In his discussion of domestic legal proceedings, for example, Calvin maintained that it would be "impossible for anyone to proceed justly with a case at law, however good his cause," unless he were to bear toward his adversary the same "love and benevolence [that he would] if the business at issue had already been amicably transacted and settled." A just litigant must act "without any thirst for revenge or desire to inflict injury, without bitterness or hate, and without taking pleasure in quarrelsomeness; on the contrary, he should be prepared to yield up his right and suffer any wrong rather than to allow his mind to be filled with enmity towards his adversary." And where "any particle of love is neglected," our case "must be contrary to our duties to God, however just it might be in itself."[34] By extension, the same principle applied to magistrates contemplating war. Magistrates must not be "carried away by anger, or hatred, or implacable severity" but must have "compassion on our common nature . . . even in those whose crimes they punish."[35]

So important was this principle to Calvin that he offered further instructions on how to apply it. The key, Calvin thought, was to keep two crucial distinctions in mind. First was the classic Augustinian distinction between internal dispositions and external acts. We may love the sinner "in the secrecy of the soul," Calvin writes, in such a way that love animates all we do, even while our external acts appear harsh.[36] Second, Calvin thought, we can distinguish between love of the sinner and hatred of his sin. "We hate the evil in him while nevertheless loving the person," he wrote to one reader who pressed him on this point.[37] In fact, love of our fellows requires us to hate the evil that sometimes overtakes them.

These considerations of right intention lead naturally to conclusions about the way Christians should treat their enemies *in bello*. For it is precisely because we love our fellow man that we are limited in what we can do. But here Calvin was inconsistent. On the one hand, he argued that certain basic humanitarian gestures should be extended even to the most implacable foes. For example, no matter how violent the enemy or how inimical their beliefs may be to the dogmas of the true church, they should never be denied water, fire, or the common elements of this world. More generally, they should never be denied the "services of humanity" while being persecuted with iron and sword.[38] On the other hand, Calvin argued repeatedly that no consideration should be given to such humanitarian gestures when the honor of God or the security of the church is in question.[39] He thought the question "whether it is lawful to overcome an enemy by wiles and stratagem" was naive, not only because a good commander could often remove the need for violence by means of such techniques, but also because once war had passed beyond the criteria of just cause, it seemed "beyond all controversy that the usual methods of conquering may be lawfully employed." The only restriction Calvin insisted upon in this connection was that once a truce or treaty of peace had been pledged, there could be no violation. To allow otherwise would in effect make peace much more difficult to attain.[40] Calvin, then, ends up in a position similar to Luther's, practically speaking, on the matter of *jus in bello*, even though he has a much more developed discussion of enemy love. So while Luther and Calvin agree on the potentiality for harshness in war, they differ insofar as Calvin insists that the soul of the soldier be animated by nothing other than love.

Disobeying and Deposing

The final chapter of Calvin's *Institutes* concludes with a discussion of resisting tyrants. Ultimately, Calvin believed that it was licit for subjects to depose unjust rulers. Thus, the entire *Institutes* ends, surprisingly, on a note of civil disobedience if not outright revolt. Yet the slow and painstaking analysis that leads Calvin to this position serves to deemphasize and delimit the doctrine of revolution that comes into view, as does the way Calvin concludes the discussion. Scholars therefore differ on the relative weight to place upon Calvin's teaching. According to one commentator, the final pages of the *Institutes* "unbarred the gate" and allowed "a phalanx of champions of the people's rights" to "storm the bastions."[41] At the other extreme, it has been argued that Calvin was really rather conservative on matters of revolution and that "when due weight" is given to the overall thrust of his argument, it is clear that he "remained firmly anchored to the Pauline doctrine of absolute nonresistance."[42] Such differences of interpretation are to be expected given the ambiguities of the text itself. Let us therefore look at Calvin's argument and consider its place in the broader history of just war reflection.

Calvin begins by insisting that subjects are duty-bound to honor and obey their magistrates as God's ministers on earth. He cites Romans 13:1 in this connection, as was conventional.[43] Magistrates are of course supposed to be shepherds of their people, guardians of justice, and defenders of the innocent, but what if they prove incompetent, unwise, and unjust? Worse, what if they "pillage homes, violate wives and maidens, slaughter the innocent and, in short, engage in . . . criminality"? Calvin answered unflinchingly that such magistrates must still be obeyed. Calvin reasoned that all rulers—good and bad alike—gain their power from God. Thus, those who govern for the public good may be understood to be "true examples and signs of God's goodness," whereas those who "govern unjustly and intemperately have been raised up by him to punish the iniquity of the people." But whatever their relative characteristics, all rulers "are equally furnished with that sacred majesty with which He has endowed legitimate authority" and must therefore be obeyed. Calvin believed that the scriptural evidence for this was simply too overwhelming to be denied.[44]

This doctrine, however, was problematic. If all those who hold power have been, by the mere fact of their power, appointed by God, then why should individuals not rise up and test their own potential power? If they succeed, their very success would demonstrate their divine mandate to rule.[45] Calvin's doctrine, it seems, was as likely to encourage revolutionary activity as it was to discourage it. He had merely reduced the difficult Thomistic question of "What is *legitimate* authority?" to the much easier question "Who has the power?"

Calvin for his part recognized this problem, but he also saw certain advantages to such revolutionary ambiguities. Perhaps God could make instruments of his people and deploy them against "the bloodstained scepters of insolent kings." God could, if he so desired, overturn unbearable tyrannies. Calvin thus turned a rather crude doctrine of legitimacy (power equals legitimacy) into a stern warning for princes: "Let princes hear and be afraid." This was not to say that subjects should routinely rise up against kings and magistrates, but then again, unusual conditions might lead them to do so, and justice could indeed be on their side.

Calvin then spelled out the ways in which God might overthrow a tyrant: (1) he could directly command one of his servants to overthrow him; (2) he could turn a frenzied mob to this purpose, even if that mob had intended something else; and (3) he could employ a foreign power to do the work. In all such cases, and whether the agents were aware of it or not, God would have empowered his servants with divine arms and a divine ordinance, and the "rebels" would not in the least have violated the sacred majesty of kings. Rather, says Calvin, they will have "subjected a lesser power by a greater, in just the same way that kings are entitled to punish their own officials."[46]

But Calvin was careful not to encourage citizens to explore such revolutionary possibilities. In the same breath as he uttered his caution to princes, he reminded subjects of their duty: "As for us, however, let us take the greatest possible care never to hold in contempt, or trespass upon, that plenitude of authority of magistrates whose majesty it is for us to venerate and which God has confirmed by the most weighty pronouncements, even when it is exercised by individuals who are wholly unworthy of it and who do their best to defile it by their wickedness." We are "not to imagine," insists Calvin, "that it is *we ourselves* who have been called upon" to inflict punishment upon our rulers. Such cautions were crucial for Calvin's position as the only check he could supply against the potentialities he had unleashed. The real danger, which Calvin must have recognized, is that individuals might suppose they had a divine mandate to use force against their rulers, when in fact they did not. The ways in which the "will of God" could be used and abused were too numerous to count. And as time went on, these became much more than mere theoretical possibilities.[47]

Calvin thus acknowledged and yet tried to discourage the possibility of divinely sanctioned revolution against tyrants. Calvin was not completely satisfied with his own position and considered a less revolutionary mode of policing tyrants: a constitutional mode. "It may be," he writes, that there are in our day certain "popular magistrates" who are established precisely to "restrain the licentiousness of kings." Calvin alludes to the ephors of Sparta, the tribunes of Rome, and the demarchs of Athens as historical examples of this power. Such constitutional checks upon higher authority seemed to Calvin both legitimate and even desirable. But was this relevant to sixteenth-century Europe? Calvin himself prescinded from making that judgment, which itself might have contributed to a "revolution" in the medieval understanding of sovereignty. But Calvin did say that if the three estates were to function in this way, then it would be "no part of my intention to prohibit" their activity. On the contrary, Calvin maintained that to fail in their duty (if it is legitimately theirs) would be to betray the people and to commit a most nefarious act of neglect.[48] To this extent, Calvin assented to the possibility of a constitutional theory of resistance. The theory was not his own but rather evolved out of Lutheran circles.[49] It was, however, available and clearly had advantages over the theory Calvin explicitly embraced, that God sometimes invites outright revolution against authorities who, on the eve of revolution, were themselves thought to be ordained by God.

Calvin's teaching on revolution was downplayed in the *Institutes* not only by the slow and painstaking way in which he spelled it out but also by the way he concluded. In his conclusion, Calvin shifts topics in order to conclude on a markedly more conservative note. He writes that when Christians, following the sound scriptural advice that one should "obey God rather than man," refuse to obey the unjust commands of a ruler, they must also bear the effects of their disobedience. At first blush, Calvin seems to say that Christians who engage in revolutionary violence must pay with their lives, but in fact he has shifted from the topic of revolution to that of mere civil disobedience—that is, from the question of resisting a ruler by force to the much less controversial question of disobeying specific unjust laws and commands.[50] The Christian who practices civil disobedience in the name of God runs the risk of severe penalties because the ruler he disobeys will remain in power to punish him. But this is not to say that Christian revolutionaries must die for their cause. On the contrary, where the revolutionary succeeds, who will be left to harm him?

Thus, Calvin concludes the *Institutes* on a misleading note, appearing to place cautionary obstacles in the way of deposing unjust rulers, when in fact he does nothing of the sort. No wonder scholars have been at odds over how to evaluate his teaching. In the end, both assessments ring true, even though they appear contradictory. Calvin does in effect "unbar the gate" for revolutionary activity, but at the same time he is conservative insofar as he downplays the possibility of divinely sanctioned revolution by considering a less tumultuous, constitutional solution and by reminding readers of the duty of Christians to suffer wrongs, even wrongs committed by kings. Calvin does not deny that revolution remains a possibility, but it is not for ordinary citizens in ordinary times to suppose they have been chosen to instigate such political upheaval.

From Calvin to the Radical Reformers

The final chapter of Calvin's *Institutes* represents a distinct voice in the ongoing just war tradition. Like all prior writers in the tradition, Calvin attempted to reconcile the tragic necessity of war with the human desire to be good, and he did so by looking to scripture as well as to tradition as a guide. Calvin's approach was unique because of his specific way of blending traditional (Catholic) ideas with Reformation ideas and of applying these to his own historical-political situation. The most distinctive feature of his just war teaching is the extent to which he allowed for "intermingling" (our term) of church and state. Although various kinds of intermingling had characterized just war doctrine in the past (Gratian's treatment of episcopal and regal power comes to mind), nothing quite like Calvin's teaching had been seen before. In Calvin, the magistrate and the church are much more intimately related than in the medieval scheme, according to which Regnum and Sacerdotium were competing, if sometimes overlapping, powers.

It is this matter—how to understand the proper relationship of church and state—that lay behind some of the most protracted differences among Reformation writers on the issue of just war. From Luther to Calvin to various kinds of Anabaptists, this question more than any other proved determinative. Consideration of this across the Reformation will also afford us the opportunity to examine the pacifist position of the Anabaptists and to see exactly how and why these particular reformers rejected the more orthodox position on just war.

In Luther's understanding of church and state, the church was entrusted with the gospel, whereas the state existed to administer the law and foster an ordered society. Lutheran theology neither equated nor conflated the two spheres.[51] For this reason, Luther referred to only one sword—the sword that belongs to the magistrate proper (cf. Romans 13)—as distinct from the notion of two swords that derived from medieval debates over the ambiguous relationship between "papal theocracy" and the magistrate. If we assume, with Reformation historian James M. Stayer, that Luther led a reform movement away from a "two swords" mode of thinking to that of "one sword," then the sixteenth-century debate over the "sword" was a distinctly Protestant phenomenon.[52]

In *On Temporal Authority*, Luther reasons that the authority of "the sword" has existed from the beginning of humankind, and that human fallenness and depravity have made it a necessity for the preservation and sustenance of an ordered community. As we have seen, Luther wrestles notably with dualisms at several levels. Christian believers must always remember that they cannot escape the essential dualism of their two citizenships in the kingdoms of God and the state. This dual identity points to the necessity of the state's authority, which will require the application of coercive force to realize the demands of justice.

Luther distinguishes himself from the "radical reformers" of his age, such as the Anabaptists, with his ability to reconcile St. Paul's teaching in Romans 13 with Jesus' Sermon on the Mount. In this regard, he remains in continuity with Augustine and Aquinas, as well as mainstream Christian thinkers to come. Based on natural law reasoning, in harmony with divine revelation as interpreted through scripture, "the sword" is required on the part of the magistrate for the benefit of society. Wherever the ruler violates the natural moral law by not applying the sword, or by applying it unjustly, his authority is undermined. It is important to note that the Christian believer, according to Luther, serves God neither by separation from the world nor by Christianization of the world but by bringing Christian motivation to bear on the world. This includes public spheres such as political deliberation and governing, which are realms that for all the magisterial Protestant reformers should not be left simply to unbelievers but rather are legitimate areas of Christian stewardship. What separates Luther from Calvin on this score is the extent to which the magistrate may act in the name of Christ and the church.

The reforms brought about by Luther's work were not confined to one geographical locale. In rather remarkable fashion, this vision for reform spread. Nowhere was this rate of change more pronounced than in the Swiss territories to the south, where reformers such as Huldrych Zwingli, Conrad Grebel, Balthasar Hubmaier, Hans Hut, and Felix Manz pressed for reform in both faith and practice. Among some reformers, a chief cause of resistance was a questioning of the scriptural warrant for infant baptism. This led to a rebaptism—a "believer's baptism" as it came to be called—by some in the reform movement. In so doing, these groups were distinguishing themselves as separate communions apart from the church, since this belief was tantamount to denying the validity of their prior baptism as infants. Hence, they became known by their opponents as "Anabaptists," that is, those baptized again.

Whereas Anabaptists today tend to be rather uniform in their practice, their diversity in the earlier part of the sixteenth century is striking. Some, such as Johann Denck, taught on an inner light that was considered superior to scripture. Others, such as Thomas Müntzer, the agitator of the Peasants Revolt, were self-educated, apocalyptic mystics and revolutionaries who believed that the sword existed for the purpose of destroying the godless and that the Old Testament episodes in which Yahweh had instructed the faithful to slay the wicked were paradigmatic.[53] Some like Balthasar Hubmaier believed, like Luther, that a Christian could be a ruler and that war may or may not be justified,[54] while many—if not most—Anabaptists embraced varying degrees of apolitical pacifism, not infrequently resulting in death and martyrdom.

In the radicality of early-sixteenth-century Anabaptism, there was an oscillation between the polar antitheses of pacifism and revolution. Despite these variations, most of them arrived eventually at what historian James Stayer calls a "radical apoliticism—that is, a denial that political and coercive force might achieve ethical goals given the explicit commitment to be separate from the world.[55] Unlike moderate apoliticism, radical apoliticism denies that force is necessary on occasion to preserve the commonweal.

Among the earliest—and best known—of radically apolitical groups were the Swiss Brethren and the Hutterites, who were soon joined in their extreme pacifistic stance by the Mennonites in the early 1560s. To better understand their beliefs and self-identity, we shall examine one of the earliest Anabaptist documents: the Schleitheim Confession of Faith.[56]

The Schleitheim Confession

The Schleitheim Confession is significant not for its theological detail but rather because in time it would be considered a normative Anabaptist confession[57] and because it enumerates those practices that are thought to distinguish true Christians, as embodied in Anabaptism, from the world. It was adopted in February 1527 under the title "Brotherly Union of a Number of Children of God concerning Seven Articles" (*Brüderlich Vereinigung etlicher Kinder Gottes/sieben Artickel betreffend*[58]) as the fruit of a synod called by the Swiss Brethren at the village of Schleitheim. The Brethren, under the leadership of Michael Sattler, a former Benedictine monk, had been influenced by reform efforts in and around Zürich. Their synod was aimed at discussing seven specific matters of the free-church movement that were thought to be of critical importance to their faith and practice.[59] These matters of faith stressed the separation of true believers from "the world." The confession was an attempt, if not to codify and consolidate creedal convictions, at least to formulate belief and practice in such a way as to (a) address those supposed "fringe" elements that deviated from Anabaptist belief and/or (b) emphasize what was shared by all Anabaptist groups. The degree to which the confession is representative of Anabaptism continues to be debated today among scholars of its own tradition;[60] nevertheless, for our own purposes we shall assume the significance of the confession as a charter document and the crystallization point of early Anabaptism.[61]

What is noteworthy about the confession is its oppositional tone and emphasis. Pronounced antagonism rather than differentiation undergirds the articles of faith. Correlatively, the chief argument being set forth appears to be that of separation from the world. In the introduction, the document reads, "We who have been and shall be separated from the world in everything . . . [are] completely at peace." And in the fourth article, we read:

> We are agreed on separation: A separation shall be made from the evil and from the wickedness which the devil planted in the world; in this manner, simply that we shall not have fellowship with them [the wicked] and not run with them in the multitude of their abominations. . . . Since all who do not walk in the obedience of faith, and have not united themselves with God so that they wish to do His will, are a great abomination before God, it is not possible for anything to grow or issue from them except abominable things. For truly all creatures are in but two classes,

> good and bad, believing and unbelieving, darkness and light, the world and those who have come out of the world, God's temple and idols, Christ and Belial; and none can have part with the other.[62]

Indeed, the clear thrust of the Confession is that the Brethren are to be unified in their separation.

The sixth and longest of the seven articles of the confession concerns "the sword." There is a dualism in the confession's formulation of what is required of true Christian believers. On the one hand, the sword is "ordained of God," "guards and protects the good," and is "ordained to be used by the worldly magistrates." On the other hand, it is "outside the perfection of Christ" and for this reason is not to be employed by Christians. In anticipation of an objection, article 6 reasons: "Now it will be asked by many who do not recognize [this stance regarding the sword as] the will of Christ for us, whether a Christian may or should employ the sword against the wicked for the defense and protection of the good, or for the sake of love." The Brethren's reply to this question is "unanimous" and consists of a fourfold rationale:

- Christ's teaching and example point in the direction of mercy and forgiveness.

- Christ's example was not to pass judgment.

- Christ's example was not to rule as a king or prince, and in fact, Christ explicitly "forbids the [use of] the force of the sword saying 'The worldly princes lord it over them, etc. but not so shall it be with you' "[63]—an example that is supported by Paul's statement that God predestined his own to be confirmed to the image of his Son[64] and Peter's reminder that because Christ suffered, we are left with an example.[65]

- Christian citizenship is spiritual and heavenly, therefore, the work of ruling and magistracy, because it is "worldly," is out of line with their true nature.

The final point is the most substantial of the Brethren's answers to why a Christian may not employ the sword:

> Finally it will be observed that it is not appropriate for a Christian to serve as a magistrate because of these points: The government magistracy is according to the flesh, but the Christians' is according to the Spirit; their houses and dwellings remain in this world, but the Christians' are in heaven; their citizenship is in this world, but the Christians' citizenship is in heaven; the weapons of their conflict and war are carnal and against the flesh only, but the Christians' weapons are spiritual, against the fortification of the devil. The worldlings are armed with steel and iron, but the Christians are armed with the armor of God, with truth, righteousness, peace, faith, salvation and the Word of God.

The absolutist approach to the confession's dualism inevitably and inexorably breeds withdrawal from the world. On the one hand, the Swiss Brethren, as reflective of most sixteenth-century Anabaptists, were true children of the Reformation, and they agreed with Luther on one temporal sword. And yet their separation was far more radical than that of Luther, who was not apolitical. The Swiss Brethren, and the Anabaptists as a whole, derived their separation—and hence their radical apoliticism—from a particular view of Christian discipleship that issued out of their view of the world.

In fairness, it should be pointed out that this view of the world arose from their experience of intense persecution—from both the Catholic and the Protestant sides. As James Turner Johnson reminds us, neither the separatism of the Anabaptists nor their pacifism and absolute dualism between the affairs of this world and the kingdom of God were developed in a social or political vacuum. They became separatists and pacifists as a result of their attempt to distance themselves from a world in which magisterial power had been used for unjust purposes. Not having the power themselves to resist the misuse of the sword, they separated themselves for spiritual purposes, therewith renouncing for themselves any recourse to the use of the sword.[66] In fact, it was only a matter of several months after the Schleitheim synod that Michael Sattler, generally considered the author of the Schleitheim Confession, was executed in Catholic Austria. For this reason, we do well to resist attempting to understand Anabaptist views apart from their own documents and the specific religious, social, and political contexts in which these arise.[67] In the words of Roland Bainton, "The true Christian could do no other than withdraw from all political life—and in the sixteenth century the Anabaptists were compelled to withdraw from all social life."[68]

Separatist and Pacifist

By the early 1530s, separatist and pacifist themes among Anabaptists had begun to congeal. Concurrent with this development was a growing theological controversy with non-Anabaptist Protestant reformers, who viewed the Anabaptists' radicalism as being rooted in a theologically deficient understanding of the relationship of the Old Testament to the New.[69] Some of the reformed leaders, such as Calvin and Bullinger, believed that this deficiency constituted the fulcrum of the debate, but as early as 1524 Zwingli began criticizing the Anabaptist movement on this score. For Zwingli, the immediate context for construing a proper relationship between Old and New Testaments was infant baptism, and consistent with reformed thinking in the years to come, Zwingli argued that infant baptism should be understood as the New Testament parallel to the Old Testament practice of circumcision.[70]

Not only infant baptism, however, but a cluster of critically important issues—some liturgical, some ethical—hinged on how to interpret the Old Testament, including the Christian's view of the magistrate, the use of the sword, and the public sphere in general. The differences between Anabaptists and their reformed brethren are well illustrated by a disputation that occurred in 1532. In the spring of that year, Berthold Haller, a pastor and influential Protestant reformer in the city of Bern, carried on correspondence with Heinrich Bullinger, the prominent Zürich reformer, on the matter of how to engage Anabaptists. The occasion for this colorful exchange was a forthcoming disputation with a particular Anabaptist group. According to Heinold Fast, twenty learned preachers attended, in addition to delegates from the cities of Bern and Aargau.[71] From Haller's vantage point, the

Anabaptists' doctrinal peculiarity was their rejection of the authority of the Old Testament and a correlative distortion of the New, based on their claim that the "law" has been abrogated by Christ and their tendency to spiritualize Old Testament passages. How should he address this deficiency?

Bullinger advised that when disagreements between Christians arise, they must be clarified by the totality of scripture, that is, both the Old and the New Testaments together. Where Old Testament texts are said to be abrogated, one must show that these are not invalidated and at the same time expose the manner in which these texts have been misused. Pay particular attention to the manner in which *law* is used, because most of the disagreements will turn on this. Distinguish between various uses of the word *law* in scripture, as the New Testament writers—inclusive of the apostle Paul—use this word in different contexts. For example, the fact that Old Testament ceremonial law, applicable only to theocratic Israel, is annulled should in no way be interpreted to mean that the moral law, which is eternal and part of God's nature, is no longer valid. And recall statements in the New Testament that confirm the authoritative use of the Old Testament—statements by Jesus, by the apostles, and by the writers of the New Testament themselves. In sum, allow scripture to clarify and interpret scripture.[72]

Such was Bullinger's advice. Haller, in writing, is well aware that Bullinger had published a strong critique of Anabaptist beliefs during the previous year.[73] Haller's exchange with Bullinger, then, is of value insofar as it helps us understand one of the pressing issues that separated Anabaptists from their reformational counterparts. For this reason, John Roth has perceptively written:

> By seizing on this issue of the relationship of the Old Testament and the New Testament, Bullinger correctly identified one of the most foundational differences between the Reformers and the Anabaptist movement. At stake in the minds of the Reformers was not an abstract scholarly quibble over allegorical or tropological readings of Old Testament passages, but rather basic understandings of the sovereignty of God, the meaning of the Incarnation, the foundation of Christian ethics and the princi-

> ples of order and authority essential to a stable society. Indeed, as subsequent debates would show, virtually every distinctive Anabaptist argument—on baptism, the sword, the oath, the Christian magistracy, and so on—hinged on their insistence that the New Testament was more authoritative than the Old in matters of Christian ethics.[74]

In sum, the early sixteenth century constitutes something of a remarkable new chapter in reflection on war. While Protestant thinkers maintain a dependence on the Augustinian theory that seeks to mediate the tension between two citizenships—the earthly and the heavenly—new developments begin dramatically to alter the landscape. Rethinking the church's relationship to the sword, which has been the focus of our remarks on the Anabaptists, indicates an emerging break with medieval life and tradition. In addition, the discovery of the Americas as well as an increasingly fragmented Europe—both of which will be the focus of the next chapter—call for attention. Simultaneously confronting early-modern thinkers are the questions of how to assimilate non-Christian people-groups (viz., those in the "New World") and how to prevent international anarchy.

The magisterial reformers held to the conviction that while retribution does not belong to the church, it is not only permitted but commanded of rulers. Thus, two differentiated spheres of authority were understood to coexist in tension. How that tension was navigated differed considerably from Luther to Calvin, but the tension was maintained nevertheless. For the Swiss Brethren, and for Anabaptists in general, these two spheres were thought to be staunchly oppositional; therefore, a Christian could not be a magistrate or punish with the sword. The Reformed-Anabaptist debate in this regard came to a head in May and June of 1571 at the Frankenthal Disputation.[75] The Reformed position seemed to expose a weak spot in the general Anabaptist argument: if a Christian could not be permitted to serve in any sort of ruling capacity, the implication is that the office qua office is not of God but of the devil and therefore intrinsically evil. A further inconsistency needed clarification, based on article 6 of the Schleitheim Confession: three times in the opening paragraph of this article, the confession states that the sword is "ordained"—(1) it is "ordained of

God" even when existing "outside the perfection of Christ"; (2) in the Law the sword was "ordained" for the purpose of punishment; and (3) the same sword is presently "ordained" and "to be used by the worldly magistrates."[76] By the end of the sixteenth century, Anabaptists nevertheless maintained this stark polarity, which more or less exists to the present day.

7

Just War Thinking in the Early-Modern Period

In his classic book *Ideology, Reason, and the Limitation of War,* just war historian James Turner Johnson notes that the just war doctrine that was passed on from the late medieval period combined two notable strains of thoughts. It assumed the theological rationale that came through Ambrose, Augustine, and Aquinas, and it built upon the legal rationale drawn from Roman law.[1] In the early-modern period, these two strands recede into the background without fully disappearing, giving ground to a third component—namely, an appeal to the natural law. Justice has a deeper basis than mere religious confession because it is known through nature and intuited universally as binding on all people everywhere. Thus, the law of nature becomes a law to the nations (*ius gentium*), holding them accountable to the unchanging demands of justice. Just war principles, then, find confirmation in the natural law. What all people everywhere and at all times intuit, by means of a natural moral law, is both descriptive and prescriptive of good and evil.[2]

This shift in emphasis is mandated foremost by the gradual disintegration of the dominant synthesis that had held throughout the medieval era. By the sixteenth and seventeenth centuries, new explanations for the justness or unjustness of war were required. These were necessitated by a changing European geopolitical scene and secularizing tendencies. Consequently, a reliance on natural law united the important just war thinkers of the period—of whom Francisco de Vitoria, Francisco Suárez, and Hugo Grotius are representative and thus worthy of our attention.[3] Despite their differences—Victoria was a Dominican, Suárez a Jesuit, and Grotius a Protestant with Dutch Arminian proclivities—all three relied on the Christian just war tradition as well as on classical antecedents such as Cicero, Sallust, and Terence. The manner in which they go beyond Aquinas is multifaceted and noteworthy.[4] It can be seen, for example, in (1) the care with which they delineated just cause, (2) the possible scenario of both sides declaring relative "justness" in their cause; and (3) the pains they took to develop and impose limitations on warfare through *in bello* restraints.[5] The reasons for these and related developments are by no means hard to detect. The ages of Augustine and Aquinas differed greatly in the sort of dilemmas that needed addressing. Given the dominant cultural synthesis of the Middle Ages, theorists developed their understanding of just war explicitly from Christian religion and secondarily from natural law. This relationship, however, is reversed in the Age of Discovery and the early-modern period, presenting new challenges to just war thinkers. These challenges concerned people outside Christendom as well as those in a divided Christendom. A cluster of questions with new relevance needed to be answered: What about cultures and nations that find themselves outside Christendom? Does just war thinking apply to non-Christian peoples? Do the same just war criteria apply?

Vitoria and Suárez were united by common issues, principally, the matter of Spanish conquest in the New World, the encounter between "Christian" Spain and non-Christian peoples, and the delicate matter of balancing royal and ecclesial authority. The context in which Grotius wrote, however, was quite different. His work emerged against the backdrop of the Thirty Years War, fierce religious controversy, and the need to restrain nations at war with one another. Still, all three thinkers were united by their dependence on natural law rather than explicitly theological reasoning. All three granted more weight to the observance of *jus in bello* considerations than was previously done, building upon the *jus ad bellum* criteria their forebears had asserted. For them, it was crucial that greater evils not issue out of war than what war sought to avert. Means and ends needed to be united by a common set of moral guidelines.

Vitoria and Suárez in the Context of Spanish New World Conquest

Francisco de Vitoria had done his theological studies in Paris, where he was the beneficiary of renewed interest in Thomistic thought.[6] This renewal would serve him well, for this was also the period of Spanish discovery and conquest of the New World, and Spain was the intellectual center of Europe as well as the dominant military and colonial power. Spanish treatment of indigenous people, in war and in peace, instigated necessary debates about justice. Vitoria would play a critical role in those debates.

By the year 1510, disquieting reports had reached Spain that Native Americans were being denied basic liberty and property rights. By the 1530s, eyewitness accounts corroborated a worrisome story line: the Spanish were engaging in punitive annihilation. The challenge that confronted Vitoria, and the few who were like-minded, was the Spanish vision to colonize the new peoples of the Americas. Spain was prepared to justify war with Native Americans to possess their land and "convert" them to the Christian faith. Vitoria's task was to challenge Spanish imperial pretensions and the unjust treatment of the American Indians.

Vitoria argued in public lectures (*Relectiones*) delivered in 1539 (eventually published under the title *On the Indians and the Law of War*[7]) that neither differences of religion nor "the spirit of discovery" constitute grounds—legally, theologically, or morally—for warfare. Rather, there is only one just cause for war, and that is a wrong incurred.[8] Christian faith, he argued, cannot coerce others. Aquinas, of course, had also argued that faith cannot be coerced, and Vitoria cited him approvingly.[9] Faith spreads through preaching and reception, not by the sword. Where coercive force is permissible, according to Vitoria, the necessity must be demonstrated. For example, the Spanish may defend themselves if the Indians interfere or attempt to impede or attack them.[10] However, no war is just that inflicts unprovoked violence upon a population. Vitoria insisted that Native Americans were their own masters, having exercised their own form of governance and having had rightful ownership of property, before the Spanish arrived.[11] Even were the Native Americans to hear the Christian faith preached but not receive it, such would be no grounds for war.[12] And even were the Indians to attack the Spanish, a just response would be only a defensive one that sought to minimize loss. War is justifiable only when and where the injustice violates the natural law.

Modern minds fail to appreciate how radical and how comprehensive Vitoria's message was, to the extent that it mounts an attack on Spain as a kingdom as well as on the church and the papacy.[13] Against conventional thinking, Vitoria's argument was nothing short of scandalous: Neither the emperor nor the pope is master of the world.[14] The pope's temporal power is limited to what is absolutely necessary for the administration of spiritual things, which is to say for the administration of Christians.[15] Therefore, Vitoria argued, war with the Indians to acquire their land or to convert them to Christianity is unjust because Indians and Spaniards have equal rights.[16]

In identifying specific causes that might warrant going to war, Vitoria aligned with just war thinkers of the past, citing the three traditional reasons: defense against aggression, recovery of stolen property, and punishment for wrongdoing.[17] He was stunningly adamant in rejecting the Spanish imperial pretensions of his day. Further, he did not endorse war in the case of difference of religion, nor in forcing conversion to the faith, nor as a response to rejection of the faith. Nor was war justified to defend the expansion of empire or the magistrate's sense of vainglory.[18] What, then, constitutes just cause for conflict? For Vitoria, all that is necessary for the defense of the public good. Further, right intention in going to war needed to concern the establishment of peace and security, which promote the public good, since these are basic inviolable human needs.[19] Even if gross injustice per se were to justify going to war, justification would not be achieved if the war left surrounding nations worse off than before. Therefore, according to Vitoria, the reasonable chances for success in procuring justice must be evaluated with great sobriety.

Earlier we noted the care of early-modern just war theorists to impose limitations on warfare through *in bello* restraints. Vitoria affirmed the *in bello* requirements of proportionality and discrimination between guilty and innocent. As to the former, he contended that retribution is to be "proportionate to the offense, and vengeance ought to go no further."[20] Regarding the latter, he argued that the deliberate slaughter of the innocent is never lawful, according to natural law.[21] The only just cause of waging war, Vitoria observed, is "when harm has been inflicted." At the same time, Vitoria was mindful of collateral damage and acknowledged that preventing harm to all innocents in war was impossible. Such a situation might include the storming of a fortress in a just war with the knowledge that innocent people are inside. Prudence in such a case is therefore necessary, always with the aim of avoiding potential abuses.[22]

In addition to the specific application of just war restrictions to the New World, Vitoria addressed other relevant theoretical questions on war. He agreed with Augustine that Christians may serve as soldiers and participate in war and cites John the Baptist (Luke 3:14) to the effect that if Christian doctrine condemned war altogether, "surely the advice given in the Gospel to the men seeking salvation would have been to throw away their arms and avoid military service altogether."[23] Not only does the gospel not forbid such, but saints of the church and the natural law permit war that is justified.[24] Vitoria also argued that coercive force may be used by individuals to defend themselves and their property. Further, the prince, magistrate, or king may defend—and declare war on behalf of—the community, republic, or state. With Aquinas,[25] Vitoria stressed that authority to declare war resides with the governing authorities. The state cannot adequately protect the public weal if it cannot avenge a wrong and take measures against those who would destroy the public good, and therefore the proper ordering of human affairs allows a state to avenge wrongs.[26]

Moreover, "justness" cannot rest merely on the opinions of the prince or a few like-minded leaders, and for this reason Victoria emphasized the need for wise counsel to dispel doubts about the justness of the cause.[27] For Vitoria, "war should not be declared on the sole dictates of the prince, nor even on the opinion of the few, but on the opinion of the many, and of the wise and reliable."[28] And where relative justness appears to exist on both sides, then war should not be undertaken; mediation, rather, is the order of the day.[29] Justification for war cannot be adduced unless men really are guilty and lawlessness is established (over against ignorance and innocence). Where insufficient justification for war is found, mediation or arbitration is required. Finally, going to war must be motivated by a right intention. Vitoria insisted that the end and aim of war must be "peace and security" and "the good of the whole world."[30]

We find in Vitoria the beginnings of "international law," of the principles governing all nations that are anchored in natural moral law. Vitoria's argument is significant because it acknowledges, even before Westphalia, an international community of independent states or people-groups that have rights, territorial sovereignty, and reciprocal duties as to conduct. Unlike mainstream just war thinkers before him, Vitoria grounded the notion of just war not on Romans 13 and Christian theology per se but rather on moral obligations known through natural law reasoning.[31] He stood in continuity with Thomistic thought in understanding law as a rule or measure of human activity, observing that the word *lex* derives from the Latin *ligare*, "to bind," to "oblige." Thus, law is inherent in and reflective of human rationality, and as such it is a dictate of practical reason.[32] Similarly, he understood law to function on behalf of the common good, since the end of human nature is happiness. A ruler, therefore, may not institute laws that have no regard for the common good, because he "fulfils a public role which is itself ordained for the public good, and he is a servant of the commonwealth." Correlatively, no law should be obeyed that disregards the common good.[33]

Natural reason and law have established among the nations that certain rights, rooted in justice, are inviolable. Nature establishes a bond between all men. If principles of just war are applicable to non-Christian peoples, then the basis for justice and peace could not be narrowly "Christian." Human rights violations and justification for going to war are the same for all people everywhere; they are rooted in moral realities that are unchanging and universally applicable. Although we who are perched on the cusp of the twenty-first century can scarcely appreciate how radical this idea was, in Vitoria's day it was nothing short of revolutionary.[34]

Like Vitoria before him, Francisco Suárez taught theology at a leading university of his day.[35] Trained both as a lawyer and a theologian, Suárez addressed the subject of war as did Augustine and Aquinas—as a duty of love. This, along with his belief that the laws of war are binding on all nations, formed the main argument of his treatise on war, which is found in *De Triplici Virtute Theologica, Fide, Spe, et Charitate* (*On the Three Theological Virtues, Faith, Hope, and Charity*), published posthumously in 1621. Subsuming his reflections on war under the rubric of charity, Suárez asked whether war itself is evil, answering that it is both inevitable and not always evil, even when it is utterly susceptible to abuse. He followed Vitoria and previous thinkers in the just war tradition, holding that war is permitted by the natural law and by the gospel, the latter in no way derogating from the natural law.

To understand Suárez's view of war is to understand his view of law and the manner by which human action is meaningfully ordered. In book 2 and chapter 6 of his important work *De Legibus*, Suárez probed a series of interlocking questions in order to illuminate the moral predicates of law. His examination is at once legal and theological: What is the relationship between the dictates of human reason and the natural law? Correlatively, what is the role played by the natural law in discerning good and evil? Is the natural law prescriptive or descriptive in nature? And how are we to understand the execution of human choice, which presupposes moral freedom, over against a transcendent divine law?

Set against the backdrop of contemporary legal and theological debates, Suárez engaged differing opinions of his day. There are those, for example, who asserted that "goodness" and "badness" exist intrinsically in their objects, regardless of whether we wish to ascribe them to a God who is posited as "lawgiver." Others understood the natural law as a mirror of divine command ethics and a manifestation of the divine will. Suárez opted for a middle way, which he took to be "the position of St. Thomas as well as the common position of theologians."[36] Suárez viewed the natural law as both descriptive of good and evil and prescriptive of what is good. He found confirmation that the natural law is "law" in the strictest sense in the fact that mere cognition or beliefs existing in the human mind do not constitute law. To be cognizant of good and evil requires that there exist prior categories of good and evil by which to measure human acts.[37] Suárez insisted that certain behaviors are wrong because of their essential nature and that it is a metaphysical principle that the nature of things is immutable with respect to their essence.[38] Through right reason, human beings experience a consonance or dissonance with respect to the essential morality of human acts.[39]

Suárez's treatment of war began with the classic question: Is war intrinsically evil?[40] He answered: "While war is not evil per se, still on account of the many misfortunes which it brings in its train, it is one of those matters which is often done in an evil manner. And therefore many circumstances are required to make war righteous [justified]."[41]

Nonetheless, according to Suárez two wrong views persist among the religiously minded: (1) that it is intrinsically evil and contrary to charity to engage in war, and (2) that war is specifically forbidden to Christians on the basis of their faith.[42] His response is multifaceted, predicated on the New and the Old Testaments, as well as the teaching of the church fathers. In response to those who argued that war brings unspeakable horrors and even greater potential for evil, he granted that this is possible, but at the same time, he distinguished between a just and an unjust peace. He insisted that war per se is not opposed to peace or to loving one's enemies, because those who engage in a just war hate not people but rather those actions and depravity worthy of just punishment. Just punishment, moreover, does not eliminate forgiveness, since forgiveness is not enjoined in all situations. Punishment, therefore, may be exacted on some occasions without injustice.[43]

Among the conditions cited by Suárez as necessary for war to be just are punitive justice (i.e., righting a wrong) and the declaration thereof by a lawful authority. At the same time, he qualified legitimate authority, saying that while kings exercise sovereignty, that sovereignty is limited and does not extend to any and all parts of the world. The notion, very much alive in Suárez's day, that kings "have the power of avenging injuries done in any part of the world . . . is entirely false, and throws into confusion all the orderly distinctions of jurisdiction."[44] Neither God nor reason grants that sort of power to an individual, according to Suárez. Further, it is unjust to go to war if reparations have been ignored. In fact, if a cause is unjust, Suárez believed that the king's subjects are not compelled to fight.[45] The justness of a cause for going to war must be certain. Suárez, therefore, held that there can exist no objective justification on both sides; otherwise, insufficient cause exists to go to war in the first place. And while most rulers are not willing to submit the justness of a cause to judges for arbitration, Suárez believed this to be the prudent course in order for justness to be thoroughly examined.[46]

Suárez then shifted to the question "What is the proper mode of conducting war?" He understood just punishment as including all losses—human and otherwise—that have occurred throughout the conflict. Once undertaken, however, a war is unjust, according to Suárez, if it does not grant immunity to noncombatants. As far as possible, innocents are to be left untouched, for natural law demands that no one be killed intentionally who in fact is clearly not at fault. Those who do not bear arms are considered, in relative terms, innocent.[47] Suárez supposed that "the innocent can be distinguished from the guilty"; however, it is clear that he did not envision a scenario in which the deaths of innocents could be absolutely avoided.[48]

In his reflections on war, Suárez posed several interlocking questions requiring moral reflection. What is a just cause for war based on natural reason? Correlatively, can a Christian ruler marshal any justification for war apart from the dictates of natural reason? And is it permissible for a nation to punish another nation or people-group on the grounds that God has been (or is being) dishonored?[49] Suárez's overriding concern was the natural law and how states were to conduct themselves. Whereas civil or municipal law is alterable, based on customs and usage, the law of nature is universal and unchanging, governing how human beings as well as nations deal with one another. All aspects of justice flow from this reality. Further—in the footsteps of Vitoria—Suárez extended just war thinking to additional criteria. Aquinas had identified three: just cause, right intention, and sovereign authority. Both Vitoria and Suárez illuminated just war moral reasoning in a manner that implies further conditions—proportionality, last resort, and reasonable chance of success—which derive from the three core *ad bellum* criteria. The latter two criteria are best understood as prudential tests that assist the application of moral principles in particular situations.

Suárez subsumed his treatment of war under the rubrics of charity and the natural law, which, he stressed, are common to Christians and non-Christians. And following Aquinas,[50] he believed that not merely natural justice[51] but also the norm of charity constitutes the proper and primary motivation by which to judge whether participation in war is justifiable. Suárez reflected on war by assuming that the nations comprise an international society. The human race "always preserves a certain . . . moral and political unity," which is "enjoined by the natural precept of mutual love and mercy; a precept which applies to all, even to strangers of every nation."[52] Thus, for Suárez,

> although a given sovereign state, commonwealth, or kingdom may constitute a perfect community in itself, consisting of its own members, nevertheless, each one of these states is also, in

> a certain sense, viewed in relation to the human race, a member of the universal society; for these states when standing alone are never so self-sufficient that they do not require some mutual assistance, association, and intercourse, at times for their own greater welfare and advantage, but at other times because also of some moral necessity or need.[53]

For contemporary readers, to reflect on the ethics of war and peace in the European context five centuries removed is not without its challenges, especially as it concerns the interaction of European and Native American cultures. While the question of the status of peoples beyond the parameters of Christian religion seems archaic, even obtuse, to postmodern sensibilities, for people living in the sixteenth and seventeenth centuries it was profoundly significant. The stereotypical argument assumed today is that European arrival in the New World was accompanied by not only cultural imperialism of the worst kind but also the violation of universal human and political rights. What is often forgotten is the radical and unpopular nature (at the time) of the just war argument as advanced by Vitoria and Suárez—namely, that the moral basis upon which foundational human rights stand extends to all people in all places and at all times.

Hugo Grotius and the Law of Nations

In Hugo Grotius (1583–1645), we encounter a thinker who achieved a high level of erudition at a remarkably young age.[54] A noted classical scholar and disciple of Erasmus who studied at the University of Leiden, Grotius was a jurist, lawyer, statesman, theologian, and prolific author. Perhaps his most noteworthy work was the treatise *De Jure Belli ac Pacis* (*The Law of War and Peace*), published in 1625, which established his reputation as a pioneer in the development of international law.[55]

Grotius's writings mirror the great turbulence of the times in which he lived. The ravages of the Thirty Years War, important geopolitical shifts among the European powers, as well as intense religious controversy together helped shape the contours of Grotius's work, forming the backdrop against which to appreciate his contributions.[56] Grotius was witness to growing controversy in the early seventeenth century between Dutch Huguenots and Arminians, and it can scarcely be overstated how significant this controversy was for his intellectual development. Two of his works, *Ordinum Pietas* and *Remonstrantie* (both published in 1613), were devoted specifically to religious tensions, showing Grotius to be something of a champion of religious tolerance.[57] In his 1622 work *Apologetics*, he argued explicitly for the position that a diversity of religious views allowed for peace. In 1618, Grotius was sentenced to life in prison for his stance on religious tolerance, along with the Dutch statesman Johann Oldenbarnevelt.[58] In 1621, he escaped to France, where he spent the rest of his life in exile.[59]

While most observers concede Grotius's significance to international relations, historians and political philosophers are by no means agreed on precisely how to situate Grotius within the just war tradition.[60] Thomas Pangle and Peter Ahrensdorf, for example, regard Grotius as "the last great representative of the medieval Christian just war tradition."[61] James Turner Johnson, on the other hand, sees Grotius's influence as remarkably innovative to the extent that it "reconceived and recast" just war theory on the basis of the natural law and international norms.[62]

Both interpretations of Grotius doubtless contain a measure of truth. Pangle and Ahrensdorf are not incorrect to suggest that Grotius remained in continuity with classical just war thinking. In fact, Grotius acknowledges his debt to classical foundations (not merely Christian but also Aristotelian and Stoic, as expressed in Cicero and Seneca) both in the *Prolegomena* and throughout *De Jure*. At the same time, Johnson is accurate to observe that Grotius "reconceives and recasts" just war theory in a way that separates him from patristic and medieval theorists, for whom justification for war (represented in *ad bellum* considerations) was of paramount importance. Indeed, the development of *in bello* requirements may well be Grotius's most enduring contribution to the ethics of war and peace,[63] although his painstakingly meticulous development of just and unjust causes on the *ad bellum* side clearly sets his work apart as well.

However scholars choose to parse Grotius's historical position, there is little disagreement over the monumental significance of *De Jure Belli ac Pacis*. Grotius's purpose and vision can be sensed in the title, which represents his attempt to offer the world a "system of natural jurisprudence" as it affects nations' behavior one with another. In this system, one finds a body of moral principles rooted in the natural law that are the common fund of—and thus are applicable to—all nations.[64] The *Prolegomena* or "preliminary discourse" to *De Jure* allows no uncertainty as to the basis for such thinking. Grotius begins the work by describing "that law, which is common to many nations and rulers of nations, whether derived from nature or instituted by divine command or introduced by customs and tacit consent." Understanding the human person as "an animal of a very high order . . . that excels all other species of animals," Grotius notes that what is peculiar to humankind is "the desire of society, that is, a certain inclination to live with those of his own kind, not in any manner whatever, but peaceably, and in a community regulated according to the best of his understanding."[65] Man's innate sociability, we are left to conclude, is in accordance with the law of human "nature," and to honor this moral intuition, in Grotius's view, is wisdom and the use of right reason.[66] Such regulation is impossible apart from the notion of law, which, for Grotius, undergirds every rational and moral activity of human affairs. Thus, the three massive books comprising *De Jure* develop meticulously the interplay between the divine law, the natural law, and the *jus gentium,* the law of nations.

Grotius argued that we are schooled by reason, which finds confirmation in the accumulated wisdom of the ancients. Under divine providence, wisdom and justice are apprehended not only via Christian revelation, which expresses them most fully, but even through the knowledge that Stoics possess.[67] Aside from this interplay of the divine and the human, a great deal of the treatise is devoted to subjects that formally extend beyond "war and peace." So it would seem that for Grotius, the "laws of war and peace" are anchored in the same principles of justice that hold together all domains of civil society.[68] In the fitting words of Pangle and Ehrensdorf, Grotius's treatment of the law of war "thus blossoms at the very outset into a treatise on all the fundamental laws and rights of domestic peace, as well as war, prior to, outside of, as well as within the political society established by the social contract."[69]

A central burden of *De Jure* is to prevent unjust interference among nations—an interference that might subvert or destroy the common good of the human community.[70] This burden is summarized in Grotius's famous statement about the "extremes" in the *Prolegomena*, the work's introduction. One extreme, as he saw it, was to forbid to the Christian all use of coercive force. This, for example, was the position to which people like "our fellow countryman Erasmus" seem to be inclined.[71] On the other hand, the "utter ruthlessness" of aggressive men needs restraint, and such restraint can properly be understood as an exercise in charity.[72] Grotius concluded that justice resided somewhere in the middle: "For both extremes, therefore, a remedy must be found, that men may not believe either that nothing is allowable, or that everything is."[73] Grotius did not write to inquire whether there could possibly be rules to govern war and peace; rather, he intended to identify what those rules are.[74] These rules or norms among the nations were expressions of the natural law and had their source in divine law.[75] Implied in this moral reasoning is that war is unjust and contrary to international law in some cases while just and permissible in others.[76]

Early-modern geopolitical developments, as they are mirrored in *De Jure*, suggest that one of Grotius's enduring contributions is the extension of *jus ad bellum* criteria to *jus in bello* requirements. Medieval construals of just war thinking were based chiefly on Aquinas's three core criteria for prosecuting war—just cause, legitimate authority, and right intention. Thinkers such as Grotius, Vitoria, and Suárez extended the implications of the *ad bellum* criteria to right conduct in war. This is particularly the Grotian burden: universal moral obligation requires man to ensure adequate restraints on war so that greater evils do not arise from war itself. For example, it is never permissible to exact retribution that is disproportionate to the original offense.[77] At the beginning of book 3, which is devoted chiefly to *in bello* considerations, Grotius states what for him is a moral first principle: "In things of a moral nature . . . those means which conduce to a certain end . . . do assume the very nature of that end."[78] For this reason, Grotius painstakingly attempted to specify what means of prosecuting war are just and unjust and to catalog and qualify just and unjust causes of war, which required him to delineate alternatives for avoiding war.

While Grotius acknowledged that the sources that give rise to war are as numerous as those that produce lawsuits, he affirmed the three traditional justifications for war—self-defense, recovery of stolen property, and punishment. But to the traditional justifications, he added a fourth: a perceived threat or danger of injury,[79] suggesting that a party need not wait until after a catastrophe to respond justly.[80] What's more, his understanding of self-defense is significant: the "right" of self-defense arises "directly and immediately" from "the care of our own preservation, which nature recommends to every one, and not [merely] from the injustice or crime of the aggressor."[81] As evidence thereof, Grotius pointed to several scenarios. For instance, if one is attacked by another man or by a wild animal, he may defend himself, just as he might do the same if a madman were to attack him. In the same vein, a soldier who bears arms with good intentions is justified in self-defense. Nature confirms this self-preserving response as proper and just.

Unlawful causes of war, according to Grotius, are multitudinous and thus receive greater discussion than just causes in *De Jure*. Grotius argued that to engage in war without justification is "brutish" and "barbarous." At first glance, some reasons for going to war might appear justified, but these "unjust" rationalizations do not pass muster when they are examined—for example, fear of the neighbor's strength, coveting and self-aggrandizement, the desire to gain political advantage, political marriages, the desire for increased or better lands, the lust for discovery and conquest, differences in social customs or lifestyle, abuse of liberties, the desire to dominate others, or vanity.[82]

But Grotius was not content merely to expose patently unjust causes of war. Those rationalizations that are "dubious" also need identifying. They are as follows: (1) when major players in decision making are not agreed on going to war;[83] (2) when political differences can be arbitrated without coercive force;[84] and (3) when both (opposing) parties claim a just cause, which again points to the need for arbitration.[85]

But what about a situation in which both sides adduce "just cause"? Here Grotius reverted to his legal background, observing that in a lawsuit both parties do not possess legal and moral right to press their case. In other words, justice cannot be served by two contrary pursuits.[86] On occasion, one party may be ignorant of what authentically constitutes justice. Such is the frequent case in judicial matters; neither party is actually "unjust" or "wicked." In such cases where no clear distinction between "just" and "unjust" can be identified in an authoritative sense, Grotius advised that the human reaction must be to forbear and exercise restraint rather than enter into conflict for the common good of the community of nations.[87] In such a case, we are to use our liberty wisely and fear greater evils that might result from war itself.[88]

Although *De Jure* is not thusly organized, Grotius identified six criteria as requisite for the justification (*jus ad bellum*) of war: just cause,[89] sovereign authority,[90] proportionality,[91] reasonable chance of success,[92] last resort,[93] and formal declaration.[94] Grotius met the condition of "right intention," identified by both Augustine and Aquinas, in his meticulous thinking about qualifying the justness of the cause. The decision to go to war can be based only on exceptional conditions. The structure of *De Jure* makes quite clear to the reader that the first three *ad bellum* criteria—just cause, right intention (implied by the severe qualification of just cause), and legitimate authority—constitute the core of Grotius's just war thinking. Only to the extent that these three elements have been met can the behavior of nations, as they enter "dispute by force,"[95] be adjudicated.

The Grotian "innovations" to the just war tradition, by which he extended the implications of just war moral reasoning into the realm of international relations via the natural law, can be readily granted. This appraisal, however, needs moderation insofar as Grotius, from the outset, confessed his debt to classical (including ancient Christian) thinking about war and peace. His justification for war was formulated in continuity with classical just war doctrine, and his moral reasoning was heavily dependent on both pre-Christian philosophical reflection on the character and contours of justice as well as Christian moral thinkers. In his particular repertoire, Aristotle, Cicero, Seneca, Ambrose, and Aquinas seem to have pride of place.[96]

Irrespective of scholars' assessment of Grotius and whether or not we wish to ascribe to him the title "father of international law," his work—and *De Jure* in particular—bestowed a certain dignity and moral status to law and to international relations at a critical time in European history.[97] While he does not envision or seek to advance a secular version of international law, as some might ascribe to him retrospectively,[98] he does nevertheless reckon with a community of nations in which "for the foreseeable future theological differences will be so great and so touchy as to make it urgent to clarify what is demanded of men prior to . . . their higher revealed duties, no matter how the latter are interpreted."[99]

To admit the legitimacy of going to war in some circumstances, as Grotius did, is not to resign oneself to the inevitable, as the cynic or the pacifist might contend. In the concluding chapter of *De Jure*, Grotius admonishes his reader[100] to "preserve faith" and "seek peace," for "by faith . . . not only is every state preserved, but that grand society of all nations is maintained. If this be taken away, says Aristotle rightly, all human correspondence ceases."[101] Moreover, according to Grotius, "it is impossible that we should have a quiet conscience, and a just confidence in the protection of heaven, unless we aim at peace in every thing we do throughout the whole course of a war."[102] To pursue the way of violence, for Grotius, is "brutish" and to be utterly condemned.[103] "War is so horrible," he muses, "that nothing but necessity, or true charity, can make it lawful."[104]

If politics is the wedding of power and morality, as someone has said, then Grotius was a model politician, whose ability to see the wedding of political authority and moral wisdom beckons us nearly four centuries removed. His painstakingly meticulous moral distinctions between "lawful" and unlawful" war, which are rooted in the basic character of justice and typify peaceable societies, are lodged at the very heart of the just war tradition, and they continue to inform us generations later.

8

John Locke

Historians of the just war tradition have paid surprisingly little attention to Locke. But it is not clear why. Locke articulated a theory of just war, aspects of which are both original and historically influential. Moreover, Locke proved extraordinarily dexterous in grounding his arguments. On the one hand, he was the quintessential secular theorist, deriving all his claims from a view of natural rights—the rights of man in a "state of nature." On the other hand, he was quite willing and able to derive claims from scriptural premises as well. And at some points, these two foundations appear seamlessly intertwined.

For instance, on secular grounds it is wrong to harm another in the state of nature, assuming no prior provocation, because "reason" teaches us that all men are equal and independent, according to Locke. On the other hand, he also held that it is wrong because men are "all the workmanship of one omnipotent and infinitely wise maker," a creator God, who sends us into the world "by his order and about his business" without subordinating one man to another or authorizing anyone to harm another.[1] Both accounts supply answers to the same question, and although they are certainly distinct, they are not necessarily incompatible. By affirming them both, Locke appealed to multiple audiences, and this perhaps accounts in large measure for his tremendous influence, even today. Locke's approach was significant because it constituted a unique and compelling manner of construing the just war tradition. Even though Locke built his teaching in part upon scriptural concepts and claims, the overall drift of his argument is secular and derived from his understanding of rights.

Aggression and Just Punishment

Locke's view of rights was evident in his definition of "aggression," the starting point of his just war theory. All men in the state of nature are by right equal and free, according to Locke; however, it is possible to forfeit this natural status if one engages in aggression. The question of what constitutes aggression was thus critical for Locke. In the *Second Treatise*, Locke writes that aggression is any attempt to force a person to part with his life, health, liberty, or possessions without consent.[2] As such it includes acts of murder and attempted murder, as well as lesser crimes such as theft and attempted theft. In fact, for Locke a thief and a murderer are scarcely different, for anyone who tries to rob another by force places his victim in a life-threatening position: "Let [the thief's] pretense be what it will, I have no reason to suppose that he who would take away my liberty would not, when he had me in his power, take away everything else."[3] For Locke, verbal threats against one's life are also acts of aggression, provided they are premeditated enough to be credible. "Force, *or a declared design of force*, upon the person of another" is aggression. And again, it is "declaring *by word or action*, not a passionate and hasty, but a sedate, settled design upon another man's life."[4] Locke views verbal threats as aggression because, as he says, anyone who publicly declares an intent to use force is, in effect, declaring war. It is entirely proper therefore to view such a person as an enemy and a menace to my self-preservation.

Locke's definition of aggression began by focusing on individuals in a state of nature, not upon nations engaged in armed conflict. But the relationship between individuals and nations was, for Locke, very close—so close that in setting out his understanding of aggression in the state of nature, he simultaneously defined aggression at the international level. In this regard, Locke's proviso that all serious threats must be "sedate" and "settled," rather than passionate and hasty, is significant. Locke did not want to suggest, as Hobbes had before him, that the state of nature is invariably warlike. Though in the final analysis Locke agreed with Hobbes that nature is so unstable that violence is often unavoidable, he nevertheless wanted to stress the underlying background of peace.[5]

Locke's theory of just punishment followed logically from his theory of aggression. Everyone in the state of nature has a right to punish aggressors, for without this right the more basic rights of self-preservation, security, and the enjoyment of community would be critically threatened. Aggressors pose a direct threat to these goods and in so doing threaten "the whole species."[6] Locke thus maintained that mankind in general or any person in particular can "restrain" aggressors or even destroy them if necessary. Yet restraint is not the only right of punishment. Locke also endorsed "reparation"—seeking recompense for the damages that aggression has caused. Whoever suffers damages is entitled to seek reparations from the aggressor; and according to Locke, "any other person who finds it just may . . . assist" the injured party until satisfaction has been had. Note that punishment in order either to restrain aggressors or to seek reparation for their crimes is, according to Locke, within the power of every individual in the state of nature. This is, at the international level, equivalent to the right of unilateral action.

However, Locke set limits to the right of punishing. No one is entitled to punish according to his "passionate heats" or according to the "boundless extravagancies of his own will" but only insofar as "calm reason and conscience" dictate.[7] Punishment must be proportional to the crime or, more accurately, to the ultimate purposes of punishment itself. In some cases, the purpose of punishment may be to deter others from committing like crimes. In these instances, punishment may not be proportionate to the individual's crime, but it is limited nonetheless by what is effective to the ends of deterrence. Here, then, is how Locke ultimately states his full doctrine: "Each transgression may be punished to that degree and with so much severity as will suffice to make it an ill bargain to the offender, give him cause to repent, and terrify others from doing the like."[8] In other words, while the right of punishing is inherent to all men in the state of nature, the exercise of the right is limited by the purposes of restraint (and hopefully reform) of the criminal, reparation for damages, and deterrence of similar crimes. When necessary, punishment may go as far as death, especially in cases where aggressors have so abandoned the laws of nature that they become like "savage beast[s]" at war with mankind.[9]

These basic arguments about the character of aggression and the rights of punishment in the state of nature supply, as it were, the foundation for Locke's account of just war. The connection between individuals and states is that states in their relations to one another share some basic characteristics with individuals in nature.[10] Both pursue certain basic goods—property, freedom, security, and community. Both encounter threats and obstacles from others. And neither can present disputes before some commonly agreed upon superior, an arbitrator or judge of some kind, since there is no such superior above them. Of course, individuals are not permanently consigned to this perilous state of affairs. They can flee the inconveniences of nature for the benefits of civil society simply by contracting with one another to establish a sovereign ruler and judge. But not so with states, which, according to Locke, are to remain forever in a state of nature vis-à-vis other states. Or if there is some possibility of escaping this less than desirable condition, Locke chose not to explore it.[11]

Because of the tightness of the analogy between individuals in nature and states in their external relations, Locke offered scant discussion of international aggression or just cause. Rather, he simply employed the language of just and unjust wars, leaving readers to draw the appropriate inferences from his treatment of the state of nature. These inferences seem to be as follows: An unjust war is an act of aggression, the use of force against another state. A just war, by contrast, is one that reacts to aggression. It may be a response to a direct attack or to an attack upon a neighbor; or it may be a response to a "sedate" and "settled" design to use force, a design that has not yet issued in an actual attack but that is thought to be credible enough to constitute aggression itself and thus warrant immediate action. In this case, the just cause would be "preemptive" or "preventative" in nature. Because Locke did not discuss just cause explicitly, it is uncertain that he would have agreed with Grotius that threats must be "imminent" before they warrant a preemptive response. But the thrust of Locke's argument, operating as it does by analogy to the state of nature, suggests that he had a looser set of standards than Grotius—in other words, it seems that for Locke any serious threat *eo ipso* constitutes a violation of the natural law and is thus an adequate justification for war. However that may be, we can say (again by analogy) that the ends or purposes of just war, for Locke, including wars of preemption, must run parallel to the natural ends of punishment. So the ends of war would include restraint of the aggressor state, the hope of reforming its conduct in the future, reparations for damages, and deterrence of other states from imitating the crime. Since these are the ends of war, the deeds of war must be conducive to these ends.[12]

Finally, in Locke's understanding of just cause, state power can never be legitimately used in matters of religion. Defending religious orthodoxy, stamping out heresy, or preventing idolatry are not just causes of war. Indeed, according to Locke such matters are not the concern of the civil magistrate at all, since force fails as a method of bringing about genuine change in people's religious beliefs. Moreover, even if force were conducive to changing beliefs, Locke doubts that such beliefs held only out of fear would be pleasing in the eyes of God and thus useful at all for salvation. Locke set out his arguments for this position in his famous *Letter Concerning Toleration*, owing a strong debt (in spirit if not in fact) to the writings of Martin Luther, Vitoria, and Suárez. Yet Locke was not merely derivative; rather, he wrote as someone who had seen the vast destruction of the Wars of Religion. He thus counseled those who would be tempted by the use force in matters of religion to reflect on "how pernicious a seed of discord and war, how powerful a provocation to endless hatred, rapines and slaughters, they thereby furnish unto mankind."[13] Locke's novelty again lies in the power of his reasoning from a state of nature. Since an individual in the state of nature has no right to use force against another for the purpose of changing religious beliefs, it follows that individuals cannot bestow this power upon governments. Therefore, the use of force in matters of religion is, for Locke, an act of aggression, pure and simple.

Rights of Conquerors

Locke plainly made extensive use of the analogy between individuals and states, but of course the analogy is not perfect. One instance in particular where it breaks down is in the allocation of responsibility for acts of aggression. For example, when an individual commits a crime, the whole individual commits it. Arguments about insanity notwithstanding, we blame or do not blame the entire person. But with states, the situation is obviously quite different. States are composed of many individuals, only some of whom are ever responsible for acts of aggression. Political or military leaders can certainly be blamed, and perhaps soldiers can be blamed as well, although this has been doubted.[14] But when it comes to average citizens, civilians, not everyone is to blame. There are always citizens whose only "crime" was to be resident in a place when an act of aggression was committed.

Although Locke did not draw attention to this point of disanalogy, his overall analysis of war shows great sensitivity to the matter—more sensitivity perhaps than any writer before him. Indeed, the vast majority of Locke's reflections on war come by way of his chapter entitled "Of Conquest," where Locke's concern is to spell out precisely what rights accrue and do not accrue to a state that conquers another state in war. Of course, no rights accrue to conquerors in an unjust war; aggressors may have power on their side but not right. According to Locke, they therefore have "no title to the subjection and obedience of the conquered."[15] But what rights accrue to conquerors over the peoples and places they conquer in a just war? Here Locke's teaching seems at first quite permissive, while in fact it turns out to be exceptionally limiting. Conquerors in a just war have the right to kill and capture enemy combatants. Moreover, because combatants fighting on the unjust side are "aggressors," which is to say, violators of the laws of nature, they necessarily forfeit their rights when they are captured, and thus they can be made into slaves.[16]

So far, Locke's teaching is perhaps shockingly permissive, but he then turns to limitations. First, conquerors have no right to harm or enslave individuals who did not participate in the war. Here Locke shows that he was aware of the breakdown in his analogy between individuals and the state. The innocent cannot be punished, only the participants. Locke distinguishes participants as those "who have actually assisted, concurred, or consented" to the unjust use of force.[17] This is perhaps not as narrow (or as practicable) as we might like. We are not accustomed today to regard the "consenters" to an unjust cause as liable to be punished, unless they took an active role in the planning, or aided and abetted in some way. But even with this qualification, Locke's teaching is far from permissive. Second, Locke maintained, in a decisive break from Vitoria,[18] that conquerors have no right when seeking reparations to seize the property or the possessions of nonparticipants. Third, conquerors have no right to seize the property or possessions even of participants in the conflict, except in order to make reparations for specific damages that were received, and provided that enough remains for any innocent family members such as a wife or children.

Locke admitted that this "will seem a strange doctrine," since it stands so directly at odds with everyday practice.[19] How common for a soldier to lift a watch or a wallet from an enemy he has killed, and yet Locke insisted that this practice must be wrong. Likewise, the state does not steal the possessions of those it incarcerates and keep them for itself. By the same token, if someone is held at gunpoint in the street, he has the right to kill or capture his assailant but not to steal his wallet or demand all his money. That "would be robbery on my side," Locke declares.[20]

Fourth, conquerors have no right at all to the land of the conquered, because the value of land (especially viewed through the lens of Locke's teaching on property, which emphasizes unbounded industry and productivity) will always be greater than any losses a conqueror could have suffered. Land, as Locke explained, can sustain generations upon generations of people in perpetuity. No amount of damage caused by war, not even the loss of many lives, can compare to the value of land.

And finally, Locke maintained that conquerors have no right of dominion over the people they conquer. Though they have the right to kill or enslave the actual participants in the conflict, they have no right to rule over their wives or children. By what right, indeed, could a conqueror deprive an innocent people of self-government? All nonparticipants must remain "free from any subjection," and if their former government is destroyed by the war, they "are at liberty to begin and erect another to themselves."[21] Moreover, should the conqueror choose to make slaves of those who did fight against him, he does not have the right to make slaves of any children who are born in slavery, for the child of a slave is as innocent as those who never took part in the conflict. No doubt, the child would be even more innocent, since he was not alive during the time of the conflict. With this set of arguments, then, Locke exposed the injustice of institutional slavery and of empire building through just wars.[22]

Doubtless, Locke's unique emphasis on the rights of conquerors stems from the broader goals of the *Second Treatise.* Locke's purpose was to defend liberty and private property from the encroachments of absolute monarchs. Because some of Locke's contemporaries had argued that the grounds of absolute kingship in England reach back to the Norman Conquest, Locke was compelled to scrutinize the "rights of conquerors" in that and every conquest more closely than was customary. Yet it is no strike against Locke that his insights arise in part from circumstance. No theorist theorizes in a vacuum. Rather, it is precisely in concrete events that feelings of justice and injustice come alive and give rise to the philosophical enterprise of attempting to explain our moral intuitions.

Resisting Tyrants: Locke versus Aquinas

A close connection between Locke's theoretical outlook and concrete political problems is also evident in his thoughts about combating tyranny in domestic political life. Tyranny, says Locke, is the exercise of power beyond right, power employed for private rather than public advantage. As such, tyranny is not limited to monarchical regimes. Democracies can be tyrannical too, but Locke's anxieties concerned monarchical government in particular, given the context in which he wrote. He contended that a good king allows his power to be limited by law and that where law ends, tyranny begins.

Locke's teaching on what can be done about a tyrant is fascinating to consider alongside the teaching of St. Thomas Aquinas. For this reveals just how far Locke departs from medieval writers in grounding his view upon a distinctly secular conception of natural rights. According to Aquinas, the obstacles to resisting a tyrant were both scriptural and prudential in nature. Scripturally, tyranny is presented as God's wrath upon sinful subjects.[23] And prudentially, "the order of justice requires that subjects obey their superiors, else the stability of human affairs would cease."[24] This does not mean that subjects must obey a tyrant in all things, nor does it mean that tyrants are untouchable. It does mean, however, that such matters must be approached with the utmost circumspection.[25]

In Aquinas, the question of obeying this or that particular command is separate from that of resisting or deposing a tyrant. On the first matter, Aquinas distinguishes usefully between external and internal obedience. While subjects may be bound to obey a ruler in external acts, their souls remain free.[26] Even in external matters, however, Aquinas sets limits: "Man is bound to obey secular princes [only] insofar as this is required by the order of justice. Wherefore, if the prince's authority is not just but usurped, or if he commands what is unjust, his subjects are not bound to obey him, except perhaps accidentally, in order to avoid scandal or danger."[27] This amounts to a doctrine of justified disobedience but not yet a doctrine of resistance.

On the matter of resisting tyrants, Aquinas laid out the following essential considerations:

> The best offense is a good defense, as it were. In other words, governments should be set up so that tyrants are not likely to arise.[28]
>
> Not all tyrants are intolerable. This depends on the extent to which they oppress the people.[29] Of course such oppression is always offensive, but one must consider the possible outcomes of resistance, which are often "more grievous" than the tyranny itself. Attempted resistance may fail and thus enrage the tyrant even more, or it may succeed only to produce new factions and dissensions, or even a new tyrant, harsher than the former.
>
> In the case of excessive tyranny, where virtually nothing can be lost by resisting, the matter should nevertheless proceed institutionally. In other words, private individuals are not advised to depose a tyrant on their own, because such a teaching would likely be exploited by villainous subjects who find all rule burdensome, rather than adopted judiciously by the just. The public, therefore, as well as good rulers would likely be harmed by such a teaching. [Here especially we need to compare Locke.]
>
> The precise institutional options available for resisting a tyrant depend on the constitution. If the tyrant was appointed by the people, then the people can depose him. If he was appointed by a higher authority, then that authority must supply the remedy.
>
> Finally, if no institutional remedy is available, then the only option left is to appeal to God, in other words, to pray that God

> might (a) soften the tyrant's heart or (b) remove him without involving the people in sin. Aquinas cites scriptural precedent for both possibilities.[30]

However, to deserve such a release from the burdens of tyranny, the people must themselves desist from sin. And here Aquinas echoes the teaching of Augustine: "For it is by divine permission that wicked men receive power to rule as a punishment for sin."[31]

For Locke, when a ruler exceeds the authority given him by law and employs his power to the detriment of his subjects, he becomes at that moment and to that extent a tyrant; and it is the right of his subjects to resist him.[32] This seems to approximate Aquinas's teaching fairly closely, even if the language is different. Aquinas taught that to overthrow a tyrant is not sedition but a response to sedition. Locke simply transposed this into the terms of his state of nature: when a tyrant employs unjust force against his people, it is he who is guilty of rebellion or, quite literally, reviving the state of war (*rebellare*).[33] However, the difference between Locke and Aquinas is that for Locke, every subject has the right to decide for himself when the use of force is appropriate. Locke, in other words, elevated the individual right of resistance to the level of absolute right, whereas for Aquinas this depended on the regime type and one's place within it.

Even more striking is the absence in Locke of those key passages of scripture that conditioned the medieval analysis, such as Romans 13: "Let every person be subject to the governing authorities; for there is no authority except from God. . . . [and] whoever resists authority resists what God has appointed"; and 1 Peter 2:18: "Slaves, accept the authority of your masters with all deference, not only those who are kind and gentle, but also those who are harsh." Augustine and Aquinas took their bearings from these passages, as did Martin Luther just a century and a half before Locke. Locke's teaching on resisting tyrants therefore stands out, and the burden of proof would seem to be on him to explain why this radical teaching would not simply undermine political order. If subjects could disobey any command they deem unjust, what is to prevent collapse into anarchy?

Locke anticipated this question, and his reply constitutes an important chapter in the history of liberal political theory, for even though

Locke placed conditions on revolutionary activity, he nevertheless expanded the classical teaching. He argued, first, that force should be opposed to nothing except unjust force. This was his chief limiting condition. Anyone who "makes any opposition in any other case . . . draws on himself just condemnation both from God and man."[34] Second, in most normal cases of domestic politics when a party is injured by some act of government, there are established channels for redress, and wherever some institutional mode of relief exists, force against the government is not justified. Third, even in cases where appeals are blocked and no relief can be had, governments are unlikely to be overthrown, for as long as the injured party is but a minority the bulk of the people will think little of it. As regrettable as this fact is in terms of a principled concern for justice, it remains a reality that works in favor of stable government. And finally, Locke argued, people are in general so disinclined to sacrifice the benefits of civil society that even where injustices extend to great numbers of citizens, revolution is still scarcely a threat. Revolutions are simply too perilous, violent, and difficult to control in all their capricious effects for citizens to engage in them with any regularity or ease. These arguments are meant to show that the right of resisting tyrants will not, under any ordinary circumstances, compromise the structures of government. Compared to Aquinas, Locke is quite radical because he begins with an unqualified right of individuals to resist tyrants and only then considers reasons why this will not, in practice, prove as dangerous as it sounds. Aquinas, by contrast, never grants the right of individuals to resist tyrants.

Locke also differs from Aquinas when it comes to the "appeal to heaven" (cf. the fifth of Aquinas's considerations). In fact, Locke seems to have Aquinas's teaching directly in mind—or else the tradition of scholastic reflection inspired by Aquinas—as he infuses old words with new meaning. Here is Locke:

> Where the body of the people, or any single man, is deprived of their right, or is under the exercise of a power without right, and have no appeal on earth, there they have a liberty to appeal to heaven, whenever they judge the cause of sufficient moment. And therefore, tho' the *people* cannot be *judge*, so as to have by the constitution of that society any superior power, to determine

> and give effective sentence in the case; yet they have, by a law antecedent and paramount to all positive laws of men, reserv'd that ultimate determination to themselves, which belongs to all mankind, where there lies no appeal on earth, viz. to judge whether they have just cause to make their appeal to heaven. And this judgment they cannot part with. . . . God and nature never allowing a man so to abandon himself, as to neglect his own preservation.[35]

The difference is shocking. For Aquinas, the appeal to heaven is a prayerful appeal to God for deliverance from evil, informed as it is by the scripturally grounded assumption that God sends wicked rulers as punishment for sin. The precondition of divine deliverance is, moreover, that the people themselves amend their ways. For Locke, by contrast, the appeal to heaven is a request for God to look favorably on the work about to be done, i.e., on the use of force against the government. This becomes most clear when Locke cites the Old Testament figure of Jephtha as his exemplar.[36] Jephtha's war with the Ammonites commenced with the prayer: "The Lord the judge be judge this day between the children of Israel and the children of Ammon." He then marched his army out for battle.[37]

Locke and Aquinas, then, are a fruitful comparison in order to expose how radical Locke's teaching was. Though they agreed that tyranny is never just and that no one is, therefore, bound to obey the unjust commands of a tyrant (except insofar as prudence dictates), they differed markedly on the right of resistance. In Aquinas, this is a right that is limited to constitutionally instituted bodies, and its exercise is only just if careful thought is given to the likely consequences. In Locke the right is absolute, though consequences are likely to be considered as individuals decide whether to exercise it. Finally, in Locke the scriptural barriers to resistance are overcome by means of the natural rights teaching (ascribed in the quotation above to God himself) that men are not made to abandon their own preservation. Here, as in so many places in Locke, we find the Christian just war tradition subtly reworked to accommodate Locke's secular rights philosophy. Let us reflect, then, on the implications of Locke's secularization of the tradition.

Locke's Secularism: Possibilities and Perils

In Locke, we find a markedly more secular approach to just war thinking than in prior writers—even Vitoria, Suárez, and Grotius, who shared Locke's interest in using nature as a guide to right. Like these thinkers, Locke frequently (though not as frequently) alluded to scriptural passages and theological concepts, but unlike these thinkers, he did so primarily for rhetorical rather than theoretical purposes. Indeed, Locke's whole theory could be presented coherently without recourse to theological grounds, and such a restatement would not alter the conclusions.

In Locke, we also witness the tradition's ongoing process of differentiation. Areas that were left vague or unanalyzed by earlier writers are worked out here with greater care. Thus, for instance, when it comes to the rights and duties of conquerors, Locke's reflections constitute a marked advance. Surely just war writers prior to Locke voiced principles that had implications for the rights and duties of conquerors, but such implications were largely inchoate before Locke's pioneering analysis.

There are both positive and negative implications of recasting the Christian just war tradition into secular terms. On the positive side, with greater secularization the just war framework can be used in more universal contexts and contend more effectively against rival secular theories, such as the theory of balance of power or raison d'état. Moreover, Locke's more secular just war theory refuses to condone wars for the defense of religion, which removes one of the bloodiest, most protracted kinds of war from under the umbrella of justified use of force. Finally, the trend toward greater specification renders the tradition more relevant in practical political life. A theory that cannot tell soldiers how to distinguish between combatants and noncombatants, for example, is one that cannot have much application on a battlefield.

On the negative side, however, secularization produces a less restrictive framework, opening the door to more forms of justified violence than earlier just war writers allowed. Medieval just war writers were constrained by specific passages of scripture (Romans 13:1–7, 1 Peter 2:18, Matthew 5:9, Matthew 5:44, etc.) that had a direct impact on the way just war writers thought about "right intention" in war. Locke, however, never cited these foundational passages and also never discussed right intention. The absence of the passages and the absence of a serious reflection on intention go hand in hand.

For earlier writers, there were also theological concepts that placed limits on the frequency and urgency of war. The sense that we are but pilgrims in a fallen world, that we ourselves are sinners, that we should not insist on our rights, that we should suffer patiently under the powers God has put in place—these notions encouraged a degree of patience and willingness to suffer that is notably absent in Locke. For Locke, the presence of injustice in the world was an outrage. Whether injustice takes the form of international aggression or domestic tyranny, it is utterly unacceptable, and Locke encouraged readers to remedy it whenever and wherever possible. In short, during the transition into the modern age, the Christian framework for making sense of human suffering receded, and suffering became unbearable both for the sufferers and for observers. The impact of Locke's framework over time can perhaps be seen in the increase in what we now call humanitarian interventions, the use of force to stop human suffering. The point is not that anyone wants to suffer or to see others suffer, but rather that without a theological framework for understanding suffering, people feel compelled to put a stop to every instance of it, and this commits nations to a greater use of military force.

A related danger arising from Locke's secularization of just war thinking is that the whole framework becomes less coherent. Because for the medieval writers life on earth was not the *summum bonum* and bodily death was not the *summum malum*, death in war was not viewed as an intolerable evil.[38] If innocents were killed as a side effect of a just war, this was never regarded as the worst thing that could possibly have happened to them. In the Lockean context, however, this view becomes increasingly unacceptable. Our material life becomes more and more important and death seems increasingly final. And with these changes in perspective, war itself becomes harder and harder to justify. In terms of just war theory, the effect of this approach has been to place an increased weight on the *jus in bello* aspect of the theory. But there must come a point at which the modern, Lockean emphasis on individual rights and material well-being will undercut completely the just war framework itself. If every life is so precious that to destroy it means to suffer an immeasurable, unfathomable loss, then war becomes simply impossible to wage, even for the cause of justice. In this event, the *in bello* side of the framework will have completely swallowed the *ad bellum* side, and the result would be either an incoherent just war theory (at best) or no just war theory at all.

Here, then, are two dangers of opposite character that arise as the just war tradition is transposed into the language of secular rights. The first danger is that modern warfare will be more frequent because of the removal of certain scriptural obstacles and religious orientations. The second is that it will become less frequent because of the heightened value that secularists place on human life. That these two dangers pull in opposite directions does not necessarily imply that either one of them is not real. It rather suggests that in the modern era, we become (to the extent that we take our bearings from writers like Locke) much more conflicted about war than our forefathers were. On the one hand, armed conflict is looked upon more favorably than ever as a means of preventing human suffering, while it is frowned upon more than ever for the tragic losses it brings to human life.

9

Immanuel Kant: Beyond Just War?

Although Kant is not properly part of the just war tradition, he stands so close to the tradition while yet departing from it that comparison proves instructive. Moreover, Kant is important in light of the development of international law and organizations in the modern era. Earlier we claimed that the birth of international law owed something substantial to just war writers such as Vitoria, Suárez, Grotius, and Locke, and that the just war tradition indeed merged with international law during the early-modern period. Yet it would be wrong to infer that international norms of war and peace today derive simply from the just war tradition. Certainly some norms reflect such a heritage—for example, the Hague and Geneva Conventions, the Kellogg-Briand Pact, and the Nuremberg Principles, to name only a few—but other norms, particularly those connected with the United Nations Charter, reflect an alien influence, and that is the influence of Kant. The complex story of the entanglement and disentanglement of international law and the just war tradition therefore requires that we pay some attention to this eighteenth-century thinker. How did Kant understand war? Where exactly did he depart from the just war tradition, and why? To what extent can his approach be detected in international laws and organizations today, and what are the implications of this for the fate of the just war tradition going forward?

A Disheartening Conclusion

Kant viewed war as the great international problem. Writing at a time of unparalleled political upheaval,[1] he was alert to the horrors of war—the senseless violence, the tragic loss of life, and the potentially irreparable damage to human community. War indeed stood at odds with some of Kant's most basic convictions—his idea that man exists as "an end in himself, not merely as a means to be arbitrarily used by this or that will"; his belief that to act morally means "to act only on that maxim whereby thou canst at the same time will that it should become a universal law."[2] In practice, war could never live up to such ethical strictures. And yet it was unacceptable, Kant thought, for war to be excused on the grounds of a supposed rift between ethical theory and practice. Rather, such a rift could indicate only one of two things: either that ethical theory is flawed or that the practice of war is unethical. And so the duty of philosophers and policy makers alike is to attempt to harmonize the two spheres (theory and practice), not to perpetuate their divorce.[3]

Still, if war was immoral it was nevertheless a fact of international life, and Kant's first step was to try to understand this basic fact on its own terms. In doing so, he leaned heavily on the work of Thomas Hobbes, who defined war not merely in terms of battle (open hostilities) but also in terms of the very atmosphere in which battles might arise. War existed for Kant and Hobbes alike any time hostility was even conceivable—any time, in other words, that there was "no assurance to the contrary."[4] But how could such an assurance be had? This question led Kant to a rather disheartening conclusion. Peace, it seemed, would be possible only if the nations of the world could be brought together under the governance of law; and this in turn would require some form of union—a world union. Yet this was impossible, Kant foresaw, because such a large union would be too unmanageable and thus insecure. And if it were insecure, then there would still be "no assurance" of peace, and the logic of war would abide. It followed for Kant that the idea of "perpetual peace, the ultimate end of all international right, [was] an idea incapable of realization."[5]

But this was only the beginning of Kant's thoughts on the subject of war and peace. Indeed, his reflections would eventually lead him to reaffirm the possibility of perpetual peace. We can thus divide his thought on this subject into two parts: first, his consideration in the *Metaphysics of Morals* of the rights of war and peace in the world as it currently stands, the world as a "state of war," as it were; next, his consideration in his essay *Perpetual Peace* of the measures that would be requisite to bring about a stable peace. This is a logical, if not a chronological, division of Kant's reflections on war, and it is fascinating to consider each part in relation to the just war tradition. While the first phase will appear more realist than the just war tradition in a number of crucial respects, the second phase will appear more idealist. The just war tradition, then, stands somehow in between the different phases of Kant's thought.

Rights of War in *The Metaphysics of Morals*

Considering the rights of war and peace, Kant first inquired into the rights of states to use their subjects as soldiers in wars. The matter was difficult, Kant thought, because subjects could not be viewed as mere property, like cattle, to be moved hither and thither and slaughtered at will. Kant thus endeavored to place the deployment of soldiers in another light, deriving the practice not from any right on the part of the sovereign but rather from a duty on the part of the subjects: the duty of protecting the state. If subjects could be led to understand and embrace this duty, if they could give their free consent either in person or through their political representatives to every declaration of war, then they would remain self-determining wills rather than becoming instruments of the sovereign; and war could be waged without violating citizens' rights. Kant's famous notion that the only "right" form of constitution is the *Rechtsstaat*, or republic, is implicit in this reasoning. Only in such a state, Kant thought, were individuals treated as free, dignified, and rational beings.

But however just and secure a state may be in itself when it adopts the republican form, its outward relationship toward its neighbors remains one of lawlessness and war. A legitimate "right to make war," therefore, remained a means by which one state might prosecute its rights against another. Since states could not resort to legal proceedings when they perceived some threat or injury from another state, they were entitled to resort to war as the last remedy available. Here again, Kant echoed Hobbes when defining what constitutes a valid threat or injury. An actual act of aggression of course constitutes an injury, but one need not await open aggression. If a neighboring state so much as makes military preparations or even acquires new territory, it is perfectly legitimate to make war on the basis of *jus praeventionis* (the right of preventative attack), according to Kant.[6] Such is the logic of war under the rubric of nature: when the "balance of power" is disturbed, states may go to war. And yet it would be wrong for states to go immediately to war in response to such developments. Rather, according to Kant, they should attempt to settle their disputes first by "peaceful means"—that is, through communication with each other—and they should officially declare war only if and when more peaceful methods of conflict resolution break down. To do otherwise, Kant thought, would constitute a cause of war all its own, for to attack another state before so much as registering a complaint is "similar in form to *starting* a war."[7]

Since the foregoing is, in effect, Kant's account of *jus ad bellum*, we may pause here to consider how his teaching relates to the just war tradition. Kant touches upon familiar topics such as just cause (actual or potential threats), sovereign authority (the people through their representatives), last resort, and declaration. However, two important differences should be stressed. The first is that for Kant, just cause need not consist in an actual "wrong" committed by the opposing side. War may be waged for reasons of expediency—forestalling a problem that, if neglected, could become a threat in the future—markedly separating Kant from the just war tradition, according to which war should be waged only in response to some ethical misconduct, an outright act of aggression, or in the case of preemption, the unmistakable signs of an immediate intent to harm. This is, indeed, the line that separates just war from raison d'état or extreme realism. Kant (following Hobbes) takes a "realist" view of nature and of just cause at this point in his analysis.

Secondly, we note Kant's silence on the topic of "right intention," which was central to traditional accounts of *jus ad bellum*. The reason for the silence is not entirely clear, though one may certainly conjecture that the language of charity that marked discussions of right intention prior to Kant would have been too explicitly Christian for Kant's purposes. Perhaps he thought he needed a religiously neutral, philosophically universal way of discussing right intention, and the closest he would come to that (in this phase of his analysis) was to insist that sovereigns wage war with the good of their citizens in mind. This echoed at least one side of the classical formulation of right intention—all legitimate exercises of political authority must look to the common good and not to the satisfaction of the sovereign's own desires—but it neglected the other side, the love of one's enemy. Kant was evidently, and reasonably, unwilling to assume a relationship of charity between peoples of vastly different cultural backgrounds living in a state of war. Certainly, Kant was resistant to becoming a victim of blind optimism or idealism and was in this sense a realist, looking to human nature as it actually appeared.[8] Of course, Kant was not exclusively realist, and we shall return to the question of right intention later in this chapter, after we examine the full range of his reflections on war.

Kant next turned his attention to *jus in bello*, where he found the terrain especially difficult to map out. How can one speak at all of what is right in war when war is by definition a state of lawlessness—the suspension of all legal or quasi-legal relations? "The only possible solution," Kant thought, "would be to conduct the war in accordance with principles which would still leave states with the *possibility* of abandoning the state of nature in their external relations and of entering a state of right."[9] In other words, one should do nothing in war that might jeopardize the grounds of a future peace. From this general principle, Kant was able to deduce several specific stipulations. Wars should not be conducted as if their purpose were "to punish" the opposing side, for the very notion of punishment implied the relationship of a moral superior and a subject, and no such relationship existed between states in nature. Nor could war be conducted with the purpose of exterminating a people. Such wars could not be forgiven and thus peace would be extremely difficult to recover.[10] Moreover, all acts of a furtive or dishonest nature were illicit in war, since they too would undermine the trust necessary for future peace. For instance, states could not employ spies or prisoners or any type of assassin; nor could they spread false reports or engage in other acts of treachery.

Kant's prohibition of treachery and of procedures such as extermination echo familiar provisions of just war, and Kant even derived these conclusions from a principle that was central to just war thinking since Augustine, if not earlier (the aim of future peace).[11] However, Kant departs markedly from the just war tradition in viewing the various sides of a conflict as moral equals, denying, in other words, that one side might be fighting for justice against another side that has committed a wrong—which is the foundational condition of a just war according to the tradition. The reason for Kant's departure here stems again from the Hobbesian view of nature he adopts and from what we already observed about *jus ad bellum* in such a condition. Where there is no power to hold nations to their promises, promises are not reliable (according to Hobbes), and unreliable promises are not ultimately binding. Therefore, war may be resumed at any time, and the logic of prevention prevails. According to this conception, "just" and "unjust" have no meaning until some sovereign power can ensure that promises be kept. In the meantime, war may be reasonably waged when it seems expedient to do so. The realist tendency of the approach is evident. However, according to the just war tradition, right and wrong and just and unjust do not depend upon the existence of sovereign power to be operative.

Finally, Kant considered the "right which applies *after* a war"—what contemporary theorists label *jus post bellum*. As Locke did before him, Kant found it impermissible for victors to rob and plunder the conquered people, but Kant (unlike Locke) also found it impermissible for victors to claim any compensation for the costs of war. For Locke, war was a matter of justice. It remedied a *moral* wrong. In this sense, Locke is plainly part of the tradition stretching back to St. Augustine. But for Kant, the absence of a sovereign power in international affairs meant that wars were never properly disputes over justice but rather disputes over power, safety, and survival. Victors, according to Kant, "cannot claim compensation for the costs of the war," because "they would then have to pronounce [their] opponent unjust in waging it." But in a violent state of nature, no side can be morally blamed for waging war.

In addition to proscribing the recovery of war costs from the conquered state, Kant offered three more stipulations relating to conduct *post bellum*. First, there should be a peace treaty agreed upon by both sides. Second, all prisoners should be exchanged without ransom. And last, no defeated state could be forced to give up its civil freedom. In other words, defeated states could not be reduced to the status of a colony or have their citizens turned into slaves. Here again, Kant broke sharply from Locke, who allowed that victors in a just war could make slaves of their belligerent foes. Not only did this violate Kant's fundamental point that wars could not be punitive in nature or fought from a stance of moral superiority, but it also violated his teaching about the inherent dignity of man: no rational creature can be reduced merely to a means, a tool, to be manipulated by the will of other men.

Following Kant's discussion of the "rights of war" in the *Metaphysics of Morals*, Kant remarks briefly on the "rights of peace." The rights of peace, as Kant describes them, include the right to remain at peace when neighbors go to war. In other words, no state can coerce another state to break its neutrality.[12] The rights of peace also include the right to seek some guarantee that peace will be maintained once it is concluded and the right to form alliances or confederate leagues for communal defense. But here lay the problem with which Kant began—the "disheartening conclusion" referred to above. What could possibly constitute an adequate "guarantee" that peace would be maintained? Again, without some kind of world government, organized to adjudicate international disputes and equipped with sufficient power to implement its judgments, what guarantee could there be except the unreliable words of the opposing side? And yet "covenants without swords," as Thomas Hobbes wrote, "are but words, and of no strength to secure a man at all."[13] There seemed to be no hope for perpetual peace among nations, each with its own autonomy and power.

A Plan for Perpetual Peace

Kant attempted to solve this problem in an essay of 1795 entitled *Perpetual Peace: A Philosophical Sketch*. He began by accepting two basic facts. The first was that the fundamental character of human beings could not be changed. In other words, the prospects for perpetual peace could not be made to hinge upon some longed-for transformation of humans into peace-loving, peace-promoting creatures.[14] Second, Kant accepted the fact that the established system of free, sovereign states (the Westphalian system) was here to stay. Sovereign power could neither vanish altogether nor be ceded into the hands of some "world government" that was expected to rule the globe. The latter notion was particularly abhorrent to Kant. A world government—even *if* it could come into being—would almost certainly cause more problems than it was designed to remedy. Either it would prove incapable of governing so vast a territory with the alertness and sensitivity governance requires, or it would so streamline and centralize political power that it would become a dreaded despotism, a death knell to the very liberty and peace Kant desired.[15] Kant's solution would thus have to proceed by some other course than the one leading to world government.

The course finally offered by Kant was not one to be followed quickly. He thought the process would take centuries at the very least. In fact, he was not even sure it was possible. But he did operate on the basis of a philosophically grounded hope that it was possible. The possibility of perpetual peace could not be demonstrated, according to Kant, by observing nature. Nothing in the particular deeds of states or the relations among them suggested that perpetual peace was likely. But, Kant insisted, "it [is] our duty to promote it,"[16] because while the possibility of perpetual peace could not be proved, its impossibility could not be proven either. And in such cases, Kant argued, it is reasonable for a person "to ask whether it is *in his interest to assume* one or the other possibility as a hypothesis." Kant continued:

> [We *can*] have a duty to act in accordance with the idea of such an end, even if there is not the slightest theoretical probability of its realization, provided that there is no means of demonstrating that it cannot be realized. Now, moral-practical reason within us pronounces the following irresistible veto: *There shall be no war.* . . . For war is not the way in which anyone should pursue his rights. Thus it is no longer a question of whether perpetual peace is really possible or not, or whether we are not perhaps mistaken in our theoretical judgment if we assume that it is. On the contrary, we must simply act as if it could really come about (which is perhaps impossible), and turn our efforts towards realizing it. . . . And even if the fulfillment of this pacific intention were forever to remain a pious hope, we should still not be deceiving ourselves if we made it our maxim to work unceasingly towards it, for it is our duty to do so. To assume, on the other hand, that the moral law within us might be misleading, would give rise to the execrable wish to dispense with all reason and to regard our-

> selves, along with our principles, as subject to the same mechanism of nature as the other animal species.[17]

Reason pronounces a veto—*no war!*—and our duty is to act in accordance with the dictates of reason. Was Kant the victim of "blind optimism" after all? Not exactly. His position was not quite optimistic, because Kant didn't believe unequivocally that perpetual peace could be reached.[18] Nor was it blind, because Kant knew precisely what evidence could (and could not) be adduced in support of his hope. We shall say more below about Kant's understanding of "Providence," which also played a role here. But if he was not a blind optimist he was certainly unwilling to allow the weight of the past or doubts about the future to deter him from actively pursuing a more ethical world.

In his essay *Perpetual Peace*, Kant offers a series of "articles," in the form of a treaty, that detail some of the conditions that must be met for perpetual peace to be possible.[19] Kant divides the articles into two sections: six "preliminary articles" and three "definitive articles." They can be summarized as follows.

Preliminary Articles: Peace treaties are not valid if they contain secret reservations supplying material for a future war. No independent state (large or small) can be acquired by another state through inheritance, exchange, purchase, or gift. Standing armies will gradually be abolished altogether. No national debt can be contracted in connection with foreign affairs. No state shall forcibly interfere in the constitution and government of another state. Finally, no acts are allowable in war that would make mutual confidence impossible during a future time of peace. *Definitive Articles*: The civil constitution of every state shall be republican. The rights of nations shall be based on a federation of free states. And cosmopolitan rights shall be limited to conditions of universal hospitality.

We limit our remarks here to the first two definitive articles, which are by far the most important. Why did Kant suppose that the civil constitution of every state must be republican before world peace could be secure? There were two reasons. First, the republican constitution, wherein the legislative power was distinct from the executive power and whereby the people were represented in the legislature, was according to Kant the only constitution compatible with the principles of freedom and right. Consequently, all other constitutions would be unstable and possibly violent. Thus, before perpetual peace could be secure, all states must attain to a rightful and stable constitution.[20] Second, Kant thought that republican states were less likely to make war than other types of regimes because of the role the people would play:

> If, as is inevitably the case under this constitution, the consent of the citizens is required to decide whether or not war is to be declared, it is very natural that they will have great hesitation in embarking on so dangerous an enterprise. For this would mean calling down on themselves all the miseries of war, such as doing the fighting themselves, supplying the costs of war from their own resources, painfully making good the ensuing devastation, and, as the crowning evil, having to take upon themselves a burden of debt which will embitter peace itself and which can never be paid off on account of the constant threat of new wars.[21]

Kant thus thought that regimes in which the people had a significant role to play in deciding whether or not to go to war would be more pacific. This hypothesis was certainly contestable, as anyone familiar with the history of ancient Athens might recognize. But Kant was quite confident in its probability, at least in the modern context, and he has turned out to be remarkably prescient. In fact, Kant's argument has supplied the cornerstone for the modern theory (bordering on a law) that no two democracies will ever wage war against one another. Known today as the "democratic peace proposition," this theory maintains not that democracies will always see eye to eye, or that they will never find themselves on the brink of war; it maintains only that they will never cross over the brink. Of course, the theory has had its critics; but it has also proved remarkably robust upon empirical testing.[22] Moreover, this Kantian-inspired claim is precisely what has fueled the enormous effort to promote the spread of democratic governments around the world. Transition to democracy (or to "republicanism" in Kant's terms) is thought to be intrinsically good for the countries involved but also good for all existing democratic nations, since the whole international system will become more peaceful.

Kant's second definitive article—the federation of free states—has been equally influential, and we shall discuss its role in the creation of the United Nations below. Let us here consider this article in relation to the problem Kant faced at the outset of his theorizing. When Kant confronted the problem of finding a "guarantee" for international security in the *Metaphysics of Morals*, his mind (we recall) alighted upon the idea of a "world union." Yet Kant quickly rejected that idea as untenable and dangerous. The question one must ask, then, of Kant's "federation of free states" is whether it solves the original problem while avoiding the anticipated dangers of a world union. This is not an easy question to answer. The federation Kant envisaged was not to have sovereign authority over states. It was not a world government but an international organization. But could anything less than a world government supply the kind of guarantee Kant was looking for? A federation of autonomous states, as Kant describes it, has no direct means of enforcing the rule of international law. The laws and norms it ostensibly "guarantees" must be voluntarily observed, and this does not seem an adequate guarantee at all. Kant thus seems to have anticipated a change in the moral character of states if not of human nature: states would need to become voluntarily law-abiding and willing (where they were not before) to accept an imperfect guarantee that other states would abide by their word. What—we may wonder—could have been the basis of Kant's belief that such a change could occur?

The answer is supplied by Kant himself. He thought that "Providence" or "Nature" would make all the necessary changes. Of course, Providence was a religious concept, but in the context of *Perpetual Peace* Kant was anxious to stay within the bounds of human reason, not to presuppose any theoretical knowledge of transcendental affairs. In other words, Kant claimed no precise knowledge of why, how, or when perpetual peace would be achieved, or even that it would be achieved. He merely claimed that the history of human interaction pointed in the direction of perpetual peace insofar as discord could be seen constantly turning into concord (even by means of the most unlikely mechanisms), as if this were directed by some purposive plan. The examples Kant supplied were as follows. First, while peoples were once radically dissociated because of war, such that every corner of the earth was inhabited by different isolated groups, people have gradually been compelled back into relationships through commerce owing to the difficulty of sustaining life on the basis of local resources alone. Thus did nature will a degree of concord. She made humans relate peaceably, as Kant says, "whether we [were] willing to or not."[23] Second, the formation of political associations (states) suggests something similar. Human beings are by nature unruly and selfish, and yet they are forced to modify their individual behavior in order to form collective unions—namely, states governed by law because internal strife and external threats have led humans to see that their self-interest actually requires collective agreement. And finally, the case of states in the international realm suggests a similar plan. The selfish desire of every state is to dominate the whole world in order to bring about peace on its own terms. "But nature," writes Kant, "wills it otherwise." In the first place, linguistic and religious differences make it virtually impossible for the whole world to be brought under one single rule. Thus, nature constantly frustrates the megalomaniacal pretensions of despots. Then the need for commerce makes it virtually impossible for states to withdraw completely from one another's company. And, writes Kant, the "spirit of commerce . . . cannot exist side by side with war."

> Thus States find themselves compelled to promote the noble cause of peace, though not exactly from motives of morality. And wherever in the world there is a threat of war breaking out, they will try to prevent it by mediation, just as if they had entered into a permanent league for this purpose. . . . In this way, nature *guarantees* perpetual peace by the actual mechanism of human inclinations.[24]

Whether one is convinced by Kant's "guarantee" of perpetual peace or not, this was the form it took. In the next section, we discuss the extent to which this vague but inspiring guarantee has led to modern-day efforts to form international leagues and organizations. But before turning to that topic, we will pause to reflect on Kant's relationship to the just war tradition. To what extent is he in keeping with that tradition?

How one answers this question certainly depends upon which part of Kant's thinking one considers. On the one hand, there are places (especially in the *Metaphysics of Morals*) where Kant's teaching overlaps with just war principles, and this has led some scholars to situate him squarely within the tradition.[25] On the other hand, aspects of Kant's general approach to the matter of war seem to place him well outside the tradition. Kant's very definition of war, which he appropriated from Hobbes—war exists whenever conflict is possible, whenever there is no assurance to the contrary—is exactly the sort of outlook the just war tradition rejects. It in effect turns the state of nature into a permanent state of war, whereas the just war thinkers thought it possible to distinguish between states of war and peace, even in nature. This fundamental difference has implications, as we have seen, for the matter of just cause. If, as Kant thought, all international relations were more or less a state of war (absent some guarantee to the contrary), then war was more or less justifiable all the time. States did not need to wait upon an act of aggression. They could strike other states whenever they deemed this vital to their security. Again, this was not what the just war tradition maintained. Although there was (and remains) a case for preemption in the just war tradition, this was never intended to extend as far as Kant (following Hobbes, who followed Machiavelli[26]) extended it. The doctrine was always limited by some notion of "imminent danger," such as we saw in our treatment of Grotius.

Here, however, we discover not only where Kant departed from the just war tradition but also *why* he departed. Kant saw that the problem of international security led inevitably to the problem of anticipation (attacking before a presumed enemy becomes strong enough to threaten one's security) and that this in turn led to an ever-widening case for war. Kant rejected the just war approach, in other words, because he thought that one of the fundamental assumptions of the just war tradition—namely, that war could be limited by placing ethical constraints upon the actors (states)—was simply naive. The logic of security would lead states to place action above restraint every time. This is no doubt why Kant took a famous swipe at three of the best-known just war writers of the early-modern period—Hugo Grotius, Samuel von Pufendorf, and Emmerich de Vattel. "There is no instance," wrote Kant, "of a state ever having been moved to desist from its purpose by arguments supported by the testimonies of such notable men." On the contrary, observed Kant, these theorists are "dutifully quoted in *justification* of military aggression."[27] They are thus "sorry comforters all" because they write about the ethical limitations of war but have no ability whatever to ameliorate the condition of war as it actually is. Kant departed from the just war tradition, then, because he thought the problem of continual warfare required some solution the tradition had not offered and could not offer. As we have seen, Kant's attempt at a solution involved specifying the steps that would be logically and practically requisite for perpetual peace to come about. And it involved looking to Providence to take care of the overwhelming difficulty of the thing. Providence could accomplish what no individual or state ever intended to accomplish.

In Kant's intriguing reliance on Providence, we find another crucial difference between Kant and the just war tradition. The just war writers placed an enormous emphasis upon the *intention* of actors engaged in warfare. For a war to be just, the intention of the belligerents (both in going to war and in the midst of war) had to be benevolent. But, as we observed above, Kant skirted the matter of intention in his treatment of war in the *Metaphysics of Morals*, the text in which he addressed various categories of *jus ad bellum* and *jus in bello* most directly. Kant did not think that the intention of actors was a necessary or sufficient condition for the promotion of peace. Intention was no doubt significant from a moral point of view for Kant. Virtually his whole moral theory turns on the intention (or maxim) of the ethical actor. But in Kant's theory of international politics, intention could play no part, because actors could not be relied upon to be ethical in sufficient numbers, and states could not be expected to place moral scruples above national security. Thus, Providence would play the role that individual intention could not. Human beings, both individually and collectively, would remain what they were—selfish according to nature and moral according to reason. But Providence would ensure that even such selfish creatures might act unwittingly to bring about perpetual peace. Peace would be built on our selfishness, not on our better self.

Finally, we can sum up the foregoing reflections by describing what must be the root difference between Kant and the just war tradition as it was classically articulated. The root difference resides not in Kant's teaching but in the question or problem with which he was primarily concerned. The question the just war writers put to themselves was not how to stop war or even how to limit it but rather how to ensure that while engaging in war one did not sin or commit unjust deeds. The just war tradition took for granted that war would be a permanent feature of human existence on earth. Kant, by contrast, asked a different set of questions. He wanted to know how and why something as abundantly unethical as war could occur, and he wanted to know how it might be made to stop. Only in this context do his writings on war become intelligible. He does not in fact instruct readers on the ethics of war. He explains, on the one hand (in *The Metaphysics of Morals*), how war is logical under present conditions for those who engage in it and, on the other hand (in *Perpetual Peace*), how war will eventually cease, if it will ever cease at all.

Kant's emphasis on limiting and hopefully stopping war has had a marked impact on the way political theorists write about war today. Even among contemporary scholars, the just war tradition is often presented as if its goal was not the avoidance of sin (or unethical action) but rather the prevention of war. And critics have tended to praise or blame the tradition according to the extent to which it is supposed to have succeeded or failed in this somewhat alien goal.[28] Such in part has been the influence of Kant. The other aspect of Kant's enormous influence relates to the practice of international relations; and it is to this that we now turn.

Kant and the United Nations

The United Nations is sometimes described today as a Kantian institution—a deliberate attempt to pursue Kant's dream of perpetual peace by means of the definitive articles Kant outlined.[29] There is certainly evidence for this view, as we shall see. But if it is accurate, and if the United Nations in fact represents the ideal federation of free and autonomous states Kant envisaged, then the implications for the just war tradition in the twenty-first century would be enormous. Kant appears to have thought that the just war tradition would become obsolete, that it would be replaced by a system of international legal norms backed by some adequate guarantee of mutual observance. Although the United Nations does show some manifestations of Kant's influence, there is ample reason to doubt it is or ever will be the international body Kant himself imagined: first, because the UN is not composed of the proper constituent parts, and second, because it does not supply the kind of guarantee Kant himself thought necessary. So long as this is the case, Kant's hopes remain a dream, and the just war tradition remains a viable (if not the only viable) framework for thinking ethically about war.

In many ways, the United Nations is less a Kantian institution than its predecessor, the League of Nations. Established by the Treaty of Versailles in 1919–1920, the League of Nations enshrined the principle of "collective security." A sharp departure from the collective defense arrangements of the past, the collective security system was to focus its attention inward as well as outward. Members of the league would agree not merely to combine forces against external foes but also to combine forces against internal members who violated the covenant of peace. The Covenant of the League of Nations itself reads like a paraphrase of Kant's articles for perpetual peace. Members were obligated not to resort to war in their disputes prior to submitting their cases to arbitration or judicial settlement; they were required to maintain "open, just and honorable relations" and to reduce their "national armaments to the lowest point consistent with national safety and the enforcement by common action of international obligations." The penalty for violating the covenant was to be a group penalty: "the severance of all trade or financial relations, the prohibition of all intercourse [with] the nationals of the covenant-breaking state, and the prevention of all financial, commercial or personal intercourse between the nationals of the covenant-breaking state and the nationals of any other state, whether a member of the league or not."[30]

However, as thoroughly Kantian as this all sounds, the league was not completely in tune with Kant's ideas, and it failed in practice to secure peace among the members of the league. Perhaps its most significant departure from Kant's articles concerned the character of the member states. Kant was emphatic that members of the league must have republican constitutions so they would be less likely to initiate wars and would share a common set of values. This was disregarded, however, when the League of Nations admitted such countries as Nazi Germany and Stalinist Russia as members. With such a diverse body of states (and cultural values) and with the requirement that all enforcement measures be backed by unanimous approval in the council and the league assembly, it is no surprise that the league proved unable to respond to the international crises it faced. When the French occupied the Ruhr valley in Germany in 1923, the league could do nothing. Nor could it respond to the Japanese invasion of Manchuria in 1931 or to

Italy's invasion of Ethiopia in 1935. By the end of the 1930s when Japanese, Italian, and German aggression had led to the start of World War II, it was clear the league had failed in its basic purpose of preventing world war.

The United Nations, like its predecessor, was built upon Kantian hopes of securing a more peaceful world, and it too has exhibited strong Kantian leanings since its inception in 1945. To read the Charter of the United Nations is to conceive an organization that would blend the Kantian articles of peace with a host of other liberal principles, including the protection of human rights, the affirmation of gender equality, and the pursuit of social progress.[31] The maintenance of international peace and security was, according to article 1 of the charter, the organization's leading purpose. And (following Kant) the charter explicitly acknowledged the principle that all member states were equal as sovereign bodies. In other words, the organization was not to "intervene in matters which [were] essentially within the domestic jurisdiction of any state." By the same token, all members were to refrain from the "threat or use of force against the territorial integrity or political independence of any state."[32]

Learning from the failings of the League of Nations, the United Nations Charter also included unprecedented powers of enforcement. According to chapter 7, the organization had the right to employ "all necessary measures" to guarantee that the members did not violate their obligations. Not only diplomatic measures but also economic sanctions and overwhelming military force were to be within its power. As for troops and equipment, these were to come from the member states.

But despite all good intentions, the United Nations was not—in theory or in practice—the kind of organization upon which Kant himself could have pinned his hopes for peace. One reason had to do with the membership of the organization, which from the start included nondemocratic states. The other even more serious reason relates to the way the organization evolved over time.

The membership of the United Nations was never intended to be limited to states with republican constitutions. Rather, Franklin Roosevelt's idea was to construct the organization around the so-called four policemen—the United States, China, the Soviet Union, and the United Kingdom. Membership was to include all fifty states that participated in the United Nations Conference on International Organization held in San Francisco in 1945 (plus Poland, which was unable to attend), and beyond that it could be extended to "all peace-loving states."[33] Among the fifty-one original members were many nonrepublican states, including the Soviet Union, China, Cuba, Iraq, and Iran. The decision to extend membership to as many states as possible stemmed from the political needs of the time. By extending membership as broadly as possible, the United Nations stood to gain worldwide legitimacy, greater financial resources, and greater human resources, all the while lessening the threat that the organization might otherwise pose to wary non-Westerners. What it could not do, however, was fulfill Kant's first definitive article of perpetual peace, that the constitution of all states be republican in form. By 2011, with the addition of Montenegro in 2006, there were 192 United Nations member states, including virtually all internationally recognized independent states.[34]

As the United Nations evolved over time, though, it quickly became clear that the issue of membership was not the only difference separating it from the federation that Kant envisioned. In practice, the organization had difficulties from the start ensuring collective security. Unlike the League of Nations, which wisely prohibited parties in a dispute from voting in their own case, the United Nations allowed this practice. And "when coupled with the veto," notes UN scholar Jerry Pubanz, "this means that a permanent member of the Security Council can block UN action, largely excluding itself from the sanctions of collective security."[35] Moreover, because *all* the enforcement mechanisms granted under chapter 7 of the charter required the unanimity of the permanent members on the Security Council, it was virtually impossible from the start for the UN to act decisively.

Because of these problems and others, the organization has gradually come to focus less on collective security and more on other activities such as democratization efforts, the protection of human rights, and peacekeeping missions. And since these activities often prove incompatible with the Kantian prohibition on interfering in the internal affairs of sovereign states—a prohibition echoed in the UN Charter but increasingly viewed as obsolete—UN leaders have explicitly abandoned the institution's Kantian roots. A quotation from Secretary-General Kofi Annan's Millennium Summit Report of 2000 is much to the point:

> Even though the United Nations is an organization of states, the Charter is written in the name of "We the peoples. . . ." We confront a real dilemma. Few would disagree that both the defense of humanity and the defense of sovereignty are principles that must be supported. Alas, that does not tell us which principle should prevail when they are in conflict. Humanitarian intervention is a sensitive issue, fraught with political difficulty and not susceptible to easy answers. But surely no legal principle—not even sovereignty—can ever shield crimes against humanity. Where such crimes occur and peaceful attempts to halt them have been exhausted, the Security Council has a moral duty to act on behalf of the international community.[36]

Of course, humanitarian interventions, peacekeeping, and the attempt to convert weak states into functioning democracies may be more or less laudable activities. But they do require the UN to violate the sovereign integrity of member states, and when these activities come at the expense of the UN's primary function of preventing international conflict, something has gone wrong. We are no longer dealing with an organization that can supply the kind of "guarantee" Kant knew to be necessary if nations were to abandon the state of war.[37]

For many observers, the decisive failure of the United Nations came in 2002 as the United States and Britain pressed the organization to enforce its own Security Council resolutions against Iraq. Iraq had been in material breach of numerous Security Council resolutions reaching back to the end of the first Gulf War. On this point, the United Nations as a body agreed. Iraq had *not* demonstrated to the world that it had disarmed by cooperating fully with weapons inspectors, as it was required to do under Resolution 687. And a resolution (678) passed on November 29, 1990, had authorized member states to "use all necessary means to uphold and implement subsequent resolutions concerning Iraq." Legal debates raged in 2002 over the legality of individual member states employing military force against Iraq without first securing approval from the UN Security Council. But what was crucial was not the question of legality but rather the fact that the UN had failed to make member states such as the United States and the United Kingdom feel secure. Moreover, members felt insecure precisely because the UN was failing (in Kantian terms) to *guarantee* that states fulfill their promises and obligations. Thus, on September 12, 2002, President Bush posed the following question in a speech to the UN: "Are Security Council resolutions to be honored and enforced, or cast aside without consequence? Will the United Nations serve the purpose of its founding, or will it be irrelevant?"

Just as controversy raged over the question whether a single member country could take military action against Iraq, controversy also raged over the legality of preemptive military strikes, given the absence of this right in the UN Charter. (Article 51 provides only for "the inherent right of individual or collective self-defense if an armed attack occurs.") But again, the debate over legality tended to obscure the real issue at stake. When the leading international organization whose purpose is to secure its members from attack and to ensure that members live up to their promises fails in its most basic function, then the international environment is no longer one of *legal* relations properly speaking.[38] It is, in Kant's own terms, a state of war in which each state must act to secure its own safety as best it can. That the language of "preemption" surfaced so forcefully in 2003 was itself proof that states were reverting to the logic of war Kant had so carefully analyzed in the *Metaphysics of Morals.*

This brings us back to the question of the relevance of the just war tradition today. When legal relations cease to exist among states because there is no power reliable enough to guarantee them, we find ourselves back in the environment that gave rise to the just war tradition in the first place. Although just war teachings can be written down in legal codes, the tradition is not primarily a legal one; it is a tradition of moral reflection and practical reasoning.[39] As such, its salience never fades away. It supplies the criteria by which international laws and customs relating to war can be judged. And when the laws and customs themselves are thrown into confusion, it represents one of the only tools we have for bringing human conflict into the sphere of morality.

10

Contemporary Just War Thinkers

Although the just war tradition was absorbed during the early-modern period of European history into the emerging institutions and practices of international law, the process of absorption was far from perfect. Not only were alien influences often in play, such as the philosophical idealism of Immanuel Kant discussed in the previous chapter, but also, even where international law stayed true to just war ideas, it necessarily failed to capture the breadth and depth of those ideas as they emerged from the tradition itself. International law—while its advantages cannot be gainsaid—nevertheless has disadvantages when compared to the rich tradition of just war thinking. It replaces the open-ended quality of moral reflection with a more or less closed system of rules in which improvement is possible but laborious. It limits itself to consideration of what is enforceable rather than what is morally right. And it speaks in tones of metaphysical neutrality that, while no doubt useful for crossing cultural boundaries, is virtually unintelligible as a language of moral reflection.

Misgivings such as these are thematic in the writings of twentieth-century just war thinkers, who recovered the tradition afresh in order to guide thought on such newly emerging issues as nuclear deterrence, military intervention, and terrorism. These thinkers aimed at redressing lacunae in the law, viewing it as too permissive in some areas and too restrictive in others. They also aimed at resisting ideological distortions about war both in the church and in the culture at large. Thus, they wrote for multiple audiences and in markedly different ways, even though they constituted a single, coherent attempt to reintroduce the tradition of just war reflection in the modern age. In this chapter, we explore the work of five such thinkers: John Courtney Murray, Michael Walzer, William V. O'Brien, James Turner Johnson, and Jean Bethke Elshtain.

The Theological Approach of John Courtney Murray

Following World War II, Roman Catholic theologian John Courtney Murray (1904–1967) was one of the few writers to argue for the continued relevance of just war principles as articulated not in international law but in the Christian tradition. Despite the proliferation of nuclear weapons and modern warfare's inherent capacity for mass destruction, Murray still believed that the tradition could assist citizens and statesmen in reasoning about military force. In his classic *We Hold These Truths* as well as in *Morality and Modern Warfare*, Murray conversed with theologians and policy makers, attentive to Christian faith on the one hand and responsible statecraft on the other.[1]

As Murray saw it, the development of modern weapons of mass destruction gave new urgency to the moral problem of war in the 1950s. For many religious thinkers, the possibility of annihilating the human race seemed to require absolute pacifism. Murray, however, reckoned with this scenario as well as the threats of totalitarianism that made possible the political enslavement of human beings. Totalitarianism, he argued, required in principle some form of coercive response.

"There are three distinct standpoints from which it is possible to launch a discussion of the problem of war in this strange and perilous age of ours that has yet to find its name," Murray wrote in *We Hold These Truths*.[2] The first, held by many of Murray's contemporaries (and ours), is that the new potential of modern weaponry for destruction and ruin is so great that it becomes absurd to suppose modern war will be "limited" in any morally acceptable way. Therefore, it can never be justified.

According to Murray, this position in its "most respectable form" may be called "relative Christian pacifism." Relative pacifists, he observed, "are content to affirm that war has *now* become an evil that may no longer be justified, given the fact that no adequate justification can be offered for the ruinous effects of today's weapons of war."[3] However, Murray cautioned that this position did not conform to the church's historic teaching.

The second perspective, predicated upon the need to recognize in Soviet power the gravest menace to Western culture, was a secular version of "holy war" or preventive war as justifiable in the service of preserving human civilization, since the enemy was "completely unprincipled." The temptation was thus to "jettison the tradition of civilized warfare and be prepared to use any means that promises success."[4] But this conclusion, with its premises, was likewise out of step with the just war tradition and therefore unacceptable to Murray.[5]

The third approach was to put faith in the United Nations as an international organization committed by its very charter to peace. The "validity of war," it seemed, had now vanished, given the commitment of such an organization to preside over potential and actual conflicts.[6] But this viewpoint, too, struck Murray as erroneous, since the United Nations was not "a juridical organization with adequate legal authority to govern in the international community." It was "basically a power-organization," whose decisions were "natively apt to sanction injustice as well as justice." And "[i]t is not at all clear that the United Nations in its present stage of development will be able to cope justly and effectively with the underlying causes of international conflict today or with the particular cases of conflict that may arise [tomorrow]."[7]

If one adopts any of these perspectives, Murray concluded, "one will not find one's way to an integral and morally defensible position on the problem of war."[8] While all three are to be taken seriously, they are morally as well as politically deficient. Exacerbating this problem, as Murray saw it, were our cultural doubts about moral reasoning in general, the belief that there is no common "norm recognized by all as morally obligatory and therefore inviolable." But Murray was quick to counsel his readers to avoid "moral simplism," "moral skepticism," and "a flight to moral ambiguism," especially on matters of international conflict.[9] He believed instead that an informed response to the three viewpoints—

and the vexing issues they raised—was imperative: "If these questions are not carefully answered, one will have no standard against which to match the evils of war. And terror, rather than reason, will command one's judgments on the military problem."[10]

Murray's overall response began with two basic assumptions, which formed the cornerstones of his just war approach. First, the problem of war is ultimately one of "social morality." War, of course, involves power, but human beings should decide how power and morality ought to be linked to produce responsible policy. For this reason, coercive force can never be proscribed, nor can it be always prescribed. Prudence and moral discernment must be wed to political power. But it is wrong-headed and derelict to believe that individual states had no *right* to consider war. As Murray observed, "The use of force is not now a moral means for the redress of violated legal rights. The justness of the cause is irrelevant; there simply is no longer a right of self-redress; no individual state may presume to take even the cause of justice into its own hands."[11] Consequently, Murray articulated his second rudimentary assumption: going to war to repress injustice is morally admissible both in principle and in practice. Furthermore, the moral tradition of just war is deep and rich, recommending itself once again in the modern era. Here Murray gives voice to our overarching thesis that the just war tradition supplies a rich storehouse of terms, principles, and moral distinctions without which we could not reason ethically about war.

Murray next found it useful to reaffirm the church's teaching by spelling out the basic moral considerations that allow statesmen to pass "between the false extremes of pacifism and bellicism." One is to establish the justness of the cause: "war must be imposed by an obvious and extremely grave injustice." Another is noncombatant immunity, a commitment to the rights of the relatively innocent. A further condition is "the principle of proportion," by which one considers the correspondence between the damage already suffered and the damage unleashed by war to repress the injustice.[12] In this vein, Murray echoes the teaching of St. Augustine: it is not enough simply to consider "the sorrows and evils that flow from war"; there are "*greater evils* than the physical death and destruction wrought in war."[13] Thus, he insisted, it behooves us to transcend "the vulgar pacifism of sentimentalist and materialist inspiration that is so common today," since "the highest value in society is the inviolability of the order of rights and justice."[14] "Peace itself," he noted, "is the work of justice."[15]

Murray also recognized that the disuse and neglect of the traditional doctrine of just war in his own day resulted in a serious dilemma. In its place, he wrote, are "a cynical hard realism" and "a soft sentimental pacifism," both of which "are condemned by the traditional doctrine [i.e., Christian just war teaching] as false and pernicious."[16] Therefore, it was necessary both to "refute by argument the false antimony between war and morality" and to "purify the public climate of the miasma" that tended to smother the public conscience.[17] A persistent fallacy is that "war" and "peace" are "two discontinuous and incommensurable worlds of existence and universes of discourse, each with its own autonomous set of rules, 'peace' being the world of 'morality' and 'war' being the world of 'evil.'" Traditional just war moral reasoning, by contrast, "disqualifies as irrelevant and dangerous" this sort of "false dilemma," while also rejecting the prevalent notion that the big human challenge (and moral necessity) is to "abolish war" or "make peace, not war."[18] In the end, to believe as many do that "the possibility of limited war cannot be created by intelligence and energy, under the direction of a moral imperative, is to succumb to some sort of determinism in human affairs"[19]—a determinism that Murray flatly (and rightly) rejected.

Consequently, Murray demonstrated how it is possible and indeed most fruitful to consider the problem of war in continuity with the Christian tradition. That tradition, he thought, had within it a profound moral and political wisdom that could guide contemporary human affairs—a wisdom to assist modern citizens and statesmen in conceiving and formulating the appropriate terms for advancing responsible policy. However, the problem was not merely one of educating statesmen; it was also one of reeducating the church. Murray saw that the contemporary church was suffering from a vague understanding of its own just war principles, and his aim was to purify the public conscience—inside and outside the church—in order to facilitate morally responsible policy considerations.

Policy, as he reminded his readers on several occasions throughout *We Hold These Truths*, is "the meeting-place of the world of power and the world of morality."[20] Therefore, a "duty of justice" rests upon the statesman, whose nation he claims to serve. But in Murray's thinking, it also rested on all of us, who must make moral discriminations and thus "incarnate" a humane public policy on the basis of enduring moral principles.[21]

The Secular Rights Approach of Michael Walzer

Like Murray, but a generation later, Michael Walzer (born 1935) was struck by the inadequacy of American discourse about war, the contraction of what was once a rich ethical language into vastly oversimplified language of ideological extremes. Thinking and writing during the Vietnam era, Walzer observed war being described in terms of "interest," "strategy," and "security," but not in terms of moral right and wrong. It was thought that war admitted of no such consideration, or else it involved a morality all its own—one deriving from the interests of the state. In opposition to such realist assumptions was the ideology of pacifism, which maintained that wars could never be just, either because right and wrong were a matter of mere perspective (relativism), or because there was no right and wrong (nihilism), or because a policy of peace and love would always prove more effective than a policy of war (utopianism). Walzer found all such thinking reductionist. As an active opponent of the Vietnam War, he noticed that the language employed in everyday political discourse was neither the language of realism nor pacifism but precisely a language of moral right and wrong. Terms like "massacre," "atrocity," "aggression," "innocence," "humanitarian," and so on were not morally neutral, but rather they reflected deep commitments. What was needed, then, was a theoretical framework for making sense of such commitments. And in seeking such a framework, Walzer turned back to the tradition of just war thinking that had recently fallen into disuse.[22]

Published in 1977, Walzer's *Just and Unjust Wars: A Moral Argument with Historical Illustrations* has been widely acclaimed as the most important work of just war theory in the twentieth century, and the praise is well deserved.

Walzer's book is not a history of just war theory. It is an elaboration of just war principles and an attempt to apply them to specific cases of conflict in the modern era. The analysis is undertaken against the backdrop of what Walzer calls the "legalist paradigm," and one of its chief purposes is to show how just war thinking would go beyond the standards of international law. Indeed, Walzer uses his just war analysis as a standard by which to determine the adequacy of international law.

Methodologically, the work stands out for two reasons. First, it engages the difficult but necessary task of moral discrimination and, in so doing, recovers and advances the level of differentiation achieved in the just war tradition prior to the twentieth century. At every stage of his analysis, Walzer engages in the difficult work of crafting moral distinction, and this at a time when others were refusing to rise to the challenge.

Second, Walzer's method stands out for its secular philosophical character. While he does not disparage the Christian just war tradition, his first principles derive neither from scripture nor from theology but from a modern theory of rights. He is thus able to speak to many contemporary readers in a way that Christian writers cannot. Beginning with the moral language that citizens employ every day, he articulates general principles implied in that language—"rights principles"—and then applies these casuistically to historical and contemporary cases. The outcome, of course, is not identical to the outcome of Christian just war theory, but it is remarkably close. And when it departs, it does so in ways that stimulate interest and debate.

Because of the richness of Walzer's analysis—the vast intellectual terrain he covers, the many historical cases he describes, and the arresting beauty of his prose—it is possible to lose sight of his argument. But there is in fact a coherent argument running through his entire analysis, and this has been usefully adumbrated by Douglas Lackey into four essential claims:

1. Both states and persons possess moral rights. The basic rights of states are self-determination and territorial integrity; the basic rights of persons are life and liberty. Any violation of rights not justifiable in terms of the general protection of rights is wrong. States or persons may forfeit their rights as a result of their prior violations of the rights of others.

2. The use of force by one nation against another is always wrong unless the latter has already forfeited its basic rights.

3. A state forfeits its basic rights if and only if (a) it has already used force in violation of the basic rights of other states, or (b) it has threatened to use force in violation of the basic rights of other states and made preparations to carry out this threat, or (c) its ability to govern is disrupted by a secessionist movement that is representative in character, or (d) it has engaged in massive violations of basic personal rights.

4. Persons who bear arms in a war, just or unjust, forfeit their rights to life and liberty; likewise those who produce arms and the instruments of war forfeit their rights. All others retain their rights, regardless of the justice or injustice of wars being fought.[23]

This bare summary describes (1) the first principles from which Walzer's analysis proceeds, (2) his basic theory of "aggression," (3) his account of just cause, which includes not only responses to aggression (a) and (b) but also certain types of "intervention" into the domestic affairs of other states, and finally (4) Walzer's account of *jus in bello* as it pertains to the rights of individuals.

One of the most important areas of Walzer's analysis concerns interventions (3a) and (3b), because he here grapples with a problem now widely recognized by international lawyers themselves to be in need of attention—namely, that the status of international law on the matter of interventions is simply out of step with our moral intuitions and practices.[24] In international law, states are understood as possessing inviolable rights of "sovereignty" and "territorial integrity" as long as they commit no act of aggression toward other states. But interventions plainly violate this norm; they suspend the principle of sovereignty as soon as they begin. And yet interventions sometimes seem justifiable. What, then, are the moral principles that account for when they are just and when they are not?

Although Walzer respects the principle that states should never interfere in the domestic affairs of other states, he does not treat it as absolute. The principle itself derives from a set of moral values, he points out. States are entitled to determine their own affairs because they are made up of free individuals who are themselves entitled to determine their own affairs. In other words, the territorial integrity of states stems from the right of individuals to form such communities as they are willing and able to form. Drawing upon the work of John Stuart Mill, Walzer also explains the principle of nonintervention in terms of "self-help."[25] Just as individuals cannot be made virtuous by someone else, so states cannot be made virtuous from outside. States must earn their freedom; they cannot be set free. Any attempt to interfere in the domestic affairs of states is likely to do more harm than good. Such was Mill's more-or-less utilitarian argument for nonintervention.

But the principle of nonintervention admits of exceptions precisely because its aim is to protect the more fundamental principle of self-determination. Walzer puts it thus: when the value of self-determination would be better served by intervention than by nonintervention, the boundaries of a state may be crossed and the right of territorial integrity suspended. But when do such cases arise? Walzer identifies three possibilities: intervention to support a secessionist movement; intervention to offset a prior intervention by another foreign power (counter-intervention); and intervention to prevent grave harm such as genocide (humanitarian intervention). Walzer's account of these three basic types of intervention is fascinating because it reveals a secular theorist in search of the principles behind contemporary ethical intuitions and practices. If self-determination is the right of a people to become free (or not) by their own efforts, and if nonintervention is the principle guaranteeing that their efforts will not be impeded by the intrusions of an alien power, then all exceptions to the principle of nonintervention must operate on something like the following principle: "Always act so as to recognize and uphold communal autonomy."[26] In those rare cases where intervention stands a better chance than nonintervention of upholding communal autonomy, intervention may be morally justified. But even here, intervention must "be as much like nonintervention as possible."[27]

These principles have immediate implications for the way each of the three types of intervention must be justified and carried out. Of the three types, Walzer is most reserved about intervention on behalf of a secessionist movement because it has the greatest chance of backfiring, of depriving the movement of the very struggle it needs to become strong. Walzer therefore proposes a "self-help test" that secessionist movements ought to pass before they become candidates for foreign support. Secessionists must demonstrate that they represent a distinct community engaged in its own self-determination. To do so, they must command the obedience of a significant percentage of the population and establish control over a substantial portion of territory. Of course, by this time there is likely no need of foreign support. And this is precisely why Walzer hesitates to support these types of interventions. If a secessionist movement needs support, it is (ironically enough) not a secessionist movement worth supporting. This is in part the logic that led Walzer to oppose the American intervention in Vietnam. The United States intervened in Vietnam, according to Walzer, "not to fulfill commitments to another state, but to pursue policies of its own contrivance."[28]

According to Walzer, the second type of intervention is more easily justified, but its demands are somewhat unusual. When a third party—another foreign power—has already crossed territorial boundaries and interfered in a domestic struggle, then intervention may be justified to restore the local balance. Unlike most wars, however, where the purpose is to defeat the opposing side, counterinterventions aim merely to restore a degree of integrity to the struggle that had begun prior to the intervention. As an example, Walzer argues that Great Britain could have intervened (though it did not) in the Hungarian attempt to secure independence from the Hapsburg Empire in 1848–1889. Since the Russians had already been brought in from outside, this made for a pure case of counterintervention—"a national liberation movement unambiguously embodying the claims of a single, unified political community; capable at least initially of sustaining itself on the battlefield; challenged by an unambiguously foreign power; whose intervention can however be deterred or defeated without risking a general war."[29]

That the Hungarian Revolution was a "pure" case is important because it helps Walzer once again establish standards by which the war in Vietnam was unjust. Might the American action in Vietnam be construed as a legitimate counterintervention? Absolutely not, argues Walzer (at least in this book), because (a) the regime in the South had not unambiguously established itself; (b) our intervention did not unambiguously follow the intervention of a foreign power; and at any rate (c) the asymmetry of our effort suggests that we were attempting not to restore a previous balance but to win.

The final type of intervention Walzer considers, humanitarian intervention, is the easiest of all to justify on moral grounds but the hardest to find in pure form. "States don't send their soldiers into other states," Walzer remarks sardonically, "only in order to save lives."[30] Humanitarian motives are usually mixed with other motives, making the evaluation of such interventions quite complicated. Humanitarian interventions place a strict set of conditions on the actions that can be taken in a region, conditions other types of war do not require. Since the purpose of humanitarian intervention is simply to rescue, it entitles the rescuers to no special privileges, no prolonged occupation, and no right to rebuild the regime in one's own image. Although such activities often follow upon supposed humanitarian interventions (Walzer cites the American intervention in Cuba in 1898 as an example), they have no moral right behind them—or their right must be derived from something other than humanitarian intervention.

Such was Walzer's remarkably pioneering analysis of interventions. It was pioneering not because it created new categories of just cause—interventions were regarded as legitimate (e.g., by Vitoria and Suárez) long before Walzer described them as such—but rather because it confronted the poverty of contemporary international law on the topic of interventions long before international lawyers themselves began to do so. Moreover, Walzer attempted something that had never been done before, which was to articulate the underlying principles of justified intervention in a modern-day language of rights and utility (self-help). One may of course agree or disagree with the specific principles he articulates. But the broader point that needs emphasizing is that he recognized the inadequacy of international law on the topic and saw the relevance of the just war tradition as a tool for thinking through the problem afresh. It should be added that Walzer's distinct approach—his rights-based casuistic method—has breathed such new life into the just war tradition that today one finds scholars in political science departments and military academies across the country (precisely those places where realism used to reign) engaging in a more or less Walzerian approach.

Three Eclectic Approaches

The approaches employed by Murray and Walzer can be easily named because they cohere around a single prominent feature—theology in the case of Murray and rights in the case of Walzer. However, not all contemporary just war writers employ such systematic approaches, and in the next three figures we find a blend of various influences, albeit with distinct emphases and styles. William V. O'Brien, for instance, blends Christian theology, political science, and philosophy in a judicious and powerful way, yet he stands out for the emphasis he places on international law as an abiding forum for just war principles in the contemporary geopolitical world. James Turner Johnson commands a similar blend of theological and philosophical skills, yet he stands out for the historical nature of his studies as well as his interest in comparing the just war tradition across cultures. Finally, Jean Bethke Elshtain, also a theologically sensitive philosopher and ethicist, stands out both for the forceful polemical power of her writing and for her willingness to take on contemporary ideological opponents of the just war tradition in such a way that the war *within* our culture is addressed as well as the wars that should be fought abroad.

William V. O'Brien

William V. O'Brien (d. 2003), late professor of government at Georgetown University, wrote on war in such a way that his religious background was evident but not dominant. A Roman Catholic and a careful student of the just war tradition, he confronted the difficult issues of his day with an informed and disciplined mind while affirming the secular achievements of international law. The proliferation of nuclear weapons seemed to many observers during the '70s and '80s, especially in the church, to require a pacifist response—not the blanket pacifism of the religious ideologue but rather a "nuclear pacifism" which recognized that modern warfare, insofar as it involves weapons of mass destruction, must be ardently opposed. While O'Brien was sympathetic to this view, he rejected it outright and did so in a way that spoke simultaneously to Christian and secular audiences. In fact, he was as critical of some of the church's pronouncements during the '80s as he was of the culture at large.

In rejecting the pacifists' view, O'Brien accepted America's nuclear arsenal as necessary for deterrence and defense.[31] This and related themes are addressed in his *War, Deterrence, and Morality* (1967) and extended in three other important volumes: *War and/or Survival* (1969),[32] his massive *The Conduct of Just and Limited War* (1981),[33] and *The Nuclear Dilemma and the Just War Tradition* (1986).[34] O'Brien's fundamental conviction that war is a political "given" anchors much of his work. War is required for the protection of the common social order against the propensity for evil that is sewn into the nature of man. Therefore, he argued, the hope of eliminating war (nuclear or not) is utopian, dangerous and irresponsible. What was needed was not a strategy for eliminating war but rather strategies for containing it; and these were supplied in abundance by the just war tradition. In discussing moral constraints upon war, O'Brien therefore placed himself in continuity with that tradition.

O'Brien's critical response to the publication in 1983 of the U.S. Catholic bishops' pastoral letter, *The Challenge of Peace*, was important.[35] This particular document, in O'Brien's view, was "seriously flawed" for two principal reasons. First, it failed to acknowledge the threat that totalitarianism posed to the free world during the Cold War era. O'Brien chided the bishops for their inability to treat the matter of just cause and, hence, their inability to grasp the starting point of just war reasoning. Moreover, the bishops seemed to believe that, in practice, no just cause could warrant going to war in any situation. Thus, they had a dilemma. On the one hand, they wished to acknowledge the threat of evil in the world. On the other hand, they could not bring themselves to state unequivocally that such a threat should in fact be deterred. They wanted to pay lip service to the just war tradition while altering it to suit their ideological prioritizing of peace over justice. Thus, the bishops' deterrence, in the end, was "disembodied." O'Brien's exhortation to the church—and specifically to his own bishops—was to eschew idealism and return to the tradition.

In this vein, a defining feature of O'Brien's work was his meticulous delineation of both *ad bellum* and *in bello* criteria in the context of contemporary geopolitical challenges. Building upon the core criteria enunciated by Aquinas, O'Brien evaluated just cause, competent authority, and right intention in light of the nuclear dilemma. In his discussion of just cause, he acknowledged the complexity of weighing relative good against the preponderance of relative evil, without denying that such discernment is humanly impossible.[36] The motivation that produces the aim of a lasting peace (i.e., right intention) was for O'Brien none other than charity, placing him in continuity with the distinctly Christian strands of the tradition.

Because most modern debates have tended to focus on discrimination (noncombatant immunity), O'Brien found it necessary to probe the historical development of the notion. In his analysis, he treated the frequent objection that there must be an absolute prohibition against killing.[37] His position was unequivocal: neither classical just war theorists nor the church maintained an absolute prohibition against killing, and to adopt such a position is to fail to understand just war moral reasoning correctly.[38] Both common sense and the natural law suggest there are limits to our ability to anticipate—and thus guarantee—no collateral harm to others, as even analogies in the realm of domestic criminal justice illustrate. Rather, moral intention is the key qualification. Having assumed this basis for treating *ad bellum* requirements, he then explored the requirements of discrimination and proportionality in light of the problem of nuclear deterrence.[39] The upshot of O'Brien's argument was to call for a limited nuclear deterrence guided by the moral imperatives of just war doctrine.

Besides his focus on nuclear issues, what perhaps distinguished O'Brien's voice most from other twentieth-century voices in the just war tradition was his attitude toward international law. A unifying theme of the twentieth-century recovery of just war concepts was, as we have noted, a recognition that international law was a "blunt instrument" compared to the sharp distinctions of the tradition. O'Brien would certainly have agreed with this view. However, he was unique in stressing the importance of international law and the responsibility of informed citizens to help improve it. In fact, he thought people's preoccupation with nuclear war and nuclear deterrence during the '80s had led to a relative neglect of the international law as it actually stood.

> [W]hile nuclear dilemmas are naturally paramount in the minds of modern just war thinkers and authoritative Catholic spokesmen, the law of war as it pertains to conventional and, particu-

> larly, revolutionary war and counterinsurgency is the law that is being challenged constantly in the many armed conflicts being waged. The law governing these conflicts deserves more attention from modern just war doctrine.[40]

Inadequate as it may have been, the international law of war represented for O'Brien a signal achievement in the history of mankind, an achievement that needed to be preserved as well as expanded. It was thus a mistake, he thought, to allow just war thinking to address remote ethical dilemmas while neglecting the state of the law itself. In all his work, therefore, but especially in *The Conduct of Just and Limited War*, O'Brien strove to reveal the underlying kinship between positive international law and the just war tradition and to build upon that kinship moving forward.

James Turner Johnson

Another eclectic voice in the contemporary recovery of the just war tradition is James Turner Johnson, retired professor of religion at Rutgers University and author of more than a dozen books on just war. While Johnson is religiously oriented, he does not write as a theologian but as a historian of ideas, and his studies of the development of the tradition from antiquity to the present have been seminal resources for scholars and policy makers alike.[41] He also writes as a comparativist at times, setting the Western just war tradition alongside Judaic and Islamic traditions in order to stress areas of overlap and divergence.[42] And finally, he writes as a concerned citizen, attempting to use his historical and comparative knowledge in order to assess the justice of contemporary military engagements.[43]

With *Ideology, Reason, and the Limitation of War: Religious and Secular Concepts, 1200–1740* (1975), Johnson began in earnest to probe the just war tradition in order to identify whether, when, where, and how restraints and limitations on war have been applied. In this volume, Johnson is the historian. As the title suggests, he investigates the manner in which secular, legal, and theological currents helped give shape to the just war tradition in a formative period that stretches from the medieval to the early-modern era. *Just War Tradition and the Restraint of War*

(1981) might best be viewed as the companion volume to *Ideology*, since it covers a swath of history chiefly from the early sixteenth century to the late twentieth century. What makes Johnson's voice so distinct—and so important—is its peculiar blend of historical and moral-philosophical acumen. His analyses are thorough and thoughtfully crafted. And in the end, his agenda is to bring history and philosophy to bear on contemporary problems. The reader is thus enriched because of an increased awareness that just war theory is not just a "theory." Nor should it be construed as simply a "method." Rather, as Johnson wishes to impress upon the reader, it is a rich and diverse stream of moral-philosophical reflection on the complexities of war and peace. And at the heart of the tradition, from Augustine to Aquinas to Luther to Vitoria to Grotius and beyond, is the effort to reconcile two guiding moral conditions—permission and limitation.

The comparative side of Johnson's work is on display in two companion volumes coedited by John Kelsay: *Cross, Crescent, and Sword: The Justification and Limitation of War in Western and Islamic Tradition* and *Just War and Jihad: Historical and Theological Perspectives on War and Peace in Western and Islamic Traditions.* Given the notable resurgence of Islam and the political movements it has spawned, Johnson wonders whether, and to what extent, Islamic restraints on war resemble Western restraints. Viewing both traditions in historical perspective, these studies reveal many points of commonality but also profound differences on the level of initial theological assumptions.

Despite such differences, Johnson wonders whether there might be a universal consensus as to justice in war that could bridge the two divergent cultures. On Johnson's account, historical and anthropological evidence suggests that every culture has generated some analogue of just war thinking. At another level, following innovative and courageous thinkers such as Vitoria, Johnson asks whether a difference in religion is sufficient cause for war. In the Western tradition, the answer is for the most part no, especially in the modern era. In the Islamic tradition, however, the answer is yes and no. Such a conclusion is based on the theoretical (i.e., theological) foundations of the two traditions. Those of Islamic faith are required to defend their own existence as well as their duty to obey "divine law." Johnson is not inattentive to the legal and theological debates over the centuries that have occurred within Islam. Moreover, the success of Islam's territorial expansion casts new light on Qur'anic interpretations of war and peace, facilitating the transformation of warfare from a *defense* of religious belief and practice into a means by which to bring the nations under submission to Allah and divine law. Ultimately, then, holy war appears justified in the one cultural tradition, whereas it is generally condemned, with some exceptions, in the second. In appreciating the deep roots of the two traditions—for example, in comparing Jesus' and Muhammad's construal of the relationship between God and Caesar as well as the natural law tradition—one comes to a deeper appreciation of the theoretical differences that set the two traditions apart in their justification of war.

In *The Holy War Idea in Western and Islamic Traditions*,[44] Johnson builds on his past comparative studies in order to show how Western and Islamic cultures have variously defined the interrelationship of religion, statecraft, and war. Johnson appears convinced that, historically, the major interpretive streams of Islam reject the justification of war that terrorists are adducing (this volume appeared in the late 1990s). What he does not examine is the locus of authority that currently influences the interpretation of *jihad*. Even in the years since this book's publication, notable geopolitical changes have occurred that might affect his conclusions. In any event, Johnson's emphasis on the need for "fruitful dialogue"[45] is admirable. Whether such dialogue can proceed, given the vacuous nature of much interreligious dialogue, is questionable.[46]

Turning to real-world conflicts and contemporary events, Johnson's work in *Just War and the Gulf War* (1991), *Morality and Contemporary Warfare* (1999), and *The War to Oust Saddam Hussein* (2005) attempts to show the relevance of the tradition historically understood to present-day decisions. These works are important for offering readers a way of understanding military conflicts that avoids amoralism on one side or hyperlegalism on the other. The tradition is used as a vehicle for *moral* reflection and moral decision making. From this vantage point, Johnson affirmed American involvement in both Gulf Wars and in a number of humanitarian interventions while also offering cautionary reflections on matters of "limitation and restraint." He thus demonstrated concretely the ways in which the tradition can help us think in more nuanced terms about morality and war than would be possible if we simply tried to rely on our native gifts.

A final noteworthy feature of Johnson's approach to just war thinking is his critical posture toward the church when its spokesmen prove historically and theologically unsophisticated. Thus, like William V. O'Brien, Johnson has had much to say in response to *The Challenge of Peace*, published by the Catholic bishops in 1983. In fact, O'Brien and Johnson have substantively similar responses, but one point makes Johnson's response particularly forceful and unique. It is his appraisal of the following passage from the bishops' statement.

The church's teaching on war and peace establishes a strong presumption against

> war which is binding on all; it then examines when this presumption may be overridden, precisely in the name of preserving the kind of peace which protects human dignity and human rights. . . . The moral theory of the "just war" or "limited war" doctrine begins with the presumption which binds all Christians: We should do no harm. . . . How we treat our enemy is the key test of whether we love our neighbor; and the possibility of taking even one human life is a prospect we should consider in fear and trembling. How is it possible to move from these presumptions to the idea of a justifiable use of lethal force?[47]

The bishops imply that peace is the starting point for thinking about justice. The just war tradition, however, proceeds on the reverse assumption. Without justice, peace itself may be illegitimate. Just war thinking begins, in other words, not with a presumption against war but rather with a *presumption against injustice*. Therefore, anyone who categorically rules out the possibility of war or coercive force violates the presumption against injustice, which is a requirement of love rightly construed.[48] This is an abiding emphasis in Johnson's writings, and for important reasons. At the most basic level, it is a matter of accurate representation as well as moral and philosophical integrity. Many construals of just war thinking fail in this regard, particularly at the academic and theological level, proceeding mistakenly from a false starting point. Johnson's burden was, therefore, to set them straight.[49]

Jean Bethke Elshtain

A final voice in the contemporary recovery of just war thinking was the late Jean Bethke Elshtain, the former Laura Spelman Rockefeller Professor of Social and Political Ethics at the University of Chicago. In the introduction to this volume, we mentioned Elshtain's use of the tradition to assess the case for war in Iraq in 2003. We also identified her approach in various places as "Augustinian," "religio-ethical," and "eclectic." The last description is no doubt the most apt. In fact, Elshtain describes her own work as hailing "from a perspective that freely mingles theological, ethical, philosophical, and political categories." To be in conversation with Elshtain is to engage a thinker-writer who is a genuine cultural polyglot. She recognizes that her use of Christian concepts and assumptions in particular is "not what political theorists usually do."[50] But she thinks it is nevertheless necessary for proper understanding.

Despite the remarkable breadth of her interests, one detects in Elshtain a thread that weaves its way through most of her writings. She believes that the present tendency in Western thought—and American society especially—to sever political reflection from religious and ethical concerns is fraught with error. In her view, this divide is closely akin to the supposed "wall" between church and state advanced by one dominant strand of American jurisprudence. It is a divide, by no means innocuous, that requires law and politics to pose as "neutral." The problem is that no such neutrality exists. Rather, all theoretical or descriptive assessments of the polis, the civitas, or the nation-state are freighted with presuppositions of what constitutes ultimate reality. Nowhere, moreover, do we find these philosophical precommitments on display more than when we approach difficult issues such as the ordering of society or war and peace.[51]

To appreciate fully her views on civil society and the ethics of war and peace, one must appreciate her indebtedness to Christian moral thinkers of previous generations. Throughout much of Elshtain's work, the reader discovers a conscious debt—pronounced in *Who Are We?*—to the writings of Augustine,[52] Dietrich Bonhoeffer, and John Paul II. Both Bonhoeffer and John Paul affirm an anthropological dualism that is indebted to classical Christian thought, with its "two antithetical situations" and "two different states of human nature." These twin anthropological poles are "the state of integral nature," which is to say, inherent dignity and sanctity, and "the state of fallen nature." Or in more theological language: original innocence and original sin.[53]

The moral clarity advocated by Elshtain begins with truthfulness about how we approach language. Words lose their meaning as a result of inaccurate and dishonest manipulation. Therefore, "Responsibility for and toward words is a task which is intrinsically ethical."[54] Nowhere is the necessity of truthfulness in speech more evident—and more absent—than in the realm of politics. Elshtain believes that the categories of ideological political contestation become hopelessly clichéd and self-referential. Whether something is "left" or "right" is the last thing that should interest any alert and concerned citizen. One of the problems with this standard political vocabulary is that empty platitudes and tropes deflect our attention away from issues of substance, concrete dangers that require our attention in the form of policy. Further, it is the nature of ideological thinking to engage in deliberate and programmatic deflection, substituting the abstract for the specific, for the purposes of subverting the real. The ideologue, by means of his or her limitless leap into universal, utopian dogma, endeavors not to fulfill or enrich politics but to avoid it.

"Real" politics, as Elshtain describes it, is the domain of concrete responsibilities and civic duties. It is not utopian and sentimental; rather, it is tough-minded and continually aware of the "human dimension," the inherent tendency toward dignity and depravity. In this regard, Elshtain consistently displays a debt to Augustine, who serves as a guide in countering our "untrammeled self-sovereignty" and hubris.[55] Augustine alerts us to the false pride that lurks even behind good deeds and seemingly noble intentions. Pride begins with the assumption that we are the sole ground of our being. We become our own point of origin and reference; we refuse at multiple levels dependence on others around us. The upshot of this false autonomy is that we fail to acknowledge limits.

Another mark of Elshtain's work is her willingness to confront the distortions of feminist ideology concerning war. In her *Women and War*, she points out that much—though by no means all—contemporary feminism would lay the blame for war, coupled with a causal explanation for war, at the feet of men and male aggression. This reductive claim, however, appears less and less believable with thoughtful reflection. In fact, according to Elshtain, men tend to enter into war not because of sex drive or aggression but rather because of their sense of what is at stake and their ability to sacrifice.[56] Reflecting on current feminist thought in this vein, Elshtain is struck by its inability, despite its co-opting of the language of "justice," to address the problem of heinous evil when it occurs in the world. It is unable to sacrifice, unable to get beyond shrill rhetoric, unable to call forth an alternative social arrangement in which justice and mercy, charity and autonomy, can properly coexist.[57] When abominable evil occurs, "it is time to call things by their real names."[58]

War presents a case in point. For radical feminists, war is acceptable only insofar as it is directed toward men collectively as the "oppressor class." But for Elshtain, repressive feminism is itself a "greater darkness" than the darkness it purports to challenge. Feminist ideology requires that the story line of history be one of men victimizing women. Preoccupation with this presumption, however, results in several tragedies. It ends up disempowering women rather than enabling them as citizens with both rights and responsibilities. More tragically, it blinds us to the real victims who need our intercession in a fallen world. Not surprisingly, then, Elshtain has devoted a significant amount of her writing to the theme of war and peace. Justice, for her, places concrete demands on responsible citizens, calling people of goodwill to identify the truly dispossessed and to resist moral evil.[59]

One of the many strengths of Elshtain's various treatments of the just war tradition is her exposure of the overly legalist way it has come to be (mis)understood. Just war theory is typically thought to consist of seven "laws," she points out, according to which

- war must be a last resort only after all peaceful recourse has been exhausted;
- war must be a clearly defensive response against unjust attack;
- war must have as its ultimate intention the establishment of a greater peace;

- war must have a reasonable chance for victory;
- war must be declared and carried out by properly constituted governments;
- warfare must be conducted in such a way as to distinguish between combatants and noncombatants; and
- warfare must be conducted in such a way that is proportionate to the offense or injustice needing redress.[60]

As Elshtain views it, there is the dual tendency among our contemporaries either to view the above construal, with its "laws," as unrealistic—and, in practice, unattainable—or to fail to wrestle with the "human factor" in its application by means of political prudence.

Nevertheless, despite the problem of stunted stereotypes, the culture's lack of serious ethical discourse, and the human difficulty of agonizing over issues of justice, Elshtain is convinced that there is wisdom in the classical just war tradition. This repository of moral and political wisdom is necessary not only for the sake of adequate statecraft and responsible foreign policy but also for the very ordering of domestic society.[61]

Hence Elshtain's own version of the just war "story" is expressed not as a list of lawlike injunctions but as a tradition of reflection stemming from a few basic assumptions.

> One way to tell the story of just war discourse is to treat it as an authoritative tradition dotted with its own sacred texts, offering a canonical alterative to realism as received truth. Rather than beginning with Machiavelli (or, reaching back further, Thucydides), just war as continuous narrative starts with Augustine; takes up a smattering of medieval canonists; plunges into the sixteenth century with Luther as the key figure; draws in a few natural / international-law thinkers (Francisco Suárez, Francisco de Vitoria, Hugo Grotius), then leapfrogs into the era of modern nation-states. . . . With their aims of constraining collective violence, chastening *realpolitik*, and forging human identities, the

> current heirs of this way of thinking assume (1) the existence of universal moral dispositions, if not convictions—hence, the possibility of a nonrelativist ethic; (2) the need for moral judgments of who / what is aggressor / victim, just / unjust, acceptable / unacceptable, and so on; (3) the potential efficacy of moral appeals and arguments to stay the hand of force. This adds up to a vision of civic virtue, not in the classical armed sense but in a way that is equally if differently demanding.[62]

Elshtain's mention of civic virtue is not incidental. Rather, a defining feature of her just war approach is her recognition that the tradition can and should remain alive in citizens, men and women who employ just war categories in their own deliberations about war. Civic virtue requires knowledge of tradition.[63]

And this points to another prominent theme in Elshtain's work, which is patriotism. Very often today, one encounters two extreme attitudes—that of a hyperpatriotism shading into nationalism and a virulent antipatriotism that is critical of virtually everything government does. Moreover, these extreme positions seem to bear directly on how one thinks of war—in terms either of nationalist fervor or of cynical deprecation. Here again, Elshtain draws on Augustine to furnish a model for wrestling with the question of patriotism. Just as Augustine described the dual citizenship of Christians who are involved simultaneously in the city of God and the city of man, Elshtain discusses the need to embrace patriotism but also to restrain it. "Chastened patriotism" is appropriate, and for Elshtain it is "chastened" precisely because we have *two* citizenships—earthly as well as heavenly. In other words, we are at work in the world but also fundamentally oriented toward the life to come.[64] "Rejecting counsels of cynicism, they [chastened men and women] modulate the rhetoric of high patriotic purpose." They learn from the past, observing how in most societies the human tendency is to valorize particular loyalties—loyalties that might be social, cultural, political, or religious. The "chastened patriot," then, is both *devoted and detached.* Loyalties are necessary and healthy. But when they are magnified through the lens of superiority, they become dangerous. They lead toward nationalism and eventually assume the language of war. Therefore, a civic life animated by "chastened patriotism," as Elshtain construes it, has significant implications for how we think about war and peace.[65]

Elshtain offers her own conclusions about particular wars in a number of important studies, even when particular wars are not the focus of any one volume. The broader point to stress is that the various emphases of Elshtain's just war writings combine to form a powerful and distinct approach. Like John Courtney Murray and many other exponents of just war thinking in the modern age, she writes from an expressly religious perspective. But she does not write as a theologian; nor does she write for the most part as a historian of ideas, as James Turner Johnson does. Rather, Elshtain writes as a theologically and philosophically informed political commentator, attacking pernicious cultural tendencies, analyzing arguments and exposing error, identifying root issues and fundamental principles, and finally making a case for who we are and what we should be fighting for. Of course, "we are not obliged," she writes, "to defend everything we [Americans] have done, or are doing, as a country. But we do bear an obligation to defend the ideal of free citizens in a polity whose ordering principles make civic freedom and free exercise of religion available to all."[66]

Shared Assumptions

Although the writers discussed in this chapter engage the just war tradition in various ways, they share a basic commitment to its underlying assumptions—namely that war is a permanent feature of human life, that humans are by nature ethical beings who desire to act in accordance with principles of right and that, therefore, war should be waged only insofar as it can be deemed just and appropriate. These are the first principles we identified in the introduction to this volume as the foundation of just war thinking through the ages as well as the lines that separate the just war framework from the rival paradigms of realism and pacifism.

These authors also help to bear out our argument about the relevance of the just war tradition to contemporary civic debate. As the tradition was appropriated by each author in his or her own way, it supplied a largely premade framework (of terms, principles, cases, etc.) in which debates could more concretely and fruitfully occur. Therefore, the advantage of the tradition is not merely that its first principles are sound from a philosophical and theological point of view but also that it facilitates communal reflection on unresolved contemporary concerns by supplying a language in which to discuss them.

Because this language is so essential to responsible statecraft and democratic debate, we attempt in the next chapter to do for today something similar to what the writers covered in this chapter have done. We try to identify the dominant alternatives to just war thinking today and engage these dialectically in a way that reveals simultaneously their weakness and the relative benefits of the just war tradition. Perhaps it will come as a surprise that the place where we sense the most danger of cultural amnesia, where the tradition seems most apt to be forsaken, is in the contemporary church (whether Catholic or Protestant). And the reason for this amnesia appears to be (as always) the popularity of certain forms of realism and pacifism—in this case, distinctly Christian forms. We therefore identify the sources of these corrupting influences, analyze them in detail, and explain why the just war tradition should be preferred and reembraced.

11

Why Have Our Churches Lost the Tradition? Two Temptations: Christian Realism, Christian Pacifism

Present political controversy over American-led military involvement in Afghanistan and Iraq and against terrorism in general has spawned a wide interest in the Western just war tradition. Because the tradition has its roots in Christianity, in such thinkers as Augustine, Aquinas, Luther, and Calvin, and because it has been the orthodox perspective of most Christian churches (Catholic and Protestant) for centuries, one would expect the renewed interest in the tradition to be especially strong among Christian leaders. However, this has not generally been the case. To judge from what Christian leaders have been saying and writing since September 11, 2001, the reason relates to the rising popularity of two alternative ways of thinking about war (alternative both to the just war tradition and to each other)—namely, Christian realism and Christian pacifism.

The popularity of these alternatives is not new, of course. The church has always been tempted by varieties of realism and pacifism. In fact, the just war tradition emerged in critical opposition to these alternatives. Recognizing that the project of personal salvation would be ill served as much by political overactivity as by political neglect, Augustine forged a middle way, which enabled Christians to participate in some wars, under certain conditions, while taking care not to compromise their own hopes for salvation. That the just war tradition was a middle way arrived at through critical dialogue with the alternatives must be stressed, since so many Christians today seem utterly unaware of the tradition or regard it as some sort of extreme position on matters pertaining to war.

In light of this development, it seems appropriate to close the present study by attempting to reengage something of the critical dialogue that once led historical writers to the just war perspective. In other words, we want to consider realism and pacifism not in their historical manifestations but in their contemporary form and reason our way from those extremes to the more balanced position of just war. To do so, we turn to the work of Reinhold Niebuhr and John Howard Yoder, arguably the most influential Christian realist and pacifist writers of the twentieth century. Engaging each of these perspectives in turn, we attempt to show concretely how and why the just war tradition provides a middle way between these two popular extremes while remaining at once politically realistic and genuinely Christian.[1]

Niebuhr's Christian Realism

Reinhold Niebuhr will likely be familiar to most readers as a prominent Protestant theologian of the Cold War years and a staunch defender of democracy against the threat of Soviet communism. He was, interestingly enough, a Marxist and a pacifist in his early years. But by the outbreak of World War II, he had abandoned pacifism for what he called "Augustinian realism," and by 1949 he had abandoned his earlier Marxism for a distinct brand of democratic liberalism grounded in a biblical understanding of human nature. The influence of his mature ideas cannot be overstated. He is well known to have shaped the thinking of such realists as George Kennan, Hans Morgenthau, and Arthur Schlesinger, Jr.; and today he is routinely cited as influential among leading statesmen and commentators on public affairs.[2] Niebuhrian Christian realism is a force to be reckoned with.

In his mature writings, Niebuhr presented his position in international relations as itself a dialectical synthesis between extremes, with secular realism on one side and Christian idealism on the other.[3] Thus, he frequently acknowledged the basic realist insight that moral language and moral motives are never pure, that politics always involves self-interest. Yet Niebuhr does not hold, as some extreme realists do, that politics is nothing but self-interest. Niebuhr likewise acknowledges the idealist insight that "love is the law of life," that peace and justice always contain elements of self-sacrifice, and yet he does not hold (with the Christian sentimentalist) that sacrificial love can become a "simple possibility" for public policy, much less for international policy, on this side of the eschaton. That would be to adopt an idealist view whose implications point toward pacifism, and Niebuhr was emphatic in his rejection of pacifism.

In fact, the best way to explore Niebuhr's own realist stance is to observe how it emerges from his rejection of pacifism in his now classic essay "Why the Christian Church Is Not Pacifist."[4] Written during the early years of World War II, shortly after Niebuhr had abandoned his own commitment to pacifism, the essay argues that most (though not all) forms of modern pacifism are heretical. When judged by either of two standards, by the gospel's account of human nature or by the facts of human experience, modern forms of pacifism simply fail to measure up. As it happens, these two basic standards are, for Niebuhr, necessarily related. It is because the gospel's account of human nature so fully comports with and illuminates the "facts of human experience" that the gospel is authoritative.[5] In other words, the test that any theology or anthropology must pass is not a test of orthodoxy per se but one of interpretive power; and this is precisely the test that modern pacifism fails in Niebuhr's view.

With respect to the gospel, Niebuhr appealed to a sophisticated account of the human condition, which emphasizes both righteousness and *sin*.

> Christianity is a religion which measures the total dimension of human existence not only in terms of the final norm of human conduct, which is expressed in the law of love, but also in terms of the fact of sin. It recognizes that the same man who can become his true self only by striving infinitely for self-realization beyond himself is also inevitably involved in the sin of infinitely making his partial and narrow self the true end of existence. It believes, in other words, that though Christ is the true norm (the "second

> Adam") for every man, every man is also in some sense the crucifier of Christ.[6]

Because of the complexity of the human situation, the good news of the gospel can and should be understood in these two, almost contradictory, senses. On the one hand, the good news is that Christ has introduced a new "law of love" and modeled that law for the world to see. He thus offers a new power of righteousness to those who believe in him. On the other hand, the good news must entail a new promise of forgiveness, since there is a "law in our members which wars against the law that is in our mind" (Romans 7:23) and thus no one can live perfectly. The good news entails both sanctification and justification. It accounts for both our righteousness and sin. We are both Christ and his crucifier.

Against this gospel standard the anthropological outlook of much of modern pacifism appears one-sided, to be sure. It emphasizes the potential for human righteousness over the need for divine mercy, the power of love over the fact of sin. If only Christians would renounce violence more widely and love their enemies more consistently, the pacifist suggests, then human conflict might simply wither away. The kingdom of God is conceived as a historical, human possibility, awaiting only a deeper commitment of Christians to "take Christ seriously."

The erroneousness of this view is revealed not only by reference to the gospel but also by reference to historical experience. On this point, Niebuhr is characteristically brilliant:

> If we believe that the only reason men do not love each other perfectly is because the law of love has not been preached persuasively enough, we believe something to which experience does not conform. If we believe that if Britain had only been fortunate enough to have produced 30 percent instead of 2 percent of conscientious objectors to military service, Hitler's heart would have been softened and he would not have dared to attack Poland, we hold a faith which no historic reality justifies.[7]

Whatever Christian faith entails, Niebuhr insists, it does not require one to believe that self-sacrifice always, or even usually, yields politically desirable results. Indeed, historical experience suggests the exact opposite. Wherever progress has been made—for example, in the extension of civil rights to black Americans, in the enfranchisement of women, in the foiling of tyrannical schemes—it has always been made through the concerted efforts and self-assertion of those in question, not through self-denial. This is as true in the family as in politics, and it is a foolish idealism that seeks to deny it.[8] Love may indeed triumph over evil at the end of time, but in history, where human beings remain sinners, love does not solve the political problem.

The fundamental and permanent political problem, according to Niebuhr, is sin: selfishness, greed, lust for power, the assertion of self beyond the limits of fairness and justice. And what is needed to offset this problem is not love (not simply, at least) but resistance: a balance of power with power. Here lies the practical-political side of Niebuhr's realism. Because of sin (egoism), social cooperation cannot be organized upon a purely voluntary basis. Governments must coerce, and yet this necessary coercion can itself become a vehicle for sin, when it is used in selfish ways. Therefore, coercion too must be subject to coercion; power must be set against power. Were it not for government power, social life would degenerate quickly into anarchy. Were it not for checks upon government power, life would degenerate quickly into tyranny. Thus, writes Niebuhr, "the political life of man must constantly steer between the Scylla of anarchy and the Charybdis of tyranny."[9] We must indeed strive toward an ideal society in which life supports life in voluntary community. But the closest *approximation* of this ideal in a world of sinners is (realistically speaking) a "justice" in which "life is prevented from destroying life."[10]

Niebuhr's Christian realism, then, entails several related emphases: a keen awareness of human sin, a recognition of the oppressed, a sober awareness that loving one's enemies will not eliminate violence, and an appreciation for the role that coercion must play both in maintaining a just society and keeping governments in check. In the international sphere, Niebuhr's realism is in keeping with these insights. It may be said to involve two fundamental principles. One is simply that the degree of justice attained in democratic nations through the system of checks and balances is preferable to either anarchy or tyranny and that, therefore, democracies ought to be defended. This is not to say that democratic nations have attained an acceptable degree of justice, much less that they warrant an unqualified endorsement as "Christian." But they do, in Niebuhr's view, approximate the Christian ideal of loving harmony more closely than either tyranny or anarchy. Niebuhr thus views democratic civilization as a significant achievement, something worth defending. And the problem with pacifism in this regard is that it "either tempts us to make no judgments at all, or to give an undue preference to tyranny in comparison with the momentary anarchy that is necessary to overcome tyranny."[11]

The second principle of Niebuhr's international realism is that defending democratic civilization may, and almost certainly will, involve violence. This is so because there is no adequate organizing center of international politics, no international legislative, judicial, and executive powers to keep nations within their limits. If such powers could be created on an international plane (and it is not clear they could), then the sinful lust for power of one nation might be checked by the power of another within a framework of constitutional order. But in the absence of such an order, resistance to tyranny may well take the form of war. And it is Niebuhr's conviction that Christians, no less than anyone else, ought to recognize the necessity of such wars and participate in them when they are thrust upon us.

Now, it must be stressed that Niebuhr supplies no scriptural justification for Christian participation in war, and this is no accident. In fact, one cannot fully grasp the character of Niebuhr's realism without grasping the reasons for this omission. The difficulty stems from Niebuhr's understanding of the "ethic of Jesus," an understanding that owes as much to Kant, in a certain sense, as it does to the gospel.[12] According to Niebuhr, the "ethic of Jesus" is contained in a number of fundamental injunctions—"resist not evil," "love your enemies," "be not anxious for your life," "be ye therefore perfect even as your Father in heaven is perfect"—and these are taken to be "absolute" moral imperatives, which is to say they bind "without consideration of the consequences."[13] In fact, the consequences of strict adherence to these injunctions may well be disastrous for sociopolitical life. They would likely "invalidate every measure required for the maintenance of social order,"[14] such as the punishment of crime, the enforcement of law, and the protection of individual rights. But this is no strike against them in Niebuhr's view, for the scriptural arguments in favor of these injunctions are always religio-moral, never socio-moral. We are to love our enemies because God loves us, not because love might turn enemies into friends or eliminate the problem of violence. "No appeal to social consequences could ever fully justify these demands of Jesus."[15]

Not only are Jesus' demands unjustifiable in terms of social consequences; they are also impossible to fulfill. They are fit neither for sinful human beings nor for a world in which limits of time, space, and knowledge prevent one from doing all that one should. The ethic of Jesus is thus, according to Niebuhr, ultimately normative (it is the standard by which we are judged), but it is also a standard we can never meet. It is in Niebuhr's famous phrase an "impossible possibility," an ideal whose final fulfillment is possible "only when God transmutes the present chaos of this world into its final unity."[16]

Here we see the extent to which Niebuhr both is and is not Kantian in his approach to the "ethic of Jesus." There is an unmistakable Kantian flavor in an ethic that is absolute and binding regardless of consequences and that defines human freedom as the possibility of embracing its imperatives. But unlike Kant, for whom "what is true in theory must also be true in practice," Niebuhr sees an unbridgeable gap between Christian ethics and the problems of sociopolitical life.[17] The ethic of Jesus is not, Niebuhr laments, "immediately applicable to the task of securing justice in a sinful world," for it not only fails to address the immediate problem of harmonizing competing needs, desires, and wills; it also absolutely forbids the prudential measures required to protect ourselves from others.[18] All efforts to secure peace and justice in a sinful world thus involve compromises with sin and are fundamentally alien to the ethic of the kingdom in which no concession to sin is made. This does not mean, in Niebuhr's view, that the task of securing justice should be abandoned by Christians, but it does mean that we are caught up in sin the moment we take care for our earthly needs. We can and should act decisively to resist evil, but we do so without the support of the ethic of Jesus.[19]

The problem with pacifism, then, is its blindness to the depths of human sin—or to put it differently, its failure to understand the purity of Jesus' ethic. The ethic is not meant for this world. To believe that one can simply implement it and remove thereby the problem of violence is to commit two related errors. The first is the error of perfectionism, which by either underestimating the rigor of Jesus' new law or overestimating one's own righteousness asserts that the ethic can be practiced sufficiently to bring about the kingdom of God. The second is the eschatological and ontological error of attempting to immanentize a transcendent eschaton, believing that the kingdom can be achieved in this world, without fundamental ontological change.

Niebuhr says that "most modern pacifism" is heretical, although he is willing to concede that a form of pacifism that avoids these errors would have a place in the Christian fold. And he believes that pacifism can indeed avoid these errors if it would only limit its perfectionist aspirations to the private sphere, removing itself thereby from politics. For instance, the pacifism (and individual perfectionism) of the medieval ascetic or the early-modern followers of Menno Simons could offer a valuable testimony to the church, reminding it that "the true end of man is brotherhood, and that love is the law of life."[20] But as soon as this testimony becomes political and attempts to perfect not the self but the world, it attempts the impossible and threatens more harm than good. Niebuhr ultimately leaves modern pacifists with a choice: either break from the ethic of Jesus and become politically "responsible" (as the Christian realist does when necessity calls) or else attempt to live by the ethic of Jesus, to the extent that this is humanly possible, and become politically "irrelevant." There is a place for Christian pacifism, but it is not a political place. Its home is in the monastery or the withdrawn Christian community, and its value lies in its testimony to those who take the problems of politics seriously.

Yoder's Pacifism of the Messianic Community

A prolific Anabaptist writer and professor of Christian ethics at Notre Dame until his death in 1997, John Howard Yoder is widely recognized as one of the most influential pacifist writers of the century.[21] Yoder's work recommends itself too for its dialogical qualities. He wrote essays carefully engaging both Niebuhrian realism and the just war tradition in the process of illuminating and refining his own position.[22] Let us therefore examine Yoder's critique of Niebuhr as a way of understanding the grounds for his own brand of pacifism.

Interestingly, Yoder's engagement of Niebuhr has as much to do with affinities as it does with differences. To a striking extent, Niebuhr and Yoder speak a common language and recognize common problems, although slight variations in emphasis carry them to radically different conclusions. For Yoder as for Niebuhr, Jesus' Sermon on the Mount entails an absolute law of love, one that demands self-sacrifice and nonresistance without consideration for consequences.[23] Both writers, moreover, agree that nonresistance as Christ conceives it involves something altogether different from "nonviolence" as this is typically practiced today. That is, nonviolence often becomes a political strategy, a form of resistance or coercion all its own—as it was for Gandhi and his disciples. But nonresistance is no strategy at all; rather, it is an act of love in accordance with Christ's injunction "Resist not one who is evil" (Matthew 5:39) and a response to God's unconditional love for us. Finally, since both writers reject consequentialism in Christian ethics, they agree also in criticizing certain liberal Protestant forms of pacifism that became fashionable in the years surrounding World War I. For these were, Yoder admits, "over-optimistic as to the possibility of the easy solution of international problems and unaware of the depths of national selfishness and irrationality."[24]

But differences between Niebuhr and Yoder emerge on the matter of "possibilities." To what extent does Christ open new possibilities for Christians? To what extent must these remain "impossible possibilities" due to sin? One of Yoder's principal criticisms of Niebuhr (correct in our view) is that Niebuhr allows an all-too-vague notion of "impossibility" to stand in the way of Christian practice. Why, after all, is Jesus' ethic of love impossible? Is it because the individual in his freedom is unwilling to sacrifice? Or because he refuses to believe (lacking faith) that love is the law of life? Or because he lacks sufficient information, wealth, or time to love every person who needs care? Or because he lacks the power to address injustices that have become systemic? Perhaps it is all these things. But of course, these are far from identical in terms of freedom, responsibility, and guilt. In some cases, we find ourselves without freedom to act. In other cases, we can and often do act out of genuine motives of love. Niebuhr thus collapses categories together. He allows a blurring among kinds of impossibility to foster defeatism generally about the ethic of love. Because some forms of love are impossible, all forms of love are impossible.

A second major criticism concerns the effect this doctrine has on Niebuhr's ethics and politics. If the ethic of Jesus is impossible, then what will take its place? What should be the ultimate criteria of ethical action? The default criteria are, of course, natural criteria such as self-protection, economic security, and national defense. The default modes are natural modes such as coercion and prudential calculation. And these are indeed exactly what Niebuhr falls back on. When Niebuhr speaks of "approximating" the law of love, he does not mean we should attempt as much as humanly possible to "resist not one who is evil"; he means rather that by resisting evil wisely and powerfully we might contribute to a world of relative peace and justice. Moreover, when Niebuhr employs ethical concepts such as "necessity" and "responsibility," these always point to natural considerations (i.e., necessary for physical security), never the scriptural ethic of Jesus. Thus, Niebuhr "in effect rehabilitate[s] the selfish motives . . . as ethical determinants"[25] as he renders the ethic of Jesus politically otiose.

Rejecting Niebuhr's emphasis on impossibility, then, Yoder explores the many possibilities of Christian life. Focusing (as a foundation) on the concrete possibilities that Jesus himself faced in Palestine, Yoder contends that Jesus' way of life is not only normative but also politically significant and capable of being lived. What were the possibilities or options Christ faced in Palestine as the long-awaited Messiah (deliverer)? Perhaps the most tempting was what Yoder calls the "zealot option" of righteous revolutionary violence against the infidel Romans. This was, on Yoder's reading of the gospel, what tempted Christ most in the desert after his baptism and again in Gethsemane. Another option was that of withdrawal to the desert as the Essenes had done. But Christ rejects this possibility too.[26]

What he does instead is to create a new kind of community—purely voluntary, embedded within the larger political landscape, and fully committed to a new mode of life. This new community is, of course, the community of disciples, which later becomes the church; and the new way of life Jesus offers is neither simply spiritual nor purely transcendent, but one of social and political action:

> [Jesus] gave [the disciples] a new way to deal with offenders—by forgiving them . . . to deal with violence—by suffering . . . to deal

> with money—by sharing it . . . to deal with problems of leadership—by drawing upon the gifts of every member, even the most humble . . . to deal with a corrupt society—by building a new order, not smashing the old. He gave them a new pattern of relationships between man and woman, between parent and child, between master and slave, in which was made *concrete* a radical new vision of what it means to be a human person.[27]

The way Christ delivers humankind from sin and represents the kingdom of God on earth is not through "impossible possibilities" but through concrete action. Nor does Christ have nothing relevant to say about ethics and politics in the world. His is in part a sociopolitical ethic. It is true that Christ's own practice of this ethic led him eventually to the cross. But this does not in itself render the ethic of Jesus impossible. It merely renders it fit for a certain kind of person, one who truly believes that Jesus' way is the way of the kingdom or, in other words, that "Jesus is Christ and that Jesus Christ is Lord."[28]

The possibilities that Christ's new ethic opens up are not, in Yoder's view, "simple possibilities" for world politics—Yoder is not guilty of the naive optimism Niebuhr found so misguided. But they are, in Yoder's view, concrete possibilities for Christians. In order to appreciate what these possibilities entail, one must consider Yoder's ecclesiological and eschatological views.

In terms of ecclesiology, it is significant that Christ forms a community of believers, for things are possible in communities that are not possible alone. Christ does not seek out heroic individuals. He forms "a covenanting group of men and women who instruct one another, forgive one another, bear one another's burdens, and reinforce one another's witness."[29] One thinks here of the possibilities to which Christ alludes when he tells his disciples (Matthew 18:20) that "where two or three are gathered in my name, there am I in the midst of them." For Yoder, the church and the resurrection go hand in hand. The risen Lord is present in the church by means of the Holy Spirit, which fills Christ's followers. But Niebuhr entirely neglects the fact, as Yoder points out, that in the New Testament "the coming of the Spirit means the imparting of *power*, and that [this] *power* is . . . a working reality within history and especially with the church."[30]

In a related sense, the church is significant for the role it can play as a witness to the state by exhibiting its radically alternative political order. Because the church is voluntary and empowered by the Spirit, it can order its own politics according to the ethic of love. And this ordering is crucial, Yoder argues, because it prefigures the "will of God for human socialness as a whole"—it supplies a foretaste for Christians, and a witness to the world, of the coming kingdom.[31] Yoder is careful in his ecclesiology to avoid two common errors. He does not believe that the politics of the church will be perfect or free from sin; nor does he mean to suggest that the secular state will become saved or redeemed by the witness of the church. But Yoder does believe that the church, by speaking prophetically to the state on specific matters where the church has something concrete to offer, can have an impact on the state's sense of possibilities. The ethics and politics of the church are practiced (it is true) for religio-moral reasons, not for their consequences per se, but the consequences are sometimes so salutary that the church's witness can be powerful.

The possibilities Yoder sees for Christians within the church and for the church within the world are also informed by a particular eschatological view that regards the kingdom as both "here and yet not entirely here." In sharp contrast to thinkers like Niebuhr who view the kingdom as strictly transcendent, Yoder describes it as having already come but not yet in its fullness. We exist in an age between the Pentecost and the parousia, in which the new order has been ushered in by Jesus while the old order of sin still exists as well. Until Christ comes again, the earthly powers, including the state, will "struggle against the church and often appear, at least temporarily, to triumph over God and his cause."[32] But this does not mean that the victory of love over sin will take place exclusively in some transcendent realm, as Niebuhr would have it. Rather,

> sin is vanquished every time a Christian in the power of God chooses . . . obedience instead of necessity, love instead of compromise, brotherhood instead of veiled self-interest. . . . That this triumph over sin is incomplete changes in no way the fact that it is possible, and that if God calls us to deny ourselves, accept suffering, and love our neighbors that too is possible. This possibility passes by the way of the cross, and therefore is "foolishness to

> the Greeks and a scandal to the Jews, but to them that believe it is the wisdom of God and the power of God."[33]

The task of individual Christians is to practice the ethic of the kingdom: to love as Christ loved, serve as Christ served, and suffer as Christ suffered. Such a life will seem scandalous in the eyes of the world because the world is fallen and its eyes are full of sin. It will seem "imprudent" and "irresponsible" because the world defines prudence and responsibility in terms of natural (fallen) desires. But this is the life Christ calls his followers to live, and God is in control of history.

Yoder's Christology, ecclesiology, and eschatology all work together to stress the possibilities of Christian ethics. Thus, while Yoder and Niebuhr begin from similar premises—the absolute ethic of Jesus—they end up in radically different places on the question of pacifism. For Yoder, individual Christians and the church in general can and should be pacifist. The individual should be pacifist because killing is contrary to Christ's injunctions to love enemies, to resist not one who is evil, and to turn the other cheek; and also because the ethic of Jesus is an "ethic of testimony," a way of communicating through deeds that the love of God knows no "enemies."[34] The church for its part should be pacifist, too, not only because it is composed of individual Christians who must support one another in their witness, but also because the church itself has a role to play as witness: what does it "say" about the body of Christ when the church condones wars in which Christians kill Christians?[35] The name Yoder chooses for his distinct brand of nonresistance is the "pacifism of the messianic community." It is "messianic" because it finds its foundation and its enablement in the teachings, passion, and resurrection of Christ. It requires "community" because only in shared life can Christians experience a foretaste of God's kingdom.[36]

In the end, Yoder's position essentially drives a wedge through the alternatives Niebuhr had earlier posed. Where Niebuhr had insisted that Christians must choose between political responsibility (realism) and political irrelevance (personal pacifism), Yoder argues that pacifism represents a new form of political responsibility and relevance. Pacifism is relevant to the body politic of Christ, to the social organization of the kingdom. And Christians are responsible when they act in ways pleasing to God. These are indeed the only kinds of relevance and responsibility that matter for Yoder.[37] In a sense, then, Yoder takes Niebuhr's inconsistent Kantianism and makes it consistent. It is not enough that Christians simply recognize the absolute ethic of Jesus only to discard it in practical matters. We must also practice Christ's ethic as that which defines freedom, responsibility, and relevance in a new way.[38] It is true, of course, that the immediate consequences of this ethic are uncertain: "We cannot sight down the barrel of suffering love to see how it will hit its target."[39] But if we truly believe that Jesus is Christ and that God is in control of history, why should we live by any other norm?

Love and Ethical Judgment

Comparing these influential ethical systems to the classic just war tradition, we do well to begin by stating the obvious: the just war tradition is in essence neither realist nor pacifist. What the tradition maintains at its core is that war is sometimes necessary and sometimes also just, even from a Christian point of view, but only under specific conditions, which for the Christian must be compatible with scripture. In practical terms, it can be understood as a middle way between realism and pacifism—allowing war but limiting it. In terms of first principles, however, it is no middle way at all but a deliberate rejection of the flawed absolutism that undergirds Christian realism and pacifism alike.

Of course, there is significant common ground. It is as true for the classic authors in the just war tradition (Augustine, Aquinas, Luther, and Calvin) as it is for Niebuhr and Yoder that the ethic of Jesus is an ethic of love.[40] Christ says (echoing Leviticus 19:18 and Deuteronomy 6:5):

> You shall love the Lord your God with all your heart, and with all your soul, and with all your mind. This is the great and first commandment. And the second is like unto it; you shall love your neighbor as yourself. On these two commandments depend all the law and the prophets.[41]

Love is thus the first principle of all Christian ethics, and the duty to love is indeed absolute: it binds Christians completely and defines, without exception, everything that Christian ethics requires.

The just war tradition also acknowledges, along with Niebuhr and Yoder, the centrality of "the law" in Christian ethics. That is to say, scripture reveals not only universal principles of love but also more specific injunctions such as one finds in the Decalogue or the Sermon on the Mount. And since the law in both the Old and New Testaments seems to caution against the use of force, we find what amounts to a profound hesitation concerning war. The hesitation is evident in the very form of the classic just war sources. Aquinas, for instance, inquires "whether it is *always* sinful to wage war" or whether "*some* kind of war is lawful."[42] Luther similarly wonders "whether soldiers, *too*, can be saved."[43] In both cases, the questions are answered in the affirmative, yet the questions themselves reflect the hesitation.

The fundamental issue that distinguishes the just war tradition from other positions on war concerns not the question whether the law discourages violence (clearly it does); it concerns the question of the proper relationship between "the law" and the more abstract duty to love. In general, one may say (looking again at the last sentence in the quotation above from Matthew 22) that love stands as a universal first principle and that the law applies it or "connects it" to human action in the concrete. But to what extent or in what way are such injunctions absolute? Here lies the point of departure between the just war tradition on the one hand, and both Niebuhr and Yoder on the other. For Niebuhr and Yoder alike, the law itself is regarded as universal and absolute in the full sense—completely binding, exceptionless, and necessary regardless of the consequences. To "resist not one who is evil," for example, is always and everywhere precisely what love requires. The universal principle and the "connecting principles" of the law share the same absolute status.

Just war writers beginning with Augustine are familiar with this temptation,[44] but they reject it, because they will not allow the simple equation of love with nonresistance. And it has also to do (interestingly enough) with what scripture does not teach on the matter of force; scripture does not address itself to every situation in which Christians find themselves. Let us examine these claims more closely.

As Augustine points out, resistance and even force can sometimes be an act of love. This is a fact parents may know well.[45] One may go so far as to say that force is sometimes the most appropriate act of love in certain situations. For as sinners, we frequently find ourselves exceeding bounds—those of others as well as of our own true freedom. We do things we wish we had not done and in some cases would be grateful to encounter resistance from loving parents, friends, or even strangers. Does scripture rule out the possibility of such love-directed force? Far from ruling it out, the gospel supplies an example of it, and this is the example of Christ and the money changers. Christ himself uses force in resisting evil; he turns the tables over (Matthew 21:12; Mark 15:19; Luke 19:45–48) and casts the moneychangers out of the Temple with a whip (John 2:13–17). If the ethic of Jesus entails an absolute prohibition on resistance and force, what sense could be made of this act?[46]

There is another way in which scripture seems to qualify the principle of nonresistance. The Apostle Paul in Romans 13 calls upon Christians to "be subject to the governing authorities," authorities who do not "bear the sword in vain" but serve God in executing wrath upon the wrongdoer. And a similar injunction is found in 1 Peter 13–14: "Be subject for the Lord's sake to every human institution, whether it be to the emperor who is supreme, or to governors as sent by him to punish those who do wrong and to praise those who do right." Now the duty to be subject to the governing authority, political authority, stems ultimately from our fundamental commitment to love God and neighbor. For the political authorities "have been instituted by God" for our good; they foster peace by punishing wrongdoers and praising those who do right. But these authorities also involve themselves and their subjects in the use of force. Obedience to the authorities may conflict, it appears, with obedience to Christ's principle to "resist not one who is evil." Readers may, of course, want to raise questions at this point about the proper extent of one's obedience to human authorities, and such questions should be raised—our obedience to human authorities should not be blind but rather conditioned always by the more universal commitment to love God and neighbor. Yet the more fundamental point is this: not only might the duty to obey political authorities sometimes involve some citizens in acts of resistance and force; it is certain to do so. Moreover, the gospel writers and even Christ himself seem to accept this fact.

To show this, the classic writers in the just war tradition all point to a number of incidents from the Gospels.[47] One was the time when soldiers came to be baptized by John the Baptist and asked him, "What shall we do?" John's reply was that the soldiers should neither throw down their weapons nor that they should abstain altogether from force but that they should "rob no one by violence" and "be content with their pay" (Luke 3:14). Another incident was Jesus' encounter with the centurion in Capernaum, who believed that Christ could heal a paralyzed servant as effortlessly as the centurion himself could command soldiers: "I am a man under authority," the centurion tells Christ, "with soldiers under me; and I say to one 'Go,' and he goes, and to another, 'Come,' and he comes" (Matthew 8:9). As Augustine points out, Christ healed the centurion's servant and praised his faith. He did not order the centurion to desert.[48] And finally, Augustine points to Cornelius the centurion of the Italian cohort, who was told by an angel that his prayers had ascended as a memorial before God. What sense could be made of these passages if one were to insist that the injunction to "resist not one who is evil" is absolute or that one must always, without exception, "turn the other cheek"? The gospel itself frustrates such an absolute rendering of Christ's injunctions.[49]

The problem can be seen from another angle as well, if we consider (following ethicist Paul Ramsey) a scenario that does not quite occur in scripture: "It was a work of charity," writes Ramsey, "for the Good Samaritan to give help to the man who fell among thieves"; but then, Ramsey wonders, "what do you think Jesus would have made the Samaritan do if he had come upon the scene while the robbers were still at their fell work?"[50] The question is significant because it reveals in a striking way that while Jesus taught his disciples to turn the other cheek, he did not enjoin them to "lift up the face of another oppressed man for *him* to be struck again on *his* other cheek."[51] What, then, are Christians to do when in their effort to love their neighbor they find the neighbor under attack and in desperate need of aid? Does love not require Christians to help—and if the thieves will not desist, then to defend the victim from harm? (Consider James 2:14–17 in this connection.)[52] Surely Christ's Sermon on the Mount was not intended to bar Christians from such obvious requirements of love.

While the duty to love, then, is always absolute, the injunctions to turn the other cheek and to resist not one who is evil are not absolute but rather must be applied judiciously according to the more fundamental requirements of love. Christian ethics involves *judgment*, not simply the application of law. It is true, of course, that at times—for example, in war—the judgments Christians must make are extremely perilous, the risk of error very great. But the risks and dangers do not negate the obligation to judge and to act in accordance with love.

Neither Niebuhr nor Yoder

Here is precisely where the just war tradition breaks not only from Christian pacifism but also from Niebuhrian realism, and the break is not merely pragmatic. It is fundamentally a break in theological understanding, in assessing what Christian love requires. We readily acknowledge that partial truth resides in the positions of both Niebuhr and Yoder. And we recognize that, in the end, Niebuhr was closer to the just war position than Yoder, given the willingness on Niebuhr's part (and to his credit) to resist totalitarianism. At the same time, we discern faulty assumptions regarding Christian ethics and Jesus' teaching that are at work in the thinking of both Niebuhr and Yoder—assumptions that are theologically inconsistent with the Christian moral tradition and divergent from classical just war thinking. These assumptions have to do with the nature and necessity of coercive force in the course of normal human affairs. Perhaps the greatest confusion caused by both Niebuhr and Yoder is found among Christian pacifists, who mistakenly assume that "just war theory" was incubated in a "Constantinian" religio-cultural climate in which religious believers, now that they have been "co-opted" by the state, were (reluctantly) led to find justification for coercive force against the backdrop of earlier patristic pacifist nonviolence. But this view, as we sought to demonstrate in the second chapter, is false. Furthermore, this portrait fails to discern (or acknowledge) that charity can undergird the implementation of force for the good of others. Whether or not this force, at the empirical level, can be misused is beside the point philosophically. The force of Paul Ramsey's argument still holds: neighbor-love *may* require the courageous and measured application of such force for the benefit of others, and the limitations placed upon that application of force are strictly delineated by just war criteria.

Niebuhr and Yoder, by contrast, alike insist upon an "absolute ethic of Jesus" that equates love simply with nonresistance. The broader point thus needs emphasis that the mainstream theologians of the church rooted their convictions about justified war and coercive force in the duties and moral obligations of charity and justice, not in a commitment to "nonviolence." By and large, they understood that political authority is not political authority if it has no coercive power to secure and preserve the public good. Such an acknowledgment, which is true in both domestic and international contexts, does not serve to obliterate moral discriminations; to the contrary, it upholds necessary moral distinctions that demarcate innocence and guilt, justice and injustice.

Where exactly do Niebuhr and Yoder go astray? Niebuhr, for his part, has difficulty grounding Christian love in a theologically consistent framework and in concrete circumstances. The result is that he propounds a form of radical dualism—a dualism for which he is rightly criticized by Yoder, among others. Niebuhr, nevertheless, has the virtue of intuiting (in spite of his ethical principles) a confidence in the value of democratic civilization and a belief that democratic nations are worth defending. For this he can (and has) been praised by contemporary just war theorists. Still, one looks in vain in Niebuhr's work for any discussion of just war criteria or any way of bringing war under the guidance of Christian principles. In fact, Niebuhr's realism does not even require that force be used only in response to some "wrong" on the part of the opposing side. Considerations of "balance of power" and raison d'état are nowhere ruled out. Niebuhr is thus not in the "just war" tradition in the proper sense of that term. While he believes wars can be justified, he does not limit their justification to anything resembling the classic criteria of the tradition.

Yoder, for his part, corrects Niebuhr's dualism by making Niebuhrian absolutism more consistent, as it were. He insists upon pacifism in practice, not merely in theory. But Yoder, by the same token, essentially obliterates the tensions inherent in Christian ethics as he renders one set of injunctions absolute and ignores others. He dilutes, for example, Christian obedience to the governing authorities and ignores or rejects those passages of scripture in which Christ seems to acknowledge the work of soldiers.

The just war tradition, by contrast, is a complex ethical system, no matter which approach or "voice" in that tradition one considers. From a Christian point of view, at any rate, it is complex to the extent that it takes its bearings not merely from the Sermon on the Mount but also from scripture as a whole and from the insights of natural law; moreover, it is complex because it demands that Christians exercise judgment in attempting to love God and neighbor in concrete circumstances. While it accepts as an operating premise that one should "turn the other cheek" and "resist not one who is evil," it does not misconstrue Jesus' teaching as a pattern for responsible statecraft, domestic policy, or international affairs. And in contrast to both Niebuhr and Yoder, it finds that love sometimes requires more than an absolutist rendering of these injunctions.

Notes

Chapter 1: Tradition and the Just War

1. Jimmy Carter, "Just War—or a Just War?" *New York Times,* Sunday, March 9, 2003, "Week in Review," 13.
2. Jean Bethke Elshtain, "Will It Be a 'Just War' or Just a War?" *Los Angeles Times,* February 19, 2003, B13.
3. The survey was conducted by the American Civic Literacy Program at the Intercollegiate Studies Institute. See its report *Failing Our Students, Failing America: Holding Colleges Accountable for Teaching America's History and Institutions* (Wilmington: ISI, 2007). Seniors at Harvard, Princeton, and Yale were tied at 24 percent in their ability to answer the just war question correctly—slightly higher than the national average but certainly not a cause for optimism. Our data on individual schools were supplied by ISI.
4. This burden distinguishes our study from contemporary essays in just war theory such as Michael Walzer's *Just and Unjust Wars: A Moral Argument with Historical Illustrations* (New York: Basic Books, 1977). Taking the tradition as its subject, our study has more in common with James Turner Johnson's *Ideology, Reason, and the Limitation of War: Religious and Secular Concepts: 1200–1740* (Princeton, NJ: Princeton University Press, 1975) and *Just War Tradition and the Restraint of War: A Moral and Historical Inquiry* (Princeton, NJ: Princeton University Press, 1981). However, where Johnson provides a historical narrative and traces historical influences, we attempt to offer a more detailed exegetical meditation on each author we treat. The reason for this stems from our understanding of the "permanent possibilities" of intellectual history, as discussed below.
5. See W. David Clinton, ed., *The Realist Tradition and Contemporary International Relations* (Baton Rouge, LA: Louisiana State University Press, 2007), for excellent chapter-length studies of major figures in the realist tradition; and see Jack

Donnelly, *Realism and International Relations* (Cambridge: Cambridge University Press, 2000), for a typology of realist approaches.

6. Two useful studies of the varieties of pacifism are Peter Brock, *Varieties of Pacifism: A Survey from Antiquity to the Outset of the Twentieth Century* (Syracuse, NY: Syracuse University Press, 1999), and John Howard Yoder, *Nevertheless: Varieties and Shortcomings of Religious Pacifism*, 2nd ed. (Scottdale, PA: Herald Press, 1992). James Turner Johnson, *The Quest for Peace: Three Moral Traditions in Western Cultural History* (Princeton, NJ: Princeton University Press, 1987), helpfully contrasts the just war position with certain sectarian and utopian varieties of pacifism.

7. See, e.g., John Howard Yoder, *When War Is Unjust: Being Honest in Just War Thinking* (New York: Orbis Books, 1996), 31, 50–51, 67–70.

8. See, e.g., Jonathan Barnes, "The Just War," in *The Cambridge History of Later Medieval Philosophy*, ed. Norman Kretzmann, Anthony Kenny, and Jan Pinborg (Cambridge: Cambridge University Press: 1982), 783–84.

9. Oliver O'Donovan also voices frustration with the common charge in his *The Just War Revisited* (Cambridge: Cambridge University Press, 2003), 13. We might add that the charge itself relies on the just war tradition in an undetected way: in order to claim that injustices persist in war today, one must know what counts as an injustice, which is precisely what the just war articulates.

10. Examples abound, but an especially cartoonish example of the attempt to reduce the rich and variegated medieval just war tradition to a theory is Jonathan Barnes, "The Just War," 771–84. The *X*'s and *Y*'s say it all; and not a single caveat makes the cut. Walzer's approach in *Just and Unjust Wars* is also to reduce and revise the tradition into a single (though complex) argument—the bare outline of which is well adumbrated by Douglas Lackey, "A Modern Theory of Just War," *Ethics* 92 (1982): 533–46. James Turner Johnson's work on the just war tradition—*Just War Tradition and the Restraint of War*—stands as a refreshing corrective to this tendency. Though Johnson admittedly claims that "the tradition can be expressed as a theory, if care is taken to express this theory generally and with a degree of open endedness" (xxii), the caveat says it all. Johnson's own excellent studies on diversity within the tradition reveal that the tradition actually cannot be reduced to a theory except at the most general level.

11. Walzer declares in his first preface to *Just and Unjust Wars* (xxi): "I am not going to expound morality from the ground up. Were I to begin with the foundations, I would probably never get beyond them; in any case, I am by no means sure what the foundations are. The substructure of the ethical world is a matter of deep and apparently unending controversy. Meanwhile, however, we are living in the superstructure. . . . The study of judgments and justifications in the real world moves us closer, perhaps, to the most profound questions of moral philosophy, but it does not require a direct engagement with those questions. . . . For the moment, at least, practical morality is detached from its foundations, and we must act as if that separation were a possible (since it is an actual) condition of moral life."

12. On this point, see, e.g., R. G. Collingwood, *Autobiography* (Oxford: Clarendon Press, 2002), chap. 5, "Question and Answer," and R. G. Collingwood, *An Essay on Philosophical Method* (Oxford: Clarendon Press, 1933), especially chap. 10, "Philosophy as a Branch of Literature."

13. See Michael Walzer, *Arguing about War* (New Haven, CT: Yale University Press,

2004), 155, 160–61, who rightly complains that "lastness" is too often invoked as if it were a metaphysical principle that can never be reached in real life; it is invoked "as an excuse for postponing the use of force indefinitely." But last resort really means simply this: "Look hard for alternatives before you 'let loose the dogs of war.'"

14. If tradition is understood as the transmission of something from one generation to the next (in Roman law, it was a piece of property), then the transmitted object (the *traditum*) needs to be sufficiently established for the receiver to know he has received something. We would argue that the breakthrough act of formation occurred in the work of Augustine, even while the formation was not ex nihilo but drew from the past. Augustine's importance in this regard can be verified by the extent to which later writers cited him as the initial source of their thinking on war. On this understanding of *tradition* in general, see further Edward Shils, *Tradition* (London: Faber and Faber, 1981).

15. Letter 138, "To Marcellinus," in Michael Tkacz and Douglas Kries, trans., *Augustine: Political Writings*, ed. and trans. Michael Tkacz and Douglas Kries (Indianapolis: Hackett Publishing, 1994), 209.

16. Martin Luther, *On Temporal Authority*, in *Luther and Calvin on Secular Authority*, trans. Harro Höpfl (Cambridge: Cambridge University Press, 1991), 40. Cf. Martin Luther, *Whether Soldiers Too Can Be Saved*, trans. Charles M. Jacobs and Robert C. Schultz in *Luther's Works*, American ed., 55 vols. (Philadelphia: Fortress Press; St. Louis: Concordia, 1955–86), vol. 46, 130–31.

17. John Calvin, *Institutes of the Christian Religion*, IV.20.2–3.

18. The chivalric codes for combat constitute a partial exception to this rule, as shown by James Turner Johnson, *Ideology, Reason, and the Limitation of War.*

19. John Locke, *Two Treatises of Government*, II, chap. 2.

20. John Courtney Murray, *Morality and the Modern War* (New York: The Church Peace Union, 1959); Paul Ramsey, *The Just War: Force and Political Responsibility* (Lanham, MD: Rowman & Littlefield, [1968] 1983); O'Donovan, *The Just War Revisited*; Walzer, *Just and Unjust Wars*; William V. O'Brien, *U.S. Military Intervention: Law and Morality* (Beverly Hills, CA: Sage Publications, 1979), *Law and Morality in Israel's War with the PLO* (New York: Routledge, 1991); James Turner Johnson, *Ideology, Reason, and the Limitation of War*, *The Just War Tradition and the Restraint of War*, *Morality and Contemporary Warfare* (New Haven, CT: Yale University Press, 1999); Jean Bethke Elshtain, *Just War against Terror: The Burden of American Power in a Violent World* (New York: Basic Books, 2003).

21. The secularization narrative recurs throughout the literature. See, e.g., Bruno Coppieters and Nicholas Fotion, eds., *Moral Constraints on War: Principles and Cases* (Lanham, MD: Lexington Books, 2008), 311; Reuben E. Brigety II, *Ethics, Technology, and the American Way of War: Cruise Missiles and US Security Policy* (New York: Routledge, 2007), 27ff.; and Alex J. Bellamy, *Just Wars from Cicero to Iraq* (Cambridge: Polity Press, 2006), 49.

22. James Turner Johnson has had a career-long interest in this question and has approached it more adroitly than any scholar of whom we are aware. In his recent article "Thinking Historically about Just War," *Journal of Military Ethics* 8 (2009): 246–59, he describes his view as follows: "I like to describe just war tradition as a stream that moves through history like a river, remaining the same yet putting

down some elements and picking up others as it flows, from time to time dividing into different channels and then, perhaps, recombining. As I have conceived my task, it is to describe this flow and try to make sense of it, while trying to keep the various sub-streams in contact with one another and with the mother stream."

23. Bellamy recognizes this in *Just Wars* and describes it aptly (even while his historical narrative is cast in terms of a gradual movement toward a "fully secularized" theory). "The tradition is fragmented, comprising many different sub-traditions and indeed sub-sub-traditions, . . . *none of which permanently prevail over the others*" (p. 3, emphasis added).

24. Nicholas Rengger, "On the Just War Tradition in the Twenty-First Century," *International Affairs* 78 (2002): 353–63, expresses a similar view: "A tradition of thinking can have many roots, be fed by many tributaries. . . . Traditions, at least as I understand them, do not have an 'essence' or a central core. . . . Rather, one has to understand a tradition as part of an ongoing and potentially never-ending conversation in which many different assumptions will take centre stage at various points."

25. See Cynthia Grant Shoenberger, "The Development of the Lutheran Theory of Resistance: 1523–1530," *The Sixteenth Century Journal* 8 (1977): 61–76; and "Luther and the Justifiability of Resistance to Legitimate Authority," *Journal of the History of Ideas* 40 (1979): 3–20; and W. D. J. Cargill Thompson, *Studies in the Reformation* (London: Athlone Press, 1980), 3–41.

26. We owe our understanding of differentiation in history to Eric Voegelin. See his essay "Reason: The Classic Experience," in Eric Voegelin, *Anamnesis*, trans. Gerhart Niemeyer (South Bend, IN: University of Notre Dame Press, 1978), chap. 6. We should add that we have adapted Voegelin's insight to suit our own purposes.

27. Commentators frequently list "democratization of Iraq and the Arab world" as an illegitimate casus belli cited by the Bush administration. However, this may be a misrepresentation of the administration's prewar case. Democratization was not often (if at all) cited as a just cause during the buildup to war; rather, it was cited as a prudential consideration related to outcome—i.e., is the war likely to do more good than harm? This is not to deny that some individuals inside and outside the administration would have been happy for a war in the name of democratization. For Paul Wolfowitz's position, see Peter J. Boyer, "The Believer: Paul Wolfowitz Defends His War," *New Yorker*, November 1, 2004, http://www.newyorker.com/archive/2004/11/01/041101fa_fact, and for an influential view from outside, see Fouad Ajami, "Iraq and the Arabs' Future," *Foreign Affairs* 82, no. 1 (January / February, 2003): 2–18. However, this was not Bush's or Rumsfeld's public position before the war, though it evidently became their position after Baghdad had been captured and WMD stockpiles were not found. In other words, only after the true causes of war seemed shaky in retrospect did Bush begin to spin his democratization rhetoric as a casus belli. Boyer's account in "The Believer" supports this fact, as does Robert S. Snyder, "The Myth of Preemption: More than a War Against Iraq," *Orbis* 47 (2003): 653–60, though Snyder suspects that democratization was the true, unspoken motive from the start.

Chapter 2: Early Christian Attitudes toward Soldiering and War

1. A modified form of this chapter appeared in J. Daryl Charles, "Pacifists, Patriots, or Both? Second Thoughts on Pre-Constantinian Early-Christian Attitudes toward Soldiering and War," *Logos: A Journal of Catholic Thought and Culture* 13, no. 2 (Spring 2010): 17–55.
2. Roland H. Bainton, *Christian Attitudes toward War and Peace: A Historical Survey and Critical Re-evaluation* (New York / Nashville: Abingdon, 1960), 66.
3. Ibid.
4. John Howard Yoder, *The Christian Witness to the State*, Institute of Mennonite Studies 3 (Newton, KS: Faith and Life Press, 1964; repr. Scottdale, PA: Herald Press, 2002), 56.
5. Representative are Yoder, *When War Is Unjust, The Politics of Jesus*, rev. ed. (Grand Rapids / Cambridge, UK: Eerdmans, 1994), *What Would You Do? A Serious Answer to a Standard Question* (Scottdale, PA: Herald Press, 1983), *Nevertheless*, and *The Original Revolution: Essays on Christian Pacifism* (Scottdale, PA: Herald Press, 1971).
6. Richard B. Hays, *The Moral Vision of the New Testament—Community, Cross, New Creation: A Contemporary Introduction to New Testament Ethics* (San Francisco: Harper, 1996), 318.
7. Ibid., 341.
8. Ibid., 317.
9. Robert G. Clouse, "The Christian Church and Peace through the Centuries," in E. Morris Sider and Luke Keefer Jr., eds., *A Peace Reader* (Nappanee, IN: Evangel, 2002), 73.
10. Ibid., 71.
11. Ibid.
12. Ibid., 71–72.
13. Ibid., 72.
14. Bainton's account, perhaps more than any over the past fifty years, has shaped the conventional view of the early church. What is remarkable is the degree to which this portrait of early Christian attitudes toward military service and war has achieved currency across wider Christendom—Catholic, Orthodox, and Protestant (and, as authors, one of us grew up in a Mennonite, and thus Anabaptist, context). A telling illustration of the dominant interpretation of the early church is that one is hard-pressed to identify more than several monographs published during the past one hundred years that have sought to present evidence from the fathers that the early church was *not* universally and uniformly pacifist. Exceptions are Adolf von Harnack's *Militia Christi: The Christian Religion and the Military in the First Three Centuries*, trans. D. M. Gracie (Philadelphia: Fortress, 1981), originally published in 1905 by J. C. B. Mohr under the title *Militia Christi: Die Christliche Religion und der Soldatenstand in den ersten drei Jahrhunderten*; Louis J. Swift's *The Early Fathers on War and Military Service*, Message of the Fathers of the Church, vol. 19 (Wilmington, DE: Michael Glazier, 1983); and John Helgeland, Robert J. Daly, and J. Patout Burns, *Christians and the Military: The Early Experience* (Minneapolis: Fortress, 1985).
15. Clouse, "The Christian Church and Peace," 72.

16. Ibid., 73 (emphasis added).
17. Correlatively, is Augustine to be construed as the "product" of the merger of church and state, as Clouse asserts? Is such an accurate reading of *De Civitate Dei* as well as assorted Augustinian letters? And is in fact *De Civitate Dei* a mirror of church-state conflation? The limitations of the present chapter, which focuses on pre-Constantinian fathers, prevent us from reexamining the basis of such claims.
18. Thus, for example, Roland Bainton's account of the early church as pacifist should not surprise us, given the fact of his Quaker affiliation. Similarly, Yoder's Mennonite Anabaptist convictions require of him such an interpretation. And the same might be said of Robert Clouse's confessional commitments as a leader in the Brethren Church. It is fair to say that their interpretations of early Christian history approximate what one might anticipate.
19. Justin Martyr, *First Apology* 39 (*Anti-Nicene Fathers* [*ANF*], ed. Alexander Roberts, James Donaldson, and A. Cleveland Coxe, vol. 1 [Grand Rapids, MI: Eerdmans, 1951], 176).
20. Tatian, *Tatian* 11 (*ANF*, eds. Alexander Roberts, James Donaldson, and A. Cleveland Coxe, vol. 2 [Grand Rapids, MI: Eerdmans, 1951], 69).
21. Athenagoras, *Plea for Christians* 1 (*ANF* 2.129).
22. Irenaeus, *Apostolic Preaching* 96 (accessible at www.ccel.org/ccel/irenaeus/demonstr.preaching_the_demonstration_of_the_apostolic_preaching).
23. *1 Clement* 61.1–2 (accessible at www.earlychristianwritings.com/text/1clement-lightfoot). Louis J. Swift ("War and the Christian Conscience I: The Early Years," *Aufstieg und Niedergang der römischen Welt* [*ANRW*] II.23.2, ed. H. Temporini and W. Haase [Berlin / New York: Walther de Gruyter, 1984], 843, n. 34) is surely correct to note that Clement's attitude toward the empire, following the extensive persecutions of Domitian, is nothing short of remarkable.
24. *1 Clement* 60.4.
25. E.g., Justin Martyr, *First Apology* 17.3; Athenagoras, *Plea for Christians* 37; Tertullian, *Apology* 30; and Cyprian, *To Demetrius* 20.
26. Tertullian, *Apology* 30 (*ANF* 3.42).
27. Ibid., 30, 32, and 39.
28. Ibid., 42.
29. Ibid.
30. Tertullian, *Against the Jews* 3 (*ANF* 3.154). In several of his writings, Tertullian will apply future, eschatological promise concerning "swords into plowshares," foretold by OT prophets, to the present age in Christ.
31. Tertullian, *On Idolatry* 19. As to the latter, Tertullian almost seems conflicted, unable to process the New Testament data and reconcile it with his beliefs. "Of course," he muses, "if faith comes later and finds any preoccupied with military service, their case is different, as in the instance of those whom John [the Baptist] used to receive for baptism, and of those most faithful centurions, I mean the centurion whom Christ approves, and the centurion whom Peter instructs [Cornelius]; yet, at the same time, when a man has become a believer, and faith has been sealed, there must be either an immediate abandonment of it [i.e., the military office], which has been the course with many—or all sorts of quibbling will have to be resorted to in order to avoid offending God" (*On the Military Crown,* 11 in *ANF* 3.100).

32. Ibid. (*ANF* 3.99).
33. Ibid., 12 (*ANF* 3.101).
34. Tertullian, *On Idolatry* 19.
35. Hereon see Friedrich Klingmüller, "Sacramentum," in *Paulys Real-Encyclopädie der Classischen Altertumswissenschaft*, ed. Georg Wissowa (Stuttgart: J. B. Metzler, 1895), 2.1667–74.
36. Important discussions of the military cult of the early Christian centuries are to be found in John Helgeland, "Christians and the Roman Army from Marcus Aurelius to Constantine," *ANRW* II.23.2: 149–63; Helgeland, Daly, and Burns, *Christians and the Military*; and Frances Young, "The Early Church: Military Service, War and Peace," *Theology* 92 (1989): 491–503.
37. A useful resource in this regard is the volume by military historian Paul Christopher, *The Ethics of War and Peace*, rev. ed. (Upper Saddle River, NJ: Prentice Hall, 1999), especially chaps. 1 and 2.
38. Tertullian, *On the Military Crown* 12; cf. also *On Idolatry* 16 and 19.
39. Tertullian, *On Idolatry* 18, and Tertullian, *On the Apparel of Women* (*ANF.* 4, 1.1 and 2.1–13).
40. Tertullian, *On Idolatry* 15.
41. The event is depicted on the column (arch of triumph) of Marcus Aurelius in Rome, and on coins minted by Marcus Aurelius, Jupiter is depicted hurling thunderbolts at Germanic hordes.
42. Tertullian, *Apology* 5; Tertullian, *To Scapula* 2; and Eusebius, *Church History* 4.3–5.7.
43. Historians differ as to the exact date; the range is from A.D. 171 (so, e.g., Philip Carrington, *The Early Christian Church—Vol. 2: The Second Christian Century* [Cambridge: Cambridge University Press, 1957], 224–25) to 174 (Robert M. Grant, *Augustus to Constantine: The Rise and Triumph of Christianity in the Roman World* [San Francisco: Harper & Row, 1970], 91).
44. Tertullian, *Apology* 5.
45. The Twelfth Legion had been stationed in Cappadocia (present-day eastern Turkey) before the war, where there were known to be many Christian recruits.
46. Tertullian, *Apology* 5. Pagan accounts give credit variously to the emperor himself, an Egyptian magician and pagan gods.
47. Eusebius, *Church History* 5.5. Writing shortly after the Edict of Milan (A.D. 313), Eusebius uses the words "Report has it . . ." to describe the incident involving the Twelfth Legion.
48. Helgeland, "Christians and the Roman Army," 771–72, is correct to infer that it is implausible to imagine Christians appearing all of a sudden here in the Balkans; thus, Christian participation in the army must have occurred long before the early 170s. Interpreters as divergent as Stephen Gero, "*Miles Gloriosus*: The Christian and Military Service according to Tertullian," *Church History* 39 (1970): 285–98, and Johnson, *The Quest for Peace*, 3–66, point to social factors that in plausible ways account for this shift in the second century.
49. John Helgeland, "Christians and the Roman Army A.D. 173–337," *Church History* 43 (1974): 150.
50. The degree to which Tertullian's increasingly sectarian attitudes were attributable to Montanism remains speculative, even when it is worth noting and certainly

plausible. The greater factor in Tertullian's change of attitude may well have been the influx of Christians into the military profession, which aroused Tertullian to the potential dangers therein, as Gero, "*Miles Gloriosus*," 289–91, posits.

51. On the evolution of Tertullian's views, see also Hans von Campenhausen, "Christians and Military Service in the Early Church," *Tradition and Life in the Church*, trans. A. V. Littledale (Philadelphia: Fortress, 1963), 160–67, and Stephen Gero, "*Miles Gloriosus*." Gero's essay is a highly nuanced examination of Tertullian's increasingly rigorist position.

52. Origen, *Contra Celsus* 5.33 (*ANF* 4.558).

53. Ibid., 3.7 (*ANF* 4.467).

54. Ibid. (*ANF* 4.467–68).

55. Ibid., 8.73 (*ANF* 4.667).

56. Ibid. (*ANF* 4.668).

57. Ibid.

58. Ibid.

59. Ibid.

60. *On Idolatry* 17. With Origen, Tertullian acknowledges that a considerable number of Christians were already serving in the Roman legions, but unlike Origen he concedes certain conditions under which he believes a Christian *might* possibly serve as a magistrate, provided one avoid certain idolatrous contexts, as did Joseph and Daniel in the Old Testament.

61. Clement, *Stromata* 4.7.

62. Clement, *Paedagogus* 12 (*ANF* 2.267).

63. Clement, *Protrepticus* 10.

64. Hippolytus, *Apostolic Tradition* 16.17.

65. Ibid., 16.10–22.

66. Ibid., 16.17–19.

67. Cyprian, *To Donatus* 1.6 (*ANF* 5.277).

68. Cyprian, *Treatise* 9.16 (*ANF* 5.488).

69. Cyprian, *To Demetrius* 17 and 20; cf. *To Fortunatus* 13. Swift's commentary on Cyprian ("War and the Christian Conscience," 850–51) is refreshingly nuanced.

70. Dionysius, *Fragments* 2.1 (*ANF* 6.96).

71. Ibid., 2.8 (*ANF* 6.100).

72. Lactantius, *Divine Institutes* 18 (*ANF* 7.153).

73. Ibid., 20 (*ANF* 7.187).

74. Ibid., 7 (*ANF* 7.169).

75. Lactantius, *On the Deaths of the Persecutors* 10 (*ANF* 7.304–5).

76. Ibid., 11 (*ANF* 7.305).

77. *Divine Institutes* 5.18.

78. This is vividly on display in chaps. 37–52 of *On the Deaths of the Persecutors*. See especially chap. 44.

79. Sixteenth-century Anabaptism rejected the views of Luther, Calvin, and Zwingli regarding Christian participation in the affairs of the state. An important difference, however, between Anabaptists of today, at least Anabaptist academics, and their ancestors must be pointed out. As evidenced by the sixth of seven articles of the Schleitheim Confession, penned in 1527 by the Swiss Brethren as a brief summary of Anabaptist beliefs, historic Anabaptism affirmed that the sword in the

hand of the authorities is ordained by God for the twin purposes of punishment and protection. Anabaptist theologians and ethicists today, joined by other religious pacifists, are characterized by an exceedingly apocalyptic view of the powers—far more negative than that of their forebears. So, for example, John Howard Yoder, the most influential Anabaptist theologian of the last fifty years, argues in *The Politics of Jesus* and other works that not Romans 13 but Revelation 13 is the New Testament's normative teaching on the powers. Notwithstanding the early Anabaptists' radical separation from society, and while the Schleitheim Confession expressly forbids the Christian believer to use violent force, it does *not* reject violence per se in the hand of the magistrate.

80. That political authority can be abused is beyond controversy and thus immaterial to the apostolic argument.

81. At the bare minimum, these episodes amount to an implicit legitimizing of the military calling. See Gero, "*Miles Gloriosus*," 286.

82. It is significant that Ambrose, Augustine, Aquinas, Luther, and Grotius all cite popular misinterpretation in their day of the Sermon on the Mount, and Matthew 5:38–42 in particular, among the religious. All make the distinction between personal and public grievances, between matters of the heart and matters of state. All agree that the Christian must resist evil to protect others, even when the form of this resistance will vary and depend on the particular situation. And all are concerned about the common weal, which is invigorated by Christians' civic responsibility.

83. *Institutes of the Christian Religion* 4.20.10. We are here dependent on the F. L. Battle translation (Philadelphia: Westminster Press, 1960).

84. Hugo Grotius, *The Rights of War and Peace*, ed. Richard Tuck (Indianapolis: Liberty Fund, 2005), 1.2.6–7.

85. Matthew 26:51–52 and Luke 22:49–51.

86. E.g., 1 Cor. 5:11; 6:9; 10:8, 14; Gal. 5:19–20; Col. 3:5; Eph. 5:5; 1 Pet. 4:3; and Rev. 2:14.

87. Edward A. Ryan, "The Rejection of Military Service by the Early Christians," *Theological Studies* 12 (1952): 1–32, is one of a few to have argued that the early church was not pacifist. While there is some merit to his observation that those in the early church who were strongly pacifistic tended toward theologically heterodox views (e.g., Tatian, Montanists such as Tertullian, and in some respects Origen) or heresy (e.g., Marcion), this explanation is too simplistic, failing to offer a more nuanced account of diversity among Christians.

88. For example, in the regions specified by early Christian maps as Bithynia, Pontus, and Cappadocia (i.e., present-day northern and central Turkey; cf. 1 Pet. 1:1), there were known to be many Christian recruits into the Roman army. For a sociological accounting of this phenomenon, see Johnson, *The Quest for Peace*, chap. 1.

89. The contemporary implication of this presumption against coercive force is that none may legitimately serve as policemen, law-enforcement officers, security guards, soldiers, National Guardsmen, judges, legal theorists, politicians, or policy analysts in our day.

90. Hereon see, more recently, J. Daryl Charles, *Between Pacifism and Jihad: Just War and Christian Tradition* (Downers Grove, IL: InterVarsity Press, 2005), chaps. 2–4; Charles, "Justice, Neighbor-Love, and the Just War Tradition: Christian Reflections on Just Use of Force," *Cultural Encounters* 1, no. 1 (2004): 47–67; and

Charles, "Between Pacifism and Jihad: Justice and Neighbor-Love in the Just War Tradition," *Logos: A Journal of Catholic Thought and Culture* 8, no. 4 (2005): 86–123. Relatedly, the suggestion by both Roland Bainton (*Christian Attitudes toward War and Peace,* 78–80) and John Cadoux (*The Early Christian Attitude toward War* [London: Headley Brothers, 1919], 15–16) that Christians enlisted in the army for only "peaceful" duties (presupposing that such a choice were possible) is rendered nonsensical owing to a lack of evidence. As Helgeland ("Christians and the Roman Army," 161–62) has noted, this distinction is a figment of modern imagination and not ancient realities.

91. On this issue, Paul Christopher, *The Ethics of War and Peace,* 20–22, has demonstrated the hermeneutical problems quite lucidly. For a more extensive discussion of the *lex talionis* in the context of Matt. 5:38–42, see J. Daryl Charles, "'Do Not Suppose That I Have Come . . .': The Ethic of the 'Sermon on the Mount' Reconsidered," *Southwestern Journal of Theology* 46, no. 3 (Summer 2004): 47–72.

92. Cf. Matt. 5:17: "Do not suppose that I have come to abolish the law or the prophets . . ." Biblical commentary is generally agreed that by Jesus' day, rabbinic interpretation as well as common practice mirrored a distorted interpretation of the *lex talionis,* based on financial calculations.

93. While this constitutes a subtheme in many of Yoder's writings, it receives concentrated treatment in chap. 8 of *The Christian Witness to the State,* 74–83.

94. A proper perspective on Romans 13 and Revelation 13 is that the two are not mutually exclusive—a perspective that acknowledges a certain tension. Political power is not inherently evil, even when it can be used for evil purposes.

95. Kurt Aland, "The Relation between Church and State in Early Times: A Reinterpretation," *Journal of Theological Studies* 19 (1968): 124.

96. Thus, for example, the apostolic admonition: "Show proper respect to everyone, love the brotherhood of believers, fear God, honor the king" (1 Pet. 2:17).

97. Swift, "War and the Christian Conscience," 836, n. 2.

98. Ibid., 836–37.

99. Gero, "*Miles Gloriosus,*" 289–91; Helgeland, Daly, and Burns, *Christians and the Military*; Swift, "War and the Christian Conscience," 835–68; and Swift, *The Early Fathers on War and Military Service.*

100. On the silence of the church for a century and three-quarters, Hans von Campenhausen's prescient remarks are worth noting: "For little enclaves of a fairly humble status in the peaceful interior of a well-ordered empire, where there was practically no conscription, it was easy to avoid anything to do with the army. . . . Christians were still outside the field of political responsibility. . . . But this state of affairs could not last" ("Christians and Military Service in the Early Church," 161–62).

101. Relatedly, one might make a strong case for the increased attractiveness of the military profession during the period of the early Severan emperors (late second and early third centuries), as Ramsay MacMullen, *Soldier and Civilian in the Later Roman Empire* (Cambridge: Harvard University Press, 1963), 152–77, and Gero, "*Miles Gloriosus,*" 289–91, seek to do. Following MacMullen, Gero notes several immensely important practical developments occurring during the reign of Severus that would have had far-reaching effects in terms of soldier enlistment.

For example, in addition to higher pay, soldiers were permitted to form *collegia*, marriages of soldiers were normalized, with families of soldiers being granted permission to live within the camp precincts, while frontier troops were given land of their own to develop.

102. James Turner Johnson rightly notes: "The social transformation that brought Christianity into a relation of acceptance and support of the state was . . . not simply a result of changes within the Church itself; it was also a result of changes in the larger society. Nor was it the expression of a growing moral laxity, as has often been asserted." (*The Quest for Peace*, 40–41). Even a representative of the Eastern Orthodox tradition, theologian Stanley Harakas, is willing to concede that Eusebius' exuberance for the new situation in the empire, as it influenced peace and war perspectives of the church, while it may seem foreign to the modern mind, nonetheless contained "enough benefits for the Church so as to outweigh some of the concerns which the earlier church found so ready to promote in a radically different social, religious and moral climate." These benefits included "the end of persecution, the establishment of the Church, the support for the spread of the Gospel, the eradication of heresies, and the incorporation of Christian values into the legal and social system of the Empire" (Stanley Harakas, "The Teaching on Peace in the Fathers," available at www.incommunion.org/articles/essays/peace-in-the-fathers, accessed October 14, 2011).

103. Few have pressed this particular point more lucidly than Helgeland, "Christians and the Roman Army from Marcus Aurelius to Constantine," 733–34.

104. In addition to the volumes by Swift as well as Helgeland, Daly, and Burns (see n. 14), for a reasonably balanced assessment of patristic witnesses, see also David G. Hunter, "A Decade of Research on Early Christians and Military Service," *Religious Studies Review* 18, no. 2 (1992): 87–94, and Young, "The Early Church," 491–503.

Chapter 3: Origins of the Just War Tradition: Augustine

1. Thus, in addition to the texts and authors discussed in the previous chapter, see Ambrose, *On the Duties of the Clergy* 1.27.129 and 2.7.32–39. For a useful discussion of Ambrose's reflections on war, Louis J. Swift, "St. Ambrose on Violence and War," *Transactions and Proceedings of the American Philological Association* 101 (1970): 533–43; and Christopher, *The Ethics of War and Peace*.

2. Augustine, *City of God* (hereafter, *CG*) IV.6, XIV.28. Quotations from *City of God* are from the R. W. Dyson translation (Cambridge: Cambridge University Press, 1998).

3. *CG* I.1; I.21; and VII.30; see also *Against Faustus the Manichaean* XXII.73–79. Here, it would seem, deliberation about justice is God's affair, while man is left to execute the judgment. But the history of war supplies few instances of such God-commanded violence.

4. E.g., Reinhold Niebuhr's famous essay "Augustine's Political Realism," in Reinhold Niebuhr, *Christian Realism and Political Problems* (New York: Scribner's, 1953), 119–47.

5. *CG* IV.4. Whether this fully captures Augustine's view is difficult to say, given

the prominent rhetorical dimensions of his text. It is at least worth noting that the description of kingdoms as bands of robbers appears earlier in Cyprian *Ep.* 1.6 (*ANF* 5.277) and may have become by Augustine's time a rather standard jab at the Roman tendency to equate empire with justice.
6. See *CG* 19.17.
7. Augustine, Letter 138, "To Marcellinus," in Augustine, *Augustine: Political Writings*. The Tkacz and Kries translation is the one used in these citations.
8. The inference had been made by a certain Boniface, a governor of a Roman province in Africa who had written to Augustine for advice. Augustine's reply, Letter 189, has become a classic just war document.
9. The case is similar with the soldiers who approach John the Baptist to inquire about their salvation. "Teacher, what should we do?" they ask; and John's response is not that they should throw down their weapons or change their careers, but only that they should "Rob no one by violence or by false accusation and be content with your pay" (Lk. 3:14).
10. Augustine, Letter 189, "To Boniface."
11. Augustine, Letter 138, "To Marcellinus."
12. Ibid.
13. *CG* IV.14.
14. *CG* XIX.8.
15. Augustine, Letter 138, "To Marcellinus."
16. Ibid., 206. Augustine appears to be echoing a teaching of Sallust, who writes of his "most god-fearing and righteous" Roman ancestors that they "never took anything from the vanquished except the license to do harm" (*Coniuratio Catilinae* 12.3–4). However, Augustine adapts the teaching to include spiritual wrongs (sins), whereas Sallust was concerned with political and legal wrongs.
17. Augustine is infamous among some commentators for sanctioning the persecution of heretics. This too suggests something of his willingness to countenance force against sinners. However, Augustine's reflections on religious persecution are much more complex than they are often made out to be. A chronological survey of his writings on this topic reveals both caution and a willingness to change his mind. Concerning the Donatist heresy, for example, Augustine first reached out to the Donatists, then composed a treatise against them while at the same time opposing the imperial policy of persecuting them; thereafter, he would defend the imperial policy and, finally, plead for clemency. See further Augustine's *On True Religion* XVI.31; Letter 93, "To Vincentius"; and Letter 133, "To Marcellinus." These are compiled and translated by Tkacz and Kries.
18. *CG* XIX.7.
19. *Against Faustus the Manichaean* XXII.75: Interest enim quibus causis quibusque auctoribus homines gerenda bella suscipiant: ordo tamen ille naturalis mortalium paci accommodatus hoc poscit, ut suscipiendi belli auctoritas atque consilium penes Principem sit; exsequendi autem jussa bellica ministerium milites debeant paci salutique communi.
20. Ibid.
21. See, e.g., *CG* I.8; and consider also *Against Faustus the Manichaean*, XXII.75: "It is wrong to doubt that a war which must be waged, undertaken under the authority of God, whether in order to constrain, crush, or subjugate the pride of mortals, is

undertaken rightly, since even a war which is waged out of human desire can do no harm to the incorruptible God or to his saints."
22. Ibid., emphasis added.
23. Letter 189, "To Boniface."
24. Ibid.; cf. Cicero, *De Officiis* I.34–40.
25. Ibid.
26. *Against Faustus the Manichean*, XXII.74.
27. *CG* I.11.
28. *CG* XIX.8.

Chapter 4: Just War in the Middle Ages

1. Calvin's reliance upon Gratian will be treated in a subsequent chapter. Luther was also a reader of Gratian, but his attitude became more and more hostile as he moved away from the Catholic Church. Leading up to his break in 1520, Luther publicly denounced Gratian's text and burned it. See Luther's letter to Georg Spalatin in *Letters* 1, in *Luther's Works*, vol. 48, trans. G. G. Krodel (Philadelphia: Fortress Press, 1963), 187–88.
2. Pope Benedict XV in 1917 and Pope John Paul II in 1983.
3. Some scholars have questioned the historical accuracy of these divisions. See, e.g., Stanley Chodorow, *Christian Political Theory and Church Politics in the Mid-Twelfth Century: The Ecclesiology of Gratian's Decretum* (Berkeley, CA: University of California Press, 1972), 10–16.
4. The text used here is the standard modern edition from the *Corpus Iuris Canonici*, ed. Emil Friedberg (Granz: Academicsche Druck- und Verlagsanstalt, 1959), a reprint of the Leipzig edition of 1879. The section on war has never been published in English translation. We are grateful to Heather Outland and Clint Pechacek for their assistance with the medieval Latin.
5. We have been aided in our work by two contemporary studies: Chodorow, *Christian Political Theory and Church Politics in the Mid-Twelfth Century*; and F. H. Russell, *The Just War in the Middle Ages* (Cambridge: Cambridge University Press, 1975).
6. Gratian cites Matt. 5:39; Rom. 12:19; Matt. 26:52; Deut. 32:35; Matt. 7:1; Matt. 13:30; and Deut. 32:35.
7. Cf. Russell, *The Just War in the Middle Ages*, 60.
8. The requirement that wars be officially declared was insisted upon by Cicero; see *De Re Publica* III.23. Most just war writers do not stress this condition, if they mention it at all. Gratian and (much later) Grotius stand out in this regard; see Grotius, *De Jure Belli ac Pacis* II.26.7 and III.3. The benefit of the requirement seems obvious, and one wishes it were observed more strictly today: public declaration of just causes serves at once to frustrate the waging of war for expediency's sake, to forestall misplaced criticism about the true causes of war, and to signal to the enemy (as to the world) precisely what warranted the use of force. Just as criminals today must be formally charged—and this seems a matter of right as well as a sound practice for deterrence—so too should enemies in war be told precisely why force is used against them. We are grateful to Russ Hittinger for suggesting to us the abiding importance of formal declaration.

9. Bainton, *Christian Attitudes toward War and Peace*, 106.
10. Isidore, "Repetitis Rebus," *De Republica* III.23 and 35.
11. Here is Ambrose: "He who does not keep harm off a friend, if he can, is as much in fault as he who causes it" (Ambrose, *On the Duties of the Clergy* I.36). For a host of classical references—Hebrew, Egyptian, Greek, and Roman—to similar effect, see Grotius, *De Jure Belli ac Pacis*, II.25, with the notes of Barbeyrac, Tuck, ed., *The Rights of War and Peace*. This is a doctrine that Calvin adopted centuries later.
12. C. 23, Q. 4, dict. post c. 36: "sicut et Christus corporaliter persecutus est eos, quos de templo expulit."
13. This was the message of the sermon preached by Urban II at the Council of Clermont in 1095, which inaugurated the First Crusade. Gratian quotes the sermon approvingly in Q. 5, c. 47.
14. Russell, *The Just War in the Middle Ages*, 76.
15. See, e.g., Johnson, *Ideology, Reason, and the Limitation of War*, 39.
16. See Gratian's dicta after canons 25 and 26 of Q. 4.
17. Johnson locates the beginnings of the *jus in bello* tradition in precisely this sort of thinking (that is to say, in the gradual extension of "right intention" into the conduct of the war itself), but he marks the beginning of this shift in Aquinas rather than in Gratian.
18. C. 24, Q. 3, c. 22–25; also C. 17, Q. 4, c. 29.
19. Q. 1, c. 3.
20. Q. 8, c.15; see further Russell, *The Just War in the Middle Ages*, 70.
21. C. 29 of the council reads, "We prohibit under anathema that murderous art of crossbowmen and archers, which is hateful to God, to be employed against Christians and Catholics from now on."
22. Russell, *The Just War in the Middle Ages*, 70–71.
23. Q. 8, c. 30, which comes from the eleventh council of Toledo in A.D. 675.
24. For the impossibility of serving God and the secular powers at once, see Q. 8, c. 5–6; for Nicholas I's prohibition, see c. 19.
25. Q. 8, c. 10.
26. Q. 8, dict. post c. 28.
27. Q. 5, dict. post c. 25.
28. We follow standard practice in referencing the *Summa Theologica* (hereafter, *ST*) according to its divisions into parts, subparts, questions, articles, and the various elements of the articles just noted.
29. An exception to the general rule of treating Question 40 out of context is Darrell Cole's illuminating essay "Thomas Aquinas on Virtuous Warfare," *Journal of Religious Ethics* 27 (1999): 57–80.
30. Thomas also marshals support for his position from Rom. 13:4 ("He does not bear the sword in vain: for he is God's servant, an agent of wrath to bring punishment on the wrongdoer") and from Ps. 82:4 ("Rescue the weak and needy; deliver them from the hand of the wicked"). Thus, scripture and natural law combine to support his view.
31. This echoes Aquinas's first precept of natural law, to pursue the good and avoid evil.
32. 2a, 2ae, Q. 40, a2. These points are raised in the *videtur quod*.
33. Ibid.

34. 2a, 2ae, Q. 40, a. 2, rep. obj. 3.
35. QQ. In Hept. Qu.x super Jos.
36. 2a, 2ae, Q. 40, Q. 3, *respondeo.*
37. On this point, compare Thomas's fascinating discussion of concealment in *Summa* I, Q.1, a. 9.
38. 2a, 2ae, Q. 104, a. 6.
39. 2a, 2ae, Q. 104, a. 5.
40. 2a, 2ae, Q. 104, a. 6, rep. obj. 3.
41. 1a, 2ae, Q. 96, a. 4.
42. On this point, see *ST* 2a, 2ae, Q. 42 ("On Sedition"), a. 2; and also *De Regimine Principum* (*On Kingship*). Aquinas insists that nonexcessive tyranny should be tolerated, not overthrown; and all acts of resistance against unjust rule must be "public" in character. For more on Aquinas's limited doctrine of revolution, see chap. 8.
43. Standard accounts of the "origins" of just war thinking, when they do not neglect the linkage of justice with charity in Augustinian thought, tend to gloss over the moral-theological underpinnings of this linkage.

Chapter 5: Martin Luther and the Tradition

1. Reasonably so, although, as we wish to stress here, the tendency to assimilate obscures important differences that are worth noting. For examples of assimilation, see, e.g., James Turner Johnson, "Aquinas and Luther on War and Peace: Sovereign Authority and the Use of Armed Force," *Journal of Religious Ethics* 31 (2003): 3–20; Elshtain, *Just War Against Terror,* 101; Charles, *Between Pacifism and Jihad*, 50–52; Arthur F. Holmes, ed., *War and Christian Ethics* (Grand Rapids, MI: Baker Academic, 2005), 140; and Paul Ramsey, *The Just War: Force and Political Responsibility* (Lanham, MD: Rowman & Littlefield, 1983), 261–62.
2. Though we focus primarily on the period from 1520 to 1529 (the period of Luther's boldest and most distinctive political writings), we should stress that some of Luther's positions evolved in significant ways after this time. We are indeed anxious to avoid the common tendency of ignoring these developments. On this tendency, evident for example in studies by John Finnis, Ernst Troeltsch, and Reinhold Niebuhr, see Quentin Skinner, *The Foundations of Modern Political Thought*—vol. 2: *The Age of Reformation* (Cambridge: Cambridge University Press, 1978), 74; Carter Lindberg, *Beyond Charity: Reformation Initiatives for the Poor* (Minneapolis: Fortress Press, 1993), 161–69; and more recently Gary M. Simpson, "Toward a Lutheran 'Delight in the Law of the Lord': Church and State in the Context of Civil Society," in John R. Stumme and Robert W. Tuttle, eds., *Church and State: Lutheran Perspectives* (Minneapolis: Fortress Press, 2003), esp. 20–41. In order to avoid this tendency, we take pains throughout this study to note the chief areas where Luther's position changed after the 1520s. The interested reader should also consult W. D. J. Cargill Thompson, *The Political Thought of Martin Luther* (New Jersey: Barnes and Noble, 1984), especially the final chapter.
3. For a more detailed account of Charles V's conflict with the Lutherans, see Quentin Skinner, *The Foundations of Modern Political Thought*, vol. 2: *The Age of Reform* (Cambridge: Cambridge University Press, 1978), 194–97.

4. *Luther's Works,* American ed., 55 vols. (Philadelphia: Fortress Press, 1955–86), 46:53–54 [hereafter *LW*].
5. For a further account of this evolution, see F. Edward Cranz, *An Essay on the Development of Luther's Thought on Justice, Law and Society* (Cambridge, MA: Harvard University Press, 1959), 159–73.
6. This is what happened in Münster from February 1534 until June 1535, when a group of violent millennialist Anabaptists seized the government. Known as the Münster rebellion, the attempt ended in disaster. See chap. 6 below for a fuller discussion of the Anabaptists.
7. For further discussion of Luther's understanding of the "two kingdoms" doctrine, see the classic study by W. D. J. Cargill Thompson "The 'Two Kingdoms' and the 'Two Regiments': Some Problems of Luther's *Zwei-Reiche-Lehre*," *Journal of Theological Studies* 20 (1969): 164–85.
8. In later writings (see especially his *Commentary on Psalm 82* in *LW* 13:45ff.), Luther stressed other reasons (besides restraint of the un-Christian) for Christians to embrace political life. Political authorities could, and should, perform works of righteousness. See further Gary M. Simpson, *War, Peace, and God: Rethinking the Just War Tradition* (Minneapolis: Augsburg Fortress, 2007), 80–84, which discusses the difference between "the sword" and "the scepter" as Lutheran symbols of political rule. See also Simpson, "Toward a Lutheran 'Delight in the Law of the Lord,'" 30–35, n. 23, which points out the way the image of the "bread loaf" features as a "socially generative" symbol for political rule in Luther's *Large Catechism* of 1529.
9. Luther, *On Temporal Authority.* All subsequent quotations from *On Temporal Authority* are from the Harro Höpfl translation unless otherwise noted.
10. Cf. Luther, *Whether Soldiers Too Can Be Saved, LW* 46:99.
11. Luther, *On Temporal Authority,* 10, 11–12 (emphasis added).
12. Ibid., 15.
13. Ibid., 21, 22.
14. *On Free Choice* I.5; Letter 47, "To Publicola."
15. Letter 153, trans. Wilfrid Parsons, in *Fathers of the Church,* vol. 20 (New York: Fathers of the Church, 1953), 294.
16. The doctrine of double effect, often credited to Aquinas, permits an unlawful act or occurrence if it is an accidental consequence of an otherwise good intention underlying the act itself. In his discussion of self-defense, Aquinas writes, "Nothing hinders one act from having two effects, only one of which is intended, while the other is beside the intention. Now moral acts take their species according to what is intended, and not according to what is beside the intention, since this is accidental as explained above." Of course, the doctrine of double-effect is limited by proportionality: "And yet, though proceeding from a good intention, an act may be rendered unlawful, if it be out of proportion to the end. Wherefore if a man, in self-defense, uses more than necessary violence, it will be unlawful." *ST* 2a, 2ae, Q. 64, a. 7.
17. According to *ST* 2a, 2ae, Q. 64, a. 7, it is "natural to everything to keep itself in 'being' as far as possible," and moreover, "one is bound to take *more* care of one's own life than of another's" (emphasis added). Contrast Augustine, *On Christian Doctrine,* I.27: "We ought to love another man better than our own body, because

all things are to be loved in reference to God, and another man can have fellowship with us in the enjoyment of God, whereas our body cannot; for the body only lives through the soul, and it is by the soul that we enjoy God." Trans., J. F. Shaw, *Nicene and Post-Nicene Fathers*: series I, vol. II (Peabody, MA: Hendrickson Publishers, 1994). And for a helpful discussion, see Richard B. Miller, *Interpretations of Conflict* (Chicago: University of Chicago Press, 1991), 18–23.

18. "Reluctant," *though not ultimately unwilling*. While Luther never, to our knowledge, changed his position on self-defense, it is well known that he was led by political experience to change his position (very gradually, and not easily or lightly) on other important topics related to the just use of force, especially during the final decades of his life. See Thompson, *Political Thought of Martin Luther*, 171–72; and see n. 49 below.

19. Luther, *On Temporal Authority*, 39–40.

20. Luther, *Whether Soldiers Too Can Be Saved*, 88–137.

21. Ibid., 96.

22. Luther is referring here to *public* self-defense. His objections to self-defense discussed earlier concern private self-defense.

23. Luther, *Whether Soldiers Too Can Be Saved*, 121.

24. Ibid., 125.

25. Ibid. As an example, Luther cites God's command that the Israelites make war on the Canaanites. In this instance, they were victorious. However, while God's command establishes necessity, it is not always sufficient for victory. If one fails to fight "with fear and care," one may still lose. This is how Luther explains, for instance, the defeat of the Israelites by the soldiers of Ai (Josh. 7:1–5) after God himself had ordered them to fight.

26. *Quaestiones in Heptateuchum*, bk. 7, Q. 10, in *Patrologia Latina*, vol. 34 (Gallice: Près la Barrière d'Enfer, 1841), 781.

27. Gratian, *Decretum*, Causa 23, Quaestio 2, in Friedberg, ed., *Corpus Iuris Canonici*. Gratian based his doctrine on two previous writers, Augustine and Isidore of Seville (c. 560–636). Consider also Aquinas, *ST* 2a, 2ae, Q. 40, a. 1.

28. A comparison between Luther (1483–1546) and his Spanish contemporary Francisco Vitoria (1492–1546) is instructive on this point. Like Luther (see below), Vitoria disapproved of wars whose purpose was to convert non-Christians to the faith. But unlike Luther, Vitoria preserved and even expanded the treatment of just cause he inherited from the tradition. He thus acknowledged the possibility of just wars waged for defense (including the defense of allies), restitution, retribution, and (among religious causes) the protection of the free propagation of the gospel and the protection of Christian converts from injury. When we say Vitoria expanded the tradition of just cause, we have in mind the extent to which he brought into focus the subject of "military intervention" in the affairs of other lands. He mentions military interventions to prevent religious persecution as well as interventions to save a foreign people from tyranny. See Vitoria, *On the Law of War* and *On the American Indians* in *Vitoria: Political Writings*, ed., Anthony Pagden and Jeremy Lawrance (Cambridge: Cambridge University Press, 1991).

29. *On War against the Turk*, trans. Charles M. Jacobs and Robert C. Schultz, in *LW* 46:165, 168. How should this be reconciled with Luther's claim (see above) that God may sometimes command rulers to wage war in his name? We can see three

options: (1) by the time he composed *On War against the Turk*, Luther had changed his mind; (2) he thought that God commanded wars only in the Old Testament; or (3) he thought that a divine command to wage war would not necessitate the use of a Christian banner—war, on this view, would be a strictly secular business, undertaken by a secular authority even when God commands it.

30. Gratian, *Decretum*, Causa 23, Q. 8. See also Chodorow *Christian Political Theory and Church Politics in the Mid-Twelfth Century*; and Russell, *The Just War in the Middle Ages.*

31. See Luther's letter to Georg Spalatin in *LW* 48:187–88. It should be noted that by 1530, Luther rejected his own principle that heresy is a spiritual matter not to be dealt with by force, when dealing with the Jews of Germany (see *Commentary on Psalm 82*, *LW* 13:61–67; *On the Jews and Their Lies*, *LW* 47:262–74). As Simpson writes of this regrettable development (*War, Peace, and God*, 56–57), "Because the Jews in Germany had publicly rejected Jesus' divinity and thus violated the Second Commandment against blasphemy, he [Luther] recommended to the princes that they use their office and the sword by burning Jews' synagogues and schools, destroying their houses, confiscating their books, forbidding their rabbis to teach, abolishing all rights of safe conduct, prohibiting their banking businesses, forcing them to do manual labor, and doing anything else necessary, short of killing, to 'rid' Germany of the Jews. The error and evil of Luther's violation of his 1523 theological political ethics remain beyond dispute!"

32. Martin Luther, *Against the Robbing and Murdering Hordes of Peasants* (1525), trans. Charles M. Jacobs and Robert C. Schultz, in *LW* 46, 52.

33. Luther, *Whether Soldiers Too Can Be Saved*, 125.

34. Luther, *On Temporal Authority*, 40.

35. Luther, *Against the Robbing and Murdering Hordes*, 52–53; see also *On Temporal Authority*, 9. Here Luther echoes the oft-cited maxim of Ambrose: "He who does not keep harm off a friend, if he can, is as much in fault as he who causes it" (*On the Duties of the Clergy* I.36; cf. Thomas Aquinas, *ST* IIa-IIae, Q. 60, a.6, ad. 2).

36. Luther, *On Temporal Authority*, 35–36.

37. See *ST* IIa-IIae, Q. 40, a. 1, ad. 2 (emphasis added).

38. See, e.g., *Against the Robbing and Murdering Hordes*, 53; *On War against the Turk*, 178–79.

39. As opposed to *jus ad bellum* (the justice of *going* to war). These Latin phrases are of modern coinage, even though the distinction they mark was clearly recognized in medieval just war writings.

40. Luther, *On Secular Authority*, 39–40. Harro Höpfl, in a note on this passage, supposes that Luther did not intend to condone the acts Moses there recommends, but it is difficult to find any other reason for Luther's allusion to the passage.

41. Luther, *Whether Soldiers Too Can Be Saved*, 99.

42. Ibid., 104, 99.

43. Luther, *On Secular Authority*, 40.

44. *ST* 2a-2ae, a. 42, a. 2, ad 3.

45. Luther, *Whether Soldiers Too Can Be Saved*, 105. Luther admits to some doubt on this point.

46. Ibid., 105–6, 111–12.

47. Luther tells an amusing story (ibid., 111) of a widow who prayed devoutly for

her tyrant to have a long life. When the astonished tyrant asked her why she prayed for him, she replied, "I had ten cows when your grandfather lived and ruled. He took two of them and I prayed that he might die and that your father might become lord. This is what happened, and your father took three cows. I prayed again that you might become lord, and that your father might die. Now you have taken four cows, and so I am praying for you, for now I am afraid that your successor will take the last cow and everything that I have."

48. Ibid., 108–9.

49. It must be stressed that Luther changed his position on armed resistance after the failure of the Diet of Augsburg in 1530; and we do not wish, through our focus on the 1520s, to obscure a monumental development in Luther's thought—namely, the working out of a theory of resistance. See Shoenberger, "The Development of the Lutheran Theory of Resistance: 1523–1530"; Shoenberger, "Luther and the Justifiability of Resistance to Legitimate Authority," 3–20; and Thompson, *Studies in the Reformation*, 3–41. In fact, it is now standard (see, e.g., Simpson, "Toward a Lutheran 'Delight in the Law of the Lord,'" 39–41) to differentiate three stages in this development: First, during the 1520s Luther formulated and maintained in several contexts the principle that inferiors ought never to wage war on their superiors. Next (after 1530, when the military threat against the Protestants from the emperor seemed imminent), Luther became persuaded by Gregory Brück and other Saxon jurists that armed resistance against the emperor was allowable, insofar as the law of the empire *itself* granted a right of armed resistance in cases of "atrocious" or "notorious" injury. Because the arguments here were constitutional in nature, Simpson labels this a stage of "constitutionally delimited armed resistance"; it is embodied in the Torgau Declaration of October 1530, which Luther himself composed. Finally, in December 1536, Melanchthon wrote and Luther endorsed an official "opinion" prepared for Elector John Frederick that justified armed resistance on the basis of a natural law argument (*vim vi repellere licet*, literally "it is licit to repel force with force"). Though Luther had earlier rejected this argument, and may have never been *completely* persuaded of it (see Simpson, ibid., 181, n. 45, concurring with Thompson on this point), the reasoning that supports it is compelling: "if the gospel is a spiritual teaching that does not dictate laws regarding temporal government but rather confirms just laws and values them highly," then "it follows that the gospel permits all natural and equitable protection and defense that is authorized by natural laws or else by temporal government" (Simpson, "Toward a Lutheran 'Delight in the Law of the Lord,'" 40–41). The significance of all this becomes clear when we observe (see Skinner, *Foundations of Modern Political Thought*, 206–24) that in 1550 the Lutherans who penned the Magdeburg Confession, following the trajectory of Luther's thought on armed resistance, articulated for the first time for the Protestant West a nuanced theory of the conditions under which armed resistance against a superior (in this case, the emperor) was licit. Luther's late thinking on armed resistance thus had an impact on the right of resistance in Protestant political thought.

50. Luther, *Whether Soldiers Too Can Be Saved*, 130–31.

51. Of course, one might then suffer the consequences of disobeying the temporal powers. But this Luther viewed as a legitimate act of suffering on behalf of the faith and not a sin of disobedience at all.

52. This is even clearer in the parallel passage of *On Temporal Authority*, 40, where Luther says of subjects: "As long as they do not know and cannot find out, *although they have made every effort*, they may obey without danger to their souls" (emphasis added).
53. See, e.g., Augustine, *Against Faustus the Manichaean* XXII.75: "If a just man should happen to serve as a soldier under a human king who is sacrilegious, he could rightly wage war at the king's command, maintaining the order of civic peace. For what he is commanded to do is not contrary to the sure precepts of God, or else it is not sure whether it is or not. In this latter case, perhaps the iniquity of giving the orders will make the king guilty while the rank of servant in the civil order will show the soldier to be innocent."
54. Thus, Sheldon Wolin, *Politics and Vision* (Princeton, NJ: Princeton University Press, 2004), 146: "Luther fashioned a political doctrine of stark simplicity, unrelieved by the shadows of qualification."
55. See n. 28 above. For example, in the tradition before and after Luther, we find support for humanitarian interventions as well as for the use of force against states that harbor international criminals.
56. Calvin, for his part, reverted back to a doctrine of holy war. See *Luther and Calvin on Secular Authority*, 50.
57. See further James Turner Johnson, *The Holy War Idea in Western and Islamic Traditions* (University Park: Pennsylvania State University Press, 1997), esp. chaps. 2–3.

Chapter 6: Calvin and Other Reformers

1. See Calvin's *Institutes* bk. 3, chap. 19, sec. 15; and bk. 4, chap. 20.
2. For the principle, see Luther, *On Secular Authority* and *On War against the Turk*. It must be noted that Luther sometimes (mostly in private letters) ignored his own principle, as for instance when he demanded that secular rulers repress public heresy and blasphemy, or when he took up the cudgels in the name of banning the mass. The classic source for such inconsistencies in Luther's position is Joseph Lecler, *Histoire de la Tolérance au Siècle de la Réforme* (Paris: Aubier, 1955), vol. 1, 168–75. However, these exceptions were a matter of expedience, and Luther never revised his basic principle that secular authority should concern itself exclusively with external matters and not spiritual ones. The difference between Luther and Calvin can thus be stated as follows: Calvin created a *principle* for blending the spiritual and political realms that Luther would never have allowed.
3. *Institutes* III.19.15 and IV.20.1.
4. Ibid., IV.20.2, translated by Harro Höpfl, in *Luther and Calvin on Secular Authority*, 47–86. All quotations in English from bk. 4 of the *Institutes* are taken from this volume unless otherwise noted. Höpfl's translation is especially useful in noting the major textual variants.
5. The religious purposes of government were not always stated so clearly in Calvin's work. Calvin was as capable of purely secular descriptions as religious ones. For a useful discussion of his inconsistencies (or "artfulness"), see Michael Walzer, *The Revolution of the Saints: A Study in the Origins of Radical Politics* (London: Weidenfeld and Nicolson, 1966), 45–47.

6. *Institutes* IV.20.3.
7. Ibid., IV.20.9 (emphasis added). In the preface to the *Institutes*, Calvin writes: "The king who, in ruling over his realm, does not serve God's glory, exercises not kingly rule [*regnum*] but brigandage [*latrocinium*]." Compare also Calvin's *Sermons upon the Fifth Book of Moses called Deuteronomy*, trans. Arthur Golding (London: Printed by Henry Middleton for John Harrison, 1581), sermon 4.
8. For Luther's disapproval, see *On War against the Turk*. Compare Locke's 1689 *Letter Concerning Toleration* (Indianapolis: Hackett Publishing, 1983), 44: "There is absolutely no such thing under the Gospel as a Christian commonwealth" (sed sub evangelio nulla prorsus est res publica Christiana).
9. *Institutes* IV.20.4 (emphasis added).
10. Ibid.
11. The first edition of the *Institutes* appeared in the year after the disastrous attempt on the part of radical Anabaptists to form a theocracy at Münster. Even prior to this episode, Calvin was aware of Anabaptist propaganda asserting that Christians were no longer citizens of the earthly realm and should thus have nothing to do with civil government.
12. See, e.g., his pamphlet of 1549, *A Short Instruction for to Arm All Good Christian People against the Pestiferous Errors of the Common Sect of Anabaptists*. The Anabaptist rejection of politics supplied Calvin with the backdrop for some of his most memorable anti-utopian lines: "I admit that all this [political theorizing] would be superfluous if the kingdom of God as it now exists among us put an end to this present life. But if it is the will of God that . . . such aids are necessary for our journey, then those who deprive men of them take away their human nature. As for their claim that the perfection of the Church of God must be so great as to make all other government and laws redundant, this is stupidity, for it is to imagine a perfection which can never be found in any association of human beings. The effrontery of the wicked is so great, and their evil doing so incorrigible, that [even] laws of great severity are scarcely enough to hold them in check. If not even force is enough to restrain them from wrong-doing, how would we expect them to act once they [were to] see that they could do what evils they pleased with impunity?" (*Institutes*, IV.20.4).
13. On the divine origins of political rule, Calvin ran into a difficulty; and this may explain why he pays significantly less attention in the *Institutes* to the Machiavellian view than the Anabaptist one. Political rule clearly existed prior to, and independently of, the biblical narrative. It existed among the heathen, and Calvin was far too familiar with classical authors to suppose otherwise. But how could this be squared with the political genealogy Calvin hoped to establish? Calvin's answer (stated earlier in the *Institutes*) was that God gifted political order to the heathens, whether they recognized this or not (*Institutes* II.2.16). Political association was thus *not natural* but always and everywhere a gift of God. See further, Walzer, *The Revolution of the Saints*, 31–32.
14. For a slightly exaggerated account, see John T. McNeill, "The Democratic Element in Calvin's Thought," *Church History* 18 (1949): 153–71; and Winthrop S. Hudson, "Democratic Freedom and Religious Faith in the Reformed Tradition," *Church History* 15 (1946): 177–94.
15. *Lectures on Daniel*, chap. 6, cited in McNeill, "The Democratic Element," 153.

16. *Institutes*, IV.20.8.
17. Ibid.
18. See *Institutes* IV.20.4. The thought traces back, of course, to Romans 13:1–2.
19. Ibid., IV.20.8.
20. Ibid., IV.20.10.
21. Ibid., IV.20.11.
22. Gratian, *Decretum*, Causa 23, Q. 3. Calvin knew Gratian's text well and quoted it frequently in the *Institutes*. Although his usual motives in quoting it were polemical—e.g., to illustrate the "Roman error" or the falsehood of "sophistic speculations," on which, see Alexandre Ganoczy, *The Young Calvin*, trans. David Foxgrover and Wade Provo (Philadelphia: Westminster Press, 1987), 168–78—his use of Gratian on the topic of the sword may constitute an important exception.
23. Walzer, *Revolution of the Saints*, 65, seems to err in asserting that for Calvin, "the right of Christians [to wage war] extended no further than defensive war."
24. This has some relevance to the issue of international terrorism today. If a country harbors criminals and refuses to bring them to justice, if it refuses to make amends for the crimes such criminals commit, then it opens itself up to military attack, not as a matter of self-defense but as a matter of justice. Such would be Calvin's view.
25. Calvin, *Institutes*, IV.20.11. Contrast Luther, *On Temporal Authority*, 39: "A prince must punish the wicked in such a way that he . . . does not plunge his whole country and its people into chaos for the sake of one [person's] head, and fill the land with widows and orphans."
26. Ibid., IV.20.12.
27. Exodus 32:25–29 (New Revised Standard Version).
28. *Institutes* IV.20.10.
29. See also Calvin's *Sermons upon the Fifth Book of Moses Called Deuteronomy*, sermon 194, 1202–9; and Calvin's *Commentaries on the Book of Joshua* (1565), or, in English, *A Commentarie of M. Iohn Caluine, Vpon the Booke of Iosue*, trans. William Fulke (London: Printed Thomas Dawson for George Bishop, 1578). Of particular interest are Calvin's comments on Joshua 10:40 and 7:24, where he condones acts of savagery such as executing young children who have committed no wrong, provided the Lord has commanded it. Also on this point, see the illuminating study by Michael Walzer, "Exodus 32 and the Theory of Holy War: The History of a Citation," *Harvard Theological Review* 61 (1968): 1–14.
30. John Locke, *Letter Concerning Toleration*, 42.
31. *Institutes* IV.20.10.
32. Ibid., IV.20.12. One would suppose, of course, that necessity by definition permits no escape; but the fact is that Calvin's doctrine of necessity was much more restrictive (at least as it is stated in the *Institutes*) than the classical doctrine, which did not insist upon "last resort."
33. Calvin, *Commentaries on the Book of the Prophet Daniel*, trans. Thomas Myers (Grand Rapids, MI: Eerdmans, 1948); Walzer, *Revolution of the Saints*, 40–41.
34. *Institutes* IV.20.18–19.
35. Ibid., IV.20.12.
36. Ibid., IV.20.20.
37. Letter to the duchess of Ferrara, January 24, 1564, trans. M. R. Gilchrist, in

The Letters of John Calvin, ed. Jules Bonnet (New York: B. Franklin, 1973), vol. 4, 356–57. For a useful discussion of this letter, see Daniel Pellerin, "Calvin: Militant or Man of Peace?," 46, and F. Whitfield Barton, *Calvin and the Duchess* (Louisville: John Knox Press, 1989).
38. Letter to the duchess of Ferrara, 357.
39. *Calvini Opera, Corpus Reformatorum* (Brunsvigae, apud C. A. Schwetschke et filium, 1863–1900), 7:476; 24:360; and 44:346; cited and discussed in Bainton, *Christian Attitudes toward War and Peace*, 144–47.
40. Calvin, Commentary on Joshua 8:15 in *A Commentarie of M. Iohn Caluine, Vpon the Booke of Iosue*. See further Pellerin, "Calvin: Militant or Man of Peace?," 50.
41. McNeill, "The Democratic Element in Calvin's Thought," 163.
42. Skinner, *The Foundations of Modern Political Thought—Vol. II*, 193.
43. *Institutes* IV.20.22–23.
44. Ibid., IV.20.24–28, citing Job 34:30; Hosea 13:11; Isaiah 3:4 and 10:5; Deuteronomy 28:29; Daniel 2:21 and 37; and especially 1 Samuel 8:11 and Jeremiah 27:5ff.
45. See further, Walzer, *Revolution of the Saints*, 63: Calvin "revealed that the legality of resistance was at least in part a *post facto* ascription."
46. *Institutes*, IV.20.30–31.
47. For a discussion of the more revolutionary strands of Calvinism, see Skinner, *Foundations of Modern Political Thought—Vol. II*.
48. *Institutes* IV.20.31.
49. See Skinner, *Foundations of Modern Political Thought—Vol. II*, 206–38.
50. This is why he cites Daniel's refusal to obey an ungodly law (Dan. 6:22) and refers to a passage where the Israelites are condemned for obeying an ungodly law (Hosea 5:11; cf. 1 Kings 12:30).
51. Oliver O'Donovan, *The Desire of the Nations: Rediscovering the Roots of Political Theology* (Cambridge: Cambridge University Press, 1996), chap. 6, especially 207–10, captures well the creative sense in which Luther, like Augustine, wrestled with the tensions of the two kingdoms as they interact.
52. James M. Stayer, *Anabaptists and the Sword* (Lawrence: Coronado Press, 1972), 34. The strength of Stayer's scholarship is the degree to which he attempts to situate Anabaptist beliefs—and therefore religious pacifism—in the wider context of sixteenth-century Reformation thinking.
53. This is the description of Hans-Jürgen Görtz, *Innere und Äussere Ordnung in der Theologie Thomas Müntzers* (Studies in the History of Christian Thought 2; Leyden: Brill, 1967), 10–13; see as well Günther Franz, ed., *Müntzer Schriften: Quellen und Forschungen zur Reformationsgeschichte* (Gütersloh: Gütersloher, 1968).
54. So, for example, in 1528 Hubmaier would publish a treatise under the title *Von Dem Schwert* (*On the Sword*) in which he polemicized against pacifist nonresisters. Like Luther and Zwingli, Hubmaier aimed at reform of the wider church rather than requiring a separation therefrom.
55. *Anabaptists and the Sword*, 3–4.
56. For an English translation, see John C. Wenger, "The Schleitheim Confession of Faith," *Mennonite Quarterly Review* 19 (1945): 243–53. All citations below use the Wenger translation.
57. As evidence of its widespread acceptance and normativity, Calvin subsequently

would attempt to refute it (in his *Briève instruction* 23.2; cf. also Calvin's attitude toward Anabaptism in his *Institutes,* II.10.1). Over the past several decades, there has been a lively debate among Anabaptists as to the complexity of Anabaptist origins that made pacifist nonresistance a central tenet in their faith—a debate that is beyond the scope of the present discussion. See, e.g., John Howard Yoder, "'Anabaptists and the Sword' Revisited: Systematic Historiography and Undogmatic Nonresistants," *Zeitschrift für Kirchengeschichte* 85 (1974): 126–39; James M. Stayer, Werner O. Packull and Klaus Depperman, "From Monogenesis to Polygenesis: The Historical Discussion of Anabaptist Origins," *Mennonite Quarterly Review* 49 (1975): 83–121; J. Denny Weaver, *Becoming Anabaptist* (Scottdale, PA: Herald Press, 1987); C. Arnold Snyder, *Anabaptist History and Theology* (Kitchener, ON: Pandora Press, 1995); Snyder, "The Influence of the Schleitheim Articles on the Anabaptist Movement: An Historical Evaluation," *Mennonite Quarterly Review* 63 (1989): 323–44; and Gerald Biesecker-Mast, "Anabaptist Separation and Arguments Against the Sword in the Schleitheim *Brotherly Union,*" *Mennonite Quarterly Review* 74 (2000): 381–402.

58. Reproduced in Heinrich Bohmer, ed., *Urkunden zur Geschichte des Bauernkrieges und der Wiedertäufer,* 3rd ed. (Berlin: De Gruyter & Co., 1933), 27–35.

59. These seven matters, each being addressed in the form of an article of faith, were as follows: baptism, the ban (excommunication), the breaking of bread, separation from the world, pastoral duties, the sword, and the oath (vows).

60. Some contemporary Anabaptist scholars bristle at the suggestion that their tradition, as mirrored in the Schleitheim Confession, is separatist and that the document was influential, prototypical, or separatist; rather, they would argue that documents such as the confession are a product of cultural engagement and not withdrawal. The nuances of this debate are helpfully illustrated in Gerald Biesecker-Mast's essay "Anabaptist Separation and Arguments Against the Sword in the Schleitheim Brotherly Union," 381–402.

61. This is the view of at least several contemporary Anabaptist writers—among these, for example, Beulah S. Hostetler, *American Mennonites and Protestant Movements* (Scottdale, PA: Herald Press, 1987), and Snyder, "The Influence of the Schleitheim Articles on the Anabaptist Movement," 323. The influence of Schleitheim can be seen in the 450th anniversary publication by Leonard Gross, John W. Miller, and John H. Yoder, "The Schleitheim Confession," *Gospel Herald* (February 22, 1977): 151–66, as well as the related literature of the past three decades.

62. So Biesecker-Mast, "Anabaptist Separation and Arguments against the Sword in the Schleitheim *Brotherly Union,*" 392.

63. This statement, found in the three synoptic gospels, is taken out of context by the Brethren. The purpose of Jesus' teaching here is to emphasize the attitude of being a servant to all rather than wanting to be served and "lord it over" others.

64. Rom. 8:29.

65. 1 Pet. 2:21.

66. Johnson, *The Quest for Peace,* 164–65.

67. Surely, it can be argued that with the proliferation of churches and sects that issued out of the Reformation in the early sixteenth century, arguments for religious toleration and religious freedom were severely lacking, each group, after all, professing to have a corner on revealed truth. Thus, as one reformer observed, "the

papists anathematize the Lutherans, the Lutherans anathematize the Zwinglians, the Zwinglians persecute the Anabaptists, [and] the Anabaptists anathematize all the others" (*Corpus Schwenkfeldianorum* 4.829, cited in J. Wayne Baker, "Church, State, and Dissent: The Crisis of the Swiss Reformation, 1531–1536," *Church History* 57, no. 2 [1988]: 146).

68. Bainton, *Christian Attitudes toward War and Peace*, 156. This expression of pacifism, however, is not to be equated with that of Erasmus, even when the two are roughly contemporary and when they share important common features. In what ways did the pacifism of the Anabaptist differentiate itself from that of the "Christian humanist" Desiderius Erasmus? The primary difference lies in their conception of the state. For Erasmus, the state is the result—indeed, the very product—of human sociability. Concomitantly, most ills of Erasmus's age can be seen as the result of war, which is described by Erasmus in his *Institutio* as a "disease." War is contrary to reason and ethics; it is indicative of "beasts" but inconceivable and unbecoming of Christians (*dulce bellum inexpertis*), since Christ taught us peace. While Erasmus does acknowledge the theoretical possibility that a good prince could wage war, in the end an unjust peace is always better than a just war.

69. For a very helpful overview of this controversy from the period of 1530 and beyond, see John D. Roth, "Harmonizing the Scriptures: Swiss Brethren Understandings of the Relationship between the Old and New Testament during the Last Half of the Sixteenth Century," in Werner O. Packull and Geoffrey L. Dipple, eds., *Radical Reformation Studies* (Aldershot, UK: Ashgate, 1999), 35–52.

70. This argument was set forth in a 1524 treatise with the unambiguous title *Those Who Give Cause for Rebellion*, reproduced in Leland Harder, ed., *The Sources of Swiss Anabaptism: The Grebel Letters and Selected Documents* (Scottdale, PA: Herald Press, 1985), 319.

71. Heinold Fast and John H. Yoder, "How to Deal with Anabaptists: An Unpublished Letter of Heinrich Bullinger," *Mennonite Quarterly Review* 33 (1959): 83–84. Fast provides the transcription and introduction to one of these letters of inquiry. Bullinger's letter writing to Haller is gathered in vol. 2 of Fritz Büsser et al., eds., *Heinrich Bullinger, Werke. 2: Briefwechsel* (Zürich: Theologischer Verlag, 2003); for the particular exchange leading up to the debate with the Anabaptists, see 2.127–33.

72. *Heinrich Bullinger, Werke* 2.132–33. Already in 1523, Balthasar Hubmaier, a more moderate Anabaptist who, against the stream, believed that a Christian could be a ruler or use the sword for the public good, was beginning to challenge the Anabaptist presupposition that the New Testament is superior to the Old. In a formal disputation that took place before the Zürich city council, he confessed that the Word of God must be proclaimed "as written in both Testaments," as cited in H. Wayne Pipkin and John H. Yoder, eds., *Balthasar Hubmaier, Theologian of Anabaptism* (Scottdale, PA: Herald Press, 1989), 26.

73. This treatise was published in Zürich in 1531 under the title *Von dem Unverschaempten Fraefel.*

74. Roth, "Harmonizing the Scriptures," 36.

75. For an English-language version of the exchange, see Jess Yoder, "A Critical Study of the Debate between the Reformed and the Anabaptists, Held at Frankenthal, Germany in 1571 (Ph.D. dissertation, Northwestern University, 1962), part of which is condensed in the following two essays: "The Frankenthal Debate with

the Anabaptists in 1571: Purpose, Procedure, Participants," *Mennonite Quarterly Review* 36 (1962): 14–35, and "The Frankenthal Disputation: Part II. Outcome Issues, Debating Methods," *Mennonite Quarterly Review* 36 (1962): 116–46.

76. Even Anabaptist historian C. Arnold Snyder acknowledges that Anabaptists never provided a satisfactory reply, despite subsequent attempts to defend their dualism through either a figurative or spiritualizing hermeneutic. See in particular his essay "The 'Perfection of Christ' Reconsidered: The Later Swiss Brethren and the Sword," in Werner O. Packull and Geoffrey L. Dipple, eds., *Radical Reformation Studies* (Aldershot, UK: Ashgate, 1999), 58–64; see as well Snyder, "The Influence of the Schleitheim Articles on the Anabaptist Movement: An Historical Evaluation," *Mennonite Quarterly Review* 63 (1989): 323–44.

Chapter 7: Just War Thinking in the Early-Modern Period

1. Johnson, *Ideology, Reason, and the Limitation of War*, 150–54.
2. So, for example, Francisco Suárez, *De Legibus* (hereafter *De Leg.*) 2.6, an English translation of which is found in James B. Scott, *The Spanish Origin of International Law: Lectures on Francisco de Vitoria (1480–1546) and Francisco Suarez (1548–1617)* (Washington, DC: Georgetown University Press, 1929).
3. Few have addressed this issue with the precision and historical consciousness of Johnson, in *Ideology, Reason, and the Limitation of War*, 151 ff., and *Just War Tradition and the Restraint of War*. See Thomas L. Pangle and Peter J. Ahrensdorf, *Justice among the Nations: On the Moral Basis of Power and Peace* (Lawrence, KS: University of Kansas Press, 1999), 88ff., with the corresponding endnotes for a more critical assessment of Johnson and a valuable contribution in its own right.
4. In reading Vitoria and Suárez, one quickly comes to appreciate their profound debt to the casuistry of Aquinas.
5. Johnson highlights the first two of these features and treats them as one in *Ideology, Reason, and the Limitation of War*, 178–95, although he devotes greater attention to the third elsewhere, notably in *Just War Tradition and the Restraint of War*.
6. In his teaching career, Vitoria taught the entirety of Aquinas's *Summa* three times, each cycle lasting roughly seven years.
7. These two lectures, *De Indis* and *De Jure Belli*, are combined in the translation of James Brown Scott and edited by Ernest Nys under the title *De Indis et de Iure Belli Relectiones* (New York: Wildy & Sons LTD, [repr.] 1964). For our present purposes, all citations below are drawn from the translation found in *Francisco de Vitoria—Political Writings*, ed. Anthony Pagden and Jeremy Lawrance (Cambridge: Cambridge University Press, 1991).
8. Vitoria, *De Indis* 3.1, 5; *De Jure Belli* 1.3; 2.2–3; 3.5. By analogy, Vitoria argues that Spain can no more wage war on the Indians than the pope can wage war on people who fornicate (*De Indis* 2.5).
9. So Thomas Aquinas, *Summa Theologica* (hereafter *ST*) II-II Q. 10.
10. Vitoria, *De Indis* 3.2. There is, however, no question that Vitoria favors the Christian religion in his treatment of the relationship between the Spanish and the Indians.
11. Vitoria, *De Indis* 1.3–6; 2.4; cf., however, 3.8, where Vitoria says that if it could

be shown that the Indians are "unsuited to setting up a commonwealth both legitimate and ordered in human and civil terms, then they could be lawfully invaded." Vitoria leaves it to others to actually make the argument, but in allowing for the possibility he anticipates more modern arguments for interventions in "failed states."

12. Ibid., 2.4.

13. That Vitoria's strategy is comprehensive, taking to task both the political and the ecclesiastical powers, should not give the impression that Vitoria was a disloyal Spaniard. To the contrary, he develops elaborate arguments that distinguish between legitimate and illegitimate grounds for imperialism.

14. Vitoria, *De Indis* 2.1. Victoria argues: "The emperor is not the ruler of the world."

15. Ibid., 2.2.4. In fact, even if the pope had secular power over the world (which he does not), he could not give it to secular rulers (ibid., 2.2.2). And even if the Native Americans refused to recognize the pope's dominion, this would not be grounds for war (ibid., 2.2.7). Thus, for example, Vitoria could denounce Pope Alexander VI's attempt, through the Treaty of Tordesillas (1494), to divide Native American lands between the Spanish and Portuguese governments. Vitoria's understanding of papal authority is developed at length elsewhere in his treatise *De Potestate Ecclesiastica Altera* (*On the Power of the Church*), esp. 5.1–5.

16. In the conclusion of *De Indis*, Vitoria apparently wishes to pacify some who worry that his arguments might undermine the possibilities for discovery and trade. To the contrary, he maintains, neither would necessarily suffer. But the broader point remains. As James Turner Johnson writes: "Vitoria's refusal to treat the Indians as savages little better than animals, and his insistence that they are men and to be treated as such even in the face of a conflict of cultures as severe as any in history, are manifestations of the spirit of modern international law that were only just possibly conceivable to medieval man, who knew of alien cultures only by fantasy and hearsay" (*Ideology, Reason, and the Limitation of War*, 170).

17. In Question 3 of *De Indis*, Vitoria identifies several specific scenarios relative to the Indians in which coercive intervention might be justified: (1) if the Indians interfere with the natural rights of the Spaniards to free travel and trade and to natural resources; (2) if the they forcibly obstruct the free preaching of the Christian gospel; (3) if they use force against converts; (4) if they convert to Christianity in sufficient numbers that the pope deems it necessary for them to have a Christian prince; (5) if they persist in customs or rights that cause bodily harm to the innocent among them; (6) if they voluntarily elect to become Spanish subjects; (7) if they fall into civil strife and one side calls upon the Spaniards for aid; and (8) if they prove themselves "unsuited to setting up or administering a commonwealth both legitimate and ordered in human and civil terms."

18. Vitoria, *De Indis* 2.1; *De Jure Belli* 1.3.

19. Vitoria, *De Jure Belli* 1.4.

20. Ibid., 3.9.

21. Ibid., 3.1.

22. Is there, for Vitoria, noncombatant immunity in the midst of war? Innocent people and children indeed are to be spared. May these be taken captive? Yes. May they be enslaved? No. On the matter of taking women and children captive, Vitoria

is less assertive. He notes that it is "received rule" that Christians do not become slaves as a result of war. Women and children may be held as ransom, though not as slaves in the formal sense. Children may not be killed and must, along with women, be presumed innocent. See in this regard ibid., 3.3–5.
23. Ibid., 1.1. Here he cites Augustine (cf. *Epistle* ["To Boniface"] 138).
24. Vitoria, *De Jure Belli* 1.1.
25. *ST* II-II Q. 40.
26. However, "avenging wrongs," according to Vitoria, needs severe qualification. Not every kind and degree of wrong can suffice for commencing a war (ibid., 1.3); rather, the degree of punishment ought to correspond to the measure of the offence (1.4).
27. Vitoria, *De Jure Belli* 2.1–2.
28. Ibid., 2.2.
29. Ibid., 2.3. Vitoria observes that a war that is just on both sides "could never be settled" (ibid.). It would be analogous to handling a property dispute in civil court: "the just judge would not give the whole territory to one or the other side, but would divide it between them" (ibid).
30. Ibid., 1.4 and 3.9. Vitoria's treatise ends with the following admonition: "once war has been declared for just causes, the prince should press his campaign not for the destruction of his opponents, but for the pursuit of the justice for which he fights and the defence of his homeland, so that by fighting he may eventually establish peace and security" (ibid., 3.9).
31. *Lectiones* in *ST* I-II 90–105, *De Lege* (*On Law*) nos. 121, 123, and 124.
32. Ibid., no. 121, a. 1, and no. 122, a. 1.
33. Ibid., no. 121, a. 2.
34. What contemporary assessments of sixteenth-century Spanish imperialism are inclined to ignore is the fact that in 1550, i.e., four years after Vitoria's death, Spain ordered all military activity in the New World to cease and created a commission to probe the moral claims that Vitoria had set forth regarding the Indians. *Whether or not the Spanish empire was deterred in the long run is immaterial* to our argument; we only wish to point out the effects of this influential just war thinker at a time when his message was extremely unpopular.
35. Following several teaching stints, including one in Rome, Suárez taught at the University of Salamanca (1592–97), where he had been educated, before assuming a post at the University of Portugal at Coimbra (1597–1616). Portugal, at this time, was under the domination of Spain.
36. Suárez, *De Leg.* 2.6.5. Cf. *ST* I-II Q. 71, a. 6.
37. Ibid., *De Leg.* 2.6.6.
38. Here Suárez cites Aristotle (*Nic. Eth.* 2.6), who observes, "There are some passions that by their very names are connected with depravity, such as malevolence, impudence, and envy, and a number of acts, such as adultery, theft, and murder. For all of these and others are so called because they themselves are evil."
39. Suárez, *De Leg.* 2.6.13. Thus, even "if God did not prohibit or command those things that belong to the natural law, it would nonetheless be the case that lying is bad and that honoring one's parents is good and fitting" (ibid., 2.6.14). Or in Thomistic terms, such an act deviates from the proper end for which it should be done (*ST* I-II Q. 21).

40. Suárez, *On Charity*, Disp. 13 ["On War"], sec. 1. We rely on the English translation that is found in *Selections from the Three Works of Francisco Suárez*, ed. J. B. Scott; trans. G. L. Williams et al. (London: Clarendon / Humphrey Melford, 1944), 800–815. When citing from *De Triplici Virtute Theologica* below, we use the designations *On Faith* and *On Charity.*
41. Suárez, *On Charity*, Disp. 13, sec. 1.
42. Ibid.
43. Ibid.
44. Ibid., sec. 4, no. 3.
45. Ibid., secs. 6 and 8. This does not imply the presence of any sort of full-blown doctrine of conscientious objection, as Johnson (*Ideology, Reason, and the Limitation of War*, 183–84) observes, but it does nevertheless suggest that those other than rulers bore some moral responsibility in adjudicating.
46. Suárez, *On Charity*, Disp. 13, sec. 6, no. 6.
47. Ibid., sec. 7, nos. 11–21.
48. Ibid., sec. 7, no. 15.
49. The assumption behind his reasoning is that Christians do not have dominion over the world; therefore, to each of these questions Suárez answers no. And if the zealous ruler, or the pope himself, believes that God's honor is in question and needs vindication, Suárez is unambiguous: God can avenge himself (*On Charity*, Disp. 13, sec. 5). In Suárez's argument we find the fundamental distinction between a state requiring religious practice among its own people and the coercion of religious belief upon other peoples (*On Faith*, Disp. 18, sec. 6). This difference has its grounding in the nature of the state's authority; foreigners are under a different state authority, and that authority alone is responsible for their governance. Other states or people-groups, however, must permit missionaries freedom to operate, an assumption that is on display in both *On Faith* and *On Charity.* What's more, coercing faith is forbidden by both divine and natural law, by which the unbeliever responds through reason and persuasion (*On Faith*, sec. 6, nos. 1–10).
50. *ST* II-II Q. 40.
51. Cf. in this regard Aristotle, *Politics* 1333b–1334a. In line with mainstream Christian moral thinkers through the ages, Suárez rejects the Aristotelian assumption of a natural moral elite within society who through their superior knowledge intuit justice over injustice and right over wrong.
52. Suárez, *De Leg.* 2.19.
53. Ibid.
54. Grotius entered the University of Leiden for studies at the ripe age of eleven.
55. The edition we use is Hugo Grotius, *The Rights of War and Peace*, ed. Richard Tuck.
56. Grotius could write in the *Prolegomena* to *De Jure*, "I observed throughout the Christian world a licentiousness [other translations: "lack of restraint"] in relation to war, which even barbarous races ought to be ashamed of: a running to arms upon very frivolous or rather no occasions; which being once taken up, there remained no longer any reverence for right [i.e., law], either divine or human, just as if from that time men were authorized and firmly resolved to commit all manner of crimes without restrain" (no. 29). Interestingly, Grotius died in 1645 while the Peace of Westphalia was being negotiated, only three years prior to its culmination.

57. The latter of these works was a response to several Dutch provinces that had consulted with Grotius, who served as attorney general from 1613 onward, regarding how to handle the matter of Jewish worship. Hedley Bull argues—and the evidence would seem supportive—that Grotius's greatest passion, a passion even greater than for international accord, was to see a reunion of Protestant and Catholic churches. Even at the height of the Thirty Years War, Grotius preached reconciliation of the two sides, which earned him only vilification from both sides. See "The Importance of Grotius in the Study of International Relations," in Hedley Bull et al., eds., *Hugo Grotius and International Relations* (Oxford: Clarendon, 1992), 67.
58. For a fascinating depiction of the background religious controversy that engulfed Grotius, see John Marshall, *John Locke, Toleration, and Early Enlightenment Culture* (Cambridge: Cambridge University Press, 2006), especially chaps. 4 and 11.
59. In the *Prolegomena* to *De Jure*, Grotius describes his banishment from practicing law and public service in his home country (no. 31). During the last decade of his life, Grotius served the king of France as a Swedish ambassador. Perhaps the best biography of Grotius remains W. S. M. Knight, *The Life and Works of Hugo Grotius* (London: Sweet and Maxwell, 1925). For an extensive examination of the relationship between Grotius's writings and the political history of which he was a part, see the volume edited by Bull et al., *Hugo Grotius and International Relations* (noted above).
60. An example is the long-standing debate whether it is fitting to call Grotius a "father of international law." Murray Forsyth, "The Tradition of International Law," in Terry Nardin and David Mapel, eds., *Traditions of International Ethics* (Cambridge: Cambridge University Press, 1992), 23–189, argues that he should not be so called, because he wrote "as a pious Christian" (26), whereas international law must be grounded in a "legal and secular" view of sovereignty (27).
61. Pangle and Ehrensdorf. *Justice among the Nations*, 162.
62. Johnson, *The Quest for Peace*, 201.
63. Late-medieval lawyers and theologians, following Aquinas, focused primarily on *ad bellum* matters—the authority of the prince, the justice of the cause, and the intentions of those waging war.
64. If *De Jure* is not the most original treatise on the law of nations written up to that time—and his debt to Vitoria and Suárez is quite clear—it is surely the most influential and the most systematic, as Hedley Bull, "The Importance of Grotius in the Study of International Relations," 74–75, has rightly observed. Moreover, this is in keeping with Grotius's own remark at the beginning of the *Prolegomena*: few have probed and *none have examined universally and systematically* that law which is common to the nations, whether it derives from nature, divine commands or custom (no. 1).
65. *De Jure Belli ac Pacis, Proleg.* no. 6. Citations of *De Jure* hereafter are taken from Hugo Grotius, *The Rights of War and Peace*, ed. R. Tuck.
66. Ibid., no. 18.
67. Ibid., no. 12. In Grotius's argument, all "sovereign" states are bound by international law, not merely those in "civilized," Christianized Europe.
68. Ibid., bk. 2, chap. 1, no. 9.
69. Pangle and Ehrensdorf, *Justice among the Nations*, 170.

70. This is insinuated in *Proleg.* no. 17 and developed at length in bk. 2, chap. 15.
71. Ibid., 30.
72. Charity, according to Grotius, may forbid some things that are not contrary to the strictness of law. On charity as a governing motive, see 2.1.9; 2.17.9; 2.25.3,9; 3.1.4; 3.2.6; 3.13.4. As such, "the rules of charity reach farther than those of right" (3.13.4).
73. Ibid., *Proleg.* No. 30 (our translation).
74. So, rightly, Karma Nabulsi, "Conceptions of Justice in War: From Grotius to Modern Times," in Richard Sorabji and David Rodin, eds., *The Ethics of War: Shared Problems in Different Traditions* (Aldershot, UK: Ashgate, 2006), 45.
75. This is the burden of the entirety of chap. 2 in bk. 1 of *De Jure*, which is one of the longer chapters comprising the work.
76. The nature of law, for Grotius, shows war to be morally permitted under highly qualified circumstances; war is proscribed neither by charity nor by the teaching of the New Testament nor by the natural law. Grotius writes: "By the law of nature then, which may also be called the law of nations, it is plain, that every kind of war is not to be condemned" (1.2.4).
77. 2.1.4; 2.21.10–20,28,34. Justice is understood by Grotius to require restitution or proportionate compensation (1.1.8) and to be "an equality between the offence and the punishment" (2.20.2). But because of the human propensity for error and the fact that "it is difficult to find the just balance," Grotius maintains that "we ought to be ready rather to mitigate the punishment" (2.20.36).
78. Ibid., 3.1.2.
79. Ibid., 2.1.2; cf. 2.1.5 and 2.1.16.
80. While there is great room on this point for misconstruing Grotius's conviction that preemptive action may be justified, several things need to be said. First, he emphasizes the *imminence* of the actual threat (2.1.5.1). The intentions of the aggressor must be *shown* to be destructive. Grotius readily acknowledges that much evil is done when out of fear alone people retaliate prematurely and thus unjustly. For example, merely to *believe* that an enemy intends to ambush us, poison us or entrap us is not sufficient cause to attack him preemptively, much less to kill him (ibid.).
81. Ibid., 2.1.3.
82. Ibid., 2.22.1–13.
83. Ibid., 2.23.6. Grotius cites as an example the college of priests (*feciales*) in ancient Rome whose function was to advise before the outbreak of war, and the bishops of the early church (2.23.4).
84. Ibid., 2.23.7–8.
85. Ibid., 2.23.8. Such, for Grotius, is not to argue that in actuality both sides are just; it is only to concede a *relative justness* that needs some sort of external, extraecclesial arbitration (in contrast to medieval conceptions of "justness"). In his arguments, Grotius is more judicious—one might say, more "lawyerly"—than Vitoria, who held the possibility of both parties in war being just to be morally absurd. Vitoria's position was that either there exists indisputable evidence of injustice, which justifies war, or there exists insufficient evidence to go to war. Contra Benedict Kingsbury and Adam Roberts, "Introduction: Grotian Thought in International Relations," in Hedley Bull et al., *Hugo Grotius and International*

Relations, 27, one discovers in *De Jure* genuine attempts at international adjudication. What is remarkable in this vein is the detail given to Grotius's discussion of possible arbitration as an alternative means by which to avert war. See also 3.20.46.
86. Ibid., 2.23.8.
87. Ibid., 2.24.1–3.
88. Ibid., 2.24.6.
89. Ibid., 2.24.2–5.
90. Ibid., 1.3.5–23; 1.5.1–4.
91. Ibid., *Proleg.* 8; 2.20.1–2, 32; 2.28, 32–34; 3.1.2.
92. Ibid., 2.25.4–6.
93. Ibid., 2.25.3.
94. Ibid., 3.3.5–6. Grotius acknowledges that the natural law does not require such declaration yet believes that a formal *demand* is in order, whether goods are about to be seized or war is about to commence (3.3.5.2). He writes that "a publick denunciation is required in all cases, as to those peculiar effects of a just war" (ibid.).
95. This expression derives from Cicero, on whose wisdom Grotius relies exceedingly throughout *De Jure.*
96. This is true even when he disagrees with Aristotle on the nature of virtue. He takes "the philosopher" to task for the manner in which moderation (i.e., Aristotle's "golden mean" between various extremes) is construed. This, in Grotius's line of reasoning, has important implications for how we think about justice (*Proleg.* 44–45).
97. Even G. I. A. D. Draper, "Grotius' Place in the Development of Legal Ideas about War," in Bull et al., *Hugo Grotius and International Relations*, 177–207, whose general predisposition is to diminish—unfairly, in our estimation—the individual contributions of Grotius, concedes this much in the Grotian legacy (207).
98. It is not uncommon for some to misinterpret Grotius as advancing a secular theory of natural law, on the basis of statements such as his observation in the *Prolegomena* that the natural law would be valid even if there were no God or human affairs were of no concern to God. But Alex J. Bellamy is correct to note that Grotius can locate the operation of the natural within human reason without detaching it from a theistic framework (*Just Wars: From Cicero to Iraq* [Cambridge: Polity, 2006], 71).
99. So Pangle and Ehrensdorf, *Justice among the Nations*, 171.
100. As evidenced by his closing prayer (3.25.8), Grotius intends that among his readers will be those in authority. Here he prays that the minds of those in power might be enlightened with "the knowledge of every right (= law [*juris*]), divine and human," and that they might be inspired with "the constant and dutiful sense of their being the ministers of heaven, ordained to govern men"—men "for whom, of all his creatures, God has the greatest regard and affection."
101. Ibid., 3.25.1.
102. Ibid., 3.25.2. In this vein, he cites Augustine, who maintained, "We seek not peace, to make war; but we make war, in order to establish peace" (Letter 189, "To Boniface").
103. Ibid., 3.25.2.
104. Ibid., 2.25.9.3.

Chapter 8: John Locke

1. Locke, *Two Treatises of Government*, II, § 6; cited hereafter only by section number.
2. §§ 19, 17.
3. § 18.
4. §§ 19, 16 (emphasis added).
5. A good account of Hobbesian tendencies in Locke's thought, focusing especially on his understanding of international relations, is Richard H. Cox, *Locke on War and Peace* (Oxford: Oxford University Press, 1960).
6. § 8.
7. § 8.
8. § 12.
9. § 11. This likening of extreme aggressors to beasts is a marked departure from classic (Christian) just war teaching and has dangerous implications for *jus in bello.*
10. § 14.
11. The analogy between individuals and states leads one inevitably to consider the possibility of world government. Why did Locke not discuss this? He likely thought it impossible. Thus, he writes (§ 14), "since all princes and rulers of independent governments all through the world are in a state of nature, it is plain the world never was, *nor ever will be*, without numbers of men in that state" (emphasis added). For some plausible speculations about Locke's reasons for rejecting the idea of world government, see Cox, *Locke on War and Peace*, 189–95.
12. Notice that Locke drastically narrows the traditional litany of just causes; only the effort to thwart acts of aggression counts as a just cause for Locke, whereas for earlier writers (take Vitoria, for instance), just cause might also include humanitarian intervention, or the right of the pope to order a restructuring of government in a foreign land once enough of its inhabitants are converted to the faith.
13. Locke, *Letter Concerning Toleration*, in David Wooton, ed., *Political Writings of John Locke* (New York: Mentor Books), 403.
14. See Walzer, *Just and Unjust Wars*, chaps. 18–19.
15. § 176. A difficult issue arises here. Because unjust conquerors can never establish a right over the lands they conquer, subsequent generations can always revisit the issue by overthrowing the "unjust" regime, provided they have not consented to it (see § 192). One shudders to think how many wars might be justifiable were this principle strictly applied. It was perhaps with a principle like this in mind that so many wars of secession were fought in the past century. Clearly, Locke's purpose was to *discourage* acts of aggression by showing aggressors that they can never gain permanently from their crimes; but the principle he articulates here seems likely to backfire—to encourage people to wage war on the pretext of redressing wrongs from long ago.
16. §§ 178, 180.
17. § 179.
18. *De Jure Belli* 3.2.3.
19. § 180.
20. § 182.
21. § 185.

22. This is not the place to rehearse the debate about Locke's position on slavery in the *Second Treatise* versus his position in the *Constitutions of the Carolinas.* In the *Second Treatise*, Locke sets out principles that will in time move the West away from institutionalized slavery. Whether he maintained these principles consistently in practice is a separate question. For a useful discussion, see Jeremy Waldron, *God, Locke, and Equality: Christian Foundations of John Locke's Political Thought*, 199–206.
23. "On Kingship," 6.52, where Aquinas cites Osee xiii.11: "I will give thee a king in my wrath."
24. *ST* 2a2ae, Q. 104 ("Of Obedience") a. 6.
25. For Aquinas, as for Augustine, Romans 13 stands in the background: "Let every soul be subject unto the higher powers. For there is no power but of God: the powers that be are ordained of God. Whosoever therefore resisteth the power, resisteth the ordinance of God: and they that resist shall receive to themselves damnation."
26. Ibid., reply to objection 1.
27. Ibid., reply to objection 3.
28. "On Kingship," 6.42.
29. Ibid., 5.38, 6.44.
30. Ibid., 6.51.
31. Ibid., 6.52.
32. § 202.
33. § 226. Compare Thomas Aquinas, *ST* II-II, Q. 42, article 2, reply to objection 3. Thomas anticipates Locke's point here. There is no sedition in disturbing a tyranny, because the tyrant is the seditious one. But Thomas is quick to place conditions on this teaching, chiefly that if the overthrow of a tyrant produces more chaos than the tyrant's rule itself, then right has not been done.
34. § 204.
35. § 168.
36. § 21, 176; cf. Judges 11:27.
37. Judges 11:27.
38. This is a point Augustine makes explicitly (see chap. 3); consider also Romans 14:7: "We do not live to ourselves, and we do not die to ourselves. If we live, we live to the Lord, and if we die, we die to the Lord: so then, whether we live or whether we die, we are the Lord's. For to this end Christ died and lived again, so that he might be Lord of both the dead and the living."

Chapter 9: Immanuel Kant: Beyond Just War?

1. Kant was alive and writing during the years of the French Revolution and observed how that internal struggle swelled outward to envelope virtually all of France's neighbors.
2. Immanuel Kant, *Fundamental Principles of the Metaphysics of Morals*, trans. Thomas K. Abbott (New York: Bobbs-Merrill, 1949), 45, 38. These two ideas are merged together in another of Kant's basic principles: "So act as to treat humanity, whether in thine own person or in that of any other, in every case as an end withal, never as means only" (ibid., 46).

3. See Kant, "On the Common Saying: 'This May Be True in Theory, but It Does Not Apply in Practice,'" in *Kant: Political Writings*, trans. H. B. Nisbet (Cambridge: Cambridge University Press, 1970), 61–92. We use this edition for all subsequent quotations from Kant.
4. Hobbes, *Leviathan*, pt. 1, chap. 13 (Cambridge: Cambridge University Press, [1651] 1996) ; Cf. Kant, *Perpetual Peace: A Philosophical Sketch*, first definitive article; and *Theory of Right*, § 54.
5. *Metaphysics of Morals*, § 61.
6. Ibid., § 56.
7. Ibid.
8. This may sound surprising to readers who view Kant primarily as an idealist, but in fact he was a careful student of the phenomenal and the noumenal worlds alike. See the still-useful study by Kenneth N. Waltz, "Kant, Liberalism and War," *American Political Science Review* 56 (1962): 331–40, along with Elisabeth Ellis, *Kant's Politics: Provisional Theory for an Uncertain World* (New Haven, CT: Yale University Press, 2005).
9. *Metaphysics of Morals*, § 57.
10. Kant might have reasonably listed these considerations under the heading of *jus ad bellum*, since they relate to the legitimate causes and purposes of war; but he places them under *jus in bello* apparently because they are deduced from the foundational *in bello* principle of preserving the possibility of future peaceful relations.
11. Cf. Cicero, *De Officiis* I.34–40; and Augustine, Letter 189, "To Boniface"—both discussed in chap. 3 above.
12. Accordingly, the slogan made famous by Benito Mussolini—"*O con noi o contro di noi*" ("You are either with us or against us!")—and echoed recently by American leaders on the left and right is not a praiseworthy example of international rhetoric. Senator Hillary Clinton during an interview on *CBS Evening News* with Dan Rather, September 13, 2001, remarked, "Every nation has to either be with us, or against us. Those who harbor terrorists, or who finance them, are going to pay a price." And President George W. Bush in his "Address to a Joint Session of Congress and the American People," September 20, 2001, similarly exclaimed, "Every nation, in every region, now has a decision to make. Either you are with us, or you are with the terrorists."
13. *Leviathan*, pt. 2, chap. 17.
14. See further Louis P. Pojman, "Kant's Perpetual Peace and Cosmopolitanism," *Journal of Social Philosophy* 36 (2005): 62–71. Pojman is useful in situating Kant's essay in relation to Moses Mendelssohn's earlier contention that individuals make moral progress but collectives do not. Kant thought the opposite: individuals remain basically the same over time but the species as a whole gradually comes to embody the moral law through its institutions of positive law.
15. In addition to *Metaphysics of Morals*, § 61 (cited in n. 2), see *Perpetual Peace*, First Supplement, 113–14, in *Kant Political Writings*. For his own part, the late Louis Pojman thought this was precisely where Kant went wrong: "[Kant] overestimated the importance of national sovereignty," and it is now time to "bring into being a democratic world government dedicated to peace, justice and well-being for people everywhere" (70).
16. *Perpetual Peace*, 109.

17. *Metaphysics of Morals*, "Conclusion to Part I." Kant's briefer remarks in *Perpetual Peace* seem to assume familiarity with this paragraph. In any event, it helps to illuminate Kant's position. Although the *Metaphysics of Morals* (1797) was published two years later than *Perpetual Peace* (1795), the works were certainly gestating during the same period. Kant had been thinking about political theory at least since the 1760s. He had been lecturing since 1767 on the "theory of right," which included reflections on perpetual peace.
18. Kenneth Waltz ("Kant, Liberalism and War," 340) writes: "Many liberals of Kant's time and after have looked upon war as annoyance or aberration, as something, one might say, that lies outside of history. Kant, in contrast, at once condemns war and demonstrates that its occurrence is expected rather than accidental. In the end, we are left not with a confident foretelling of 'the end of wars and the reign of international law, but with a deeper appreciation of the causes of war and the immense difficulty of doing anything about them."
19. They are necessary conditions, not *sufficient*. It would indeed be surprising (not to say risible) if Kant thought he had supplied all the steps to perpetual peace in such a short space.
20. *Perpetual Peace*, 99; cf. *Metaphysics of Morals* §52.
21. *Perpetual Peace*, 100.
22. Among critics, see, e.g., John Mearsheimer, "Back to the Future: Instability in Europe after the Cold War," *International Security* 15 (1990): 5–57, and Denny Roy, "Neorealism and Kant: No Pacific Union," *Journal of Peace Research* 30 (1993): 451–54. Noteworthy among the defenders of Kant's thesis are Michael W. Doyle, "Liberalism and World Politics," *American Political Science Review* 80 (1986): 1151–69; and George Sørensen, "Kant and Processes of Democratization: Consequences for Neorealist Thought," *Journal of Peace Research* 29 (1992): 397–414. For a statistical discussion of the democratic peace proposition, see Doyle, "Kant, Liberal Legacies and Foreign Affairs," 217, and more recently, Bruce Russett and John R. Oneal, *Triangulating Peace* (New York: W. W. Norton and Co., 2001).
23. *Perpetual Peace*, 112.
24. Ibid., 114.
25. Brian Orend, *War and International Justice* (Waterloo: Wilfrid Laurier Press, 2000), esp. chap. 2, "Kant's Just War Theory," 41–61; also Susan Shell, "Kant on Unjust War and 'Unjust Enemies': Reflections on a 'Pleonasm,'" *Kantian Review* 10 (2005): 82–102.
26. On Machiavelli's account of preemption, see the excellent study by Steven Forde, "Varieties of Realism: Thucydides and Machiavelli," *Journal of Politics* 54 (1992): 372–93, esp. p. 377: "As the ancient Romans knew, threats are always imminent of forming on the horizon. The prudent state therefore attacks preemptively, at a time of its choosing, rather than waiting for the enemy. . . . Thus [the Romans] subjugated ever-widening circles of territory until no threats remained. The Romans conquered the world out of self-defense."
27. *Perpetual Peace*, 103.
28. So Yoder, *When War Is Unjust*, 3: "What do we mean when we ask whether a system of ideas is credible? The just-war tradition presents itself as an instrument for making difficult decisions. . . . What is in question is the possibility of a negative outcome. Can the criteria function in such a way that in a particular case a

specified cause, or a specified means, or a specified strategy or tactical move could be *excluded*? Can the response ever be 'no'?" Yoder's argument is that the just war tradition fails to limit war adequately.
29. See, e.g., Fernando Tesón, *Humanitarian Intervention: An Inquiry into Law and Morality* (Irvington-on-Hudson, NY: Transnational Publishers, Inc., 1996), 238–49.
30. Covenant of the League of Nations, article 16.
31. Preamble, Charter of the United Nations.
32. Art. 2.
33. Art. 4.
34. Vatican City is the only widely recognized independent state that is not a member.
35. Pubantz, "United Nations in the Twenty-First Century," 10.
36. Kofi Annan, *We the Peoples* (New York: United Nations Department of Public Information, 2000), 48.
37. Jerry Pubantz, "The United Nations in the Twenty-First Century," 37, thus writes: "By the turn of the century the Security Council had stood Kant on his head. International organizations proved the vehicle for creating new democratic states—sometimes successfully, sometimes with little success—rather than vice versa. Collective security now was recognized to include domestic administration of failed states, organization and administration of free elections, sponsorship of civil society, defense of domestic human rights, empowerment of disadvantaged groups such as women and indigenous peoples, as well as refugee repatriation, humanitarian assistance, and the elimination of weapons of mass destruction. Terrorism and even diseases—such as HIV/AIDS, tuberculosis and malaria—were described as threats to collective security, and therefore appropriately addressed in peacekeeping operations under Chapter VII of the UN Charter."
38. Thus, Louis Pojman, "Kant's Perpetual Peace and Cosmopolitanism," *Journal of Social Philosophy* 36 (2005): 62–71, refers to the UN as a "toothless tiger" and claims that while it "may provide a forum for rhetorical persuasion on the protection of human rights, nations will violate [its] edicts . . . if they can profitably get away with doing so."
39. For an excellent articulation of this point, see Nicholas Rengger, "On the Just War Tradition in the Twenty-First Century," *International Affairs* 78 (2002): 353–63.

Chapter 10: Contemporary Just War Thinkers

1. *We Hold These Truths: Catholic Reflections on the American Proposition* (New York: Sheed and Ward, 1960); *Morality and Modern Warfare* (New York: Council on Religion and International Affairs, 1959).
2. *We Hold These Truths*, 249.
3. Ibid., 250.
4. Ibid.
5. Ibid.
6. Ibid.
7. Ibid., 250–51.

8. Ibid., 251.
9. Ibid., 252. These are Murray's terms, not ours.
10. Ibid.
11. Ibid., 256.
12. Ibid., 260–65.
13. Ibid., 261 (emphasis added); cf. Augustine, *Against Faustus the Manichean*, XXII.73ff. (discussed in chap. 3 above).
14. Ibid.
15. Ibid.
16. Ibid., 265.
17. Ibid., 265–66.
18. Ibid., 269.
19. Ibid., 271.
20. Ibid., 272.
21. Ibid., 273.
22. Walzer acknowledges that just war theory was still alive in some theology departments and among Catholic writers whose appreciation for tradition allowed the theory to retain some credibility. But it was regarded as unscientific in the leading schools of political analysis. See Walzer, "The Triumph of Just War Theory (and the Dangers of Success)," *Social Research* 69 (2002): 925–44.
23. Douglas Lackey, "A Modern Theory of Just War," *Ethics* 92, no. 3 (1982): 533–46. We have abbreviated Lackey's first point; otherwise, we are quoting.
24. In the preface to the third edition, Walzer speaks of a "large and momentous shift" that has occurred between the date of the book's first appearance (1977) and the date of the third edition (2000): "The issues that I discussed under the name 'interventions,' which were peripheral to the main concerns of the book, have moved dramatically into the center. It isn't much of an exaggeration to say that the greatest danger most people face in the world today comes from their own states, and the chief dilemma of international politics is whether people in danger should be rescued by military forces from outside." For a more recent discussion of the problem in legal terms, see J. L. Holzgrefe and Robert O. Keohane, eds., *Humanitarian Intervention: Ethical, Legal, and Political Dilemmas* (Cambridge: Cambridge University Press, 2003).
25. Walzer, *Just and Unjust Wars*, 87–91, drawing upon John Stuart Mill, "A Few Words on Non-Intervention" in Mill's *Dissertations and Discussions* (New York: Holt, 1873), vol. 3, 238–63.
26. *Just and Unjust Wars*, 90.
27. Ibid., 104.
28. Ibid., 98–99.
29. Ibid., 96.
30. Ibid., 101.
31. This is the thrust of Walzer's essay "The Failure of Deterrence and the Conduct of War," in William V. O'Brien and John Langan, eds., *The Nuclear Dilemma and the Just War Tradition* (Lexington, MA: Lexington Books, 1986), 154–97.
32. William V. O'Brien, *War and/or Survival* (Garden City: Doubleday, 1969).
33. William V. O'Brien, *The Conduct of Just and Limited War* (New York: Praeger, 1981).

34. O'Brien and Langan, *The Nuclear Dilemma and the Just War Tradition.*
35. *The Challenge of Peace: God's Promise and Our Response* (Washington, DC: United States Catholic Conference, 1983).
36. O'Brien, *The Conduct of Just and Limited War*, 498.
37. Two forms of objection are recurring, according to O'Brien. One is to maintain that *any* resort to war is incompatible with an absolute commitment to discrimination, while a second is to employ a variant of the double-effect doctrine. Strangely, the noted just war theorist contemporary to O'Brien, Paul Ramsey, came close to adopting the absolutist position, with which O'Brien strongly disagreed.
38. O'Brien, *The Conduct of Just and Limited War*, 503–4.
39. See, in particular, chap. 10 ("The Laws of War") of O'Brien's *War and/or Survival Nuclear War, Deterrence, and Morality* (Westminster: Newman Press, 1967); *The Conduct of Just and Limited War*; as well as his important essay, "The Failure of Deterrence," in Judith A. Dwyer, ed., *The Catholic Bishops and Nuclear War* (Washington, DC: Georgetown University Press, 1984), 37–63.
40. William V. O'Brien, "The International Law of War as Related to the Just War Tradition," in Terry Nardin and David Mapel, eds., *Traditions of International Ethics* (Cambridge: Cambridge University Press, 1992), 189.
41. See, e.g., his *Ideology, Reason, and the Limitation of War* and *Just War Tradition and the Restraint of War.*
42. Johnson, *The Quest for Peace*; James Turner Johnson and John Kelsay, eds., *Cross, Crescent, and Sword: The Justification and Limitation of War in Western and Islamic Tradition* (Contributions to the Study of Religion 27; Westport/London: Greenwood Press, 1990); also with John Kelsay, eds., *Just War and Jihad: Historical and Theological Perspectives on War and Peace in Western and Islamic Traditions* (Contributions to the Study of Religion 28; Westport/London: Greenwood Press, 1991); and Johnson, *The Holy War Idea in Western and Islamic Traditions.*
43. See, e.g., James Turner Johnson and George Weigel, *Just War and the Gulf War* (Washington, DC: Ethics & Public Policy Center, 1991); Johnson, *Morality and Contemporary Warfare*; and Johnson, *The War to Oust Saddam Hussein: Just War and the New Face of Conflict* (Lanham/Oxford: Rowman & Littlefield, 2005).
44. Johnson, *The Holy War Idea in Western and Islamic Traditions.*
45. Ibid., 171.
46. Hereon see J. Daryl Charles, "Regensburg Left Behind," *Touchstone* 22, no. 7 (September–October 2009): 34–39.
47. *The Challenge of Peace*, paras. 70 and 80.
48. Paul Ramsey was also acutely critical of those who argued that pacifism and just war have in common the same presumption against violence; see his *Speak Up for Just War or Pacifism* (University Park/London: Pennsylvania State University Press, 1988), 109–10. Also see in this regard J. Daryl Charles, "Presumption against War or Presumption against Injustice? The Just War Tradition Reconsidered," *Journal of Church and State* 47, no. 2 (Spring 2005): 335–69.
49. This burden is summarized very concisely in his essay "The Broken Tradition," which appeared in the Fall 1996 issue of *The National Interest.*
50. Jean Bethke Elshtain, *Who Are We? Critical Reflections and Hopeful Possibilities* (Grand Rapids/Cambridge, UK: Eerdmans, 2000), ix; cf. her introduction remarks

in *Sovereignty: God, State, and Self* (New York: Basic Books, 2008), a revised version of her Gifford Lectures.

51. A further consequence of this severance is that it has marginalized political theory in the academic, "scientific" study of politics.

52. Elshtain writes that she has been reading Augustine since she was eighteen years old, though with an ever-increasing appreciation.

53. Elshtain is struck by the fact that both Bonhoeffer and Karol Wojtyla (to become Pope John Paul II) in their own time experienced the worst of human depravity yet hoped for—and continue in their own way to call us to—the best in human aspirations. Thus, they retain their immense significance for democratic culture, not because they understood themselves as political theorists (they were not) but rather because of their insight into the human condition and the emphasis in their writings on what is enduring. A trenchant analysis of the human condition is a hallmark of both Bonhoeffer and Wojtyla, despite the fact that both are "forbiddingly complex" thinkers who never shrink from tackling the most difficult questions, as *Who Are We?* attempts to make clear.

54. Citing a Vaclav Havel speech titled "On Evasive Thinking," in *Real Politics: At the Center of Everyday Life* (Baltimore / London: The Johns Hopkins University Press, 1997), 3. Cf. her discussion of language in *Just War Against Terror*, 16–25.

55. See especially her *Augustine and the Limits of Politics* (Notre Dame: University of Notre Dame Press, 1996). For her examination of Augustine on war, see pp. 105–12 ("War and Peace: Why Augustine Still Matters").

56. Elshtain, *Real Politics: At the Center of Everyday Life*, 127, writes somewhat tongue-in-cheek: "It was a relief, then, that my own young son was probably not a beast lurking and awaiting the chance to bare his fangs and shed some blood."

57. In chap. 11 of *Real Politics*, Elshtain asks somewhat contentiously: "Why, despite all the ferment and fervor, has feminism . . . failed?" (165). The remainder of chap. 11 is devoted to her understanding of why she believes this to be so.

58. Ibid., 186.

59. Elshtain's sociological critique of feminism is most forceful in chaps. 13–19 of *Real Politics* (229–317). In *Women and War* (rev. ed.; Chicago / London: University of Chicago Press, 1995), her approach is more narrative and historical.

60. This is Elshtain's rhetorical reconstruction of *conventional thinking* about just war and not her own understanding of *jus ad bellum* and *jus in bello* criteria. See her "Epilogue: Continuing Implications of the Just War Tradition," in Elshtain, ed., *Just War Theory* (New York: New York University, 1992), 324.

61. Elshtain develops the domestic implications of just war thinking, particularly as it informs civic virtue, in *Women and War*, 149–52.

62. Elshtain, *Just War Theory*, 323–24.

63. Elshtain thus attests to the overarching thesis of this book. See also on this point the incisive essay by Michael Oakeshott, "Political Education," in *Rationalism in Politics* (Indianapolis: Liberty Fund, 1991).

64. Elshtain presupposes on the part of many of her readers some sort of religious faith.

65. Elshtain, *Women and War*, 252–53, 268.

66. Elshtain, *Just War Against Terror*, 6.

Chapter 11: Why Have Our Churches Lost the Tradition? Two Temptations: Christian Realism, Christian Pacifism

1. The absence of such a synthetic study of the just war position vis-à-vis contemporary Christian realism and pacifism is a real lacuna in the literature. Jean Bethke Elshtain's recent treatment of Niebuhr in her *Just War Against Terror* (New York: Basic Books, 2003) is an exception; but Elshtain's purpose is more to assimilate Niebuhr to the just war tradition than to differentiate him from it. See also Elshtain's forward to Eric Patterson, ed., *The Christian Realists: Reassessing the Contributions of Niebuhr and His Contemporaries* (Lanham: University Press of America, 2003).
2. See Duncan Bell, *Political Thought and International Relations* (Oxford: Oxford University Press, 2008), 9; Benedicta Cipolla, "Reinhold Niebuhr Is Unseen Force in 2008 Elections," *The Pew Forum on Religion & Public Life: Religion News* (September 27, 2007); John McCain, *Hard Call: Great Decisions and the Extraordinary People Who Made Them* (New York: Twelve, 2007), 321–38; and Frank A. Ruechel, "Politics and Morality Revisited: Jimmy Carter and Reinhold Niebuhr," *Atlanta History* 37 (1994): 19–31.
3. See especially Reinhold Niebuhr, "Augustine's Political Realism," in *Christian Realism and Political Problems* (New York: Charles Scribner's Sons, 1953); see also Niebuhr, *An Interpretation of Christian Ethics* (New York: Harper and Brothers, 1935), especially chap. 3; and Niebuhr, *The Nature and Destiny of Man*, vol. 2 (Charles Scribner's Sons, 1964), chap. 3. The best scholarly treatment of Niebuhr's realism is Robin W. Lovin, *Reinhold Niebuhr and Christian Realism* (Cambridge: Cambridge University Press, 1995). Lovin's work is particularly helpful in distinguishing among the different aspects—political, moral, and theological—of Niebuhr's overall realist outlook.
4. Originally published in 1939 as a pamphlet and later included in *Christianity and Power Politics* (New York: Charles Scribner's Sons, 1940), to which all subsequent citations refer.
5. For a recent critique of Niebuhr's anthropological-exegetical approach, see Stanley Hauerwas, *With the Grain of the Universe: The Church's Witness and Natural Theology* (Grand Rapids: Brazos Press, 2001), p. 115; see also John Howard Yoder, "Reinhold Niebuhr and Christian Pacifism," *The Mennonite Quarterly Review* 29 (April, 1955): 101–117.
6. Niebuhr, "Why the Christian Church Is Not Pacifist," 2.
7. Ibid., 6.
8. Compare on this point Niebuhr's "The Ethic of Jesus and the Social Problem," in D. B. Robertson, ed., *Love and Justice: Selections from the Shorter Writings of Reinhold Niebuhr* (Louisville: Westminster / John Knox Press), 34–35.
9. Niebuhr, "Why the Christian Church Is Not Pacifist," 14.
10. Ibid., 27.
11. Ibid., 28.
12. Niebuhr's understanding of the "ethic of Jesus" changed little over the course of his career. See, e.g., *An Interpretation of Christian Ethics*, 35–62; and *The Nature and Destiny of Man*, vol. 2, pp. 68–97. Niebuhr's remarks about the "absolute ethic of Jesus" in "Why the Christian Church Is Not Pacifist" will seem rather cryptic to

the reader unfamiliar with this theme in his broader work. See also "The Ethic of Jesus and the Social Problem," in *Love and Justice*, 29–40.

13. Niebuhr, "Why the Christian Church Is Not Pacifist," 8; *An Interpretation of Christian Ethics*, 52.

14. Niebuhr, *An Interpretation of Christian Ethics*, 47.

15. Ibid., 46.

16. Ibid., 58, 56–57.

17. Compare Immanuel Kant, "On the Common Saying: 'This May Be True in Theory, but It Does Not Apply in Practice.'"

18. Niebuhr, "Why the Christian Church Is Not Pacifist," 9; cf. *An Interpretation of Christian Ethics*, 39.

19. It should be noted that Niebuhr *does* view Christ's ethic as relevant to politics but not immediately relevant; see especially "The Relevance of an Impossible Ethical Ideal," in *An Interpretation of Christian Ethics*, 103–35; and cf. "Why the Christian Church Is Not Pacifist," 21–30. It is relevant in two senses. First, it is *the* standard that is truly normative and before which we are all condemned as sinners; here the ethic of Jesus serves as a principle of "indiscriminate criticism." Second, it is a standard according to which various human approximations can be ranked and evaluated; here it supplies a principle of "discriminate criticism." In this way, the Christian ideal of loving relationships is never a "simple possibility" in a world of human sin, but it is never irrelevant either.

20. Niebuhr, "Why the Christian Church Is Not Pacifist," 31.

21. See Craig A. Carter, *The Politics of the Cross: The Theology and Social Ethics of John Howard Yoder* (Grand Rapids: Brazos Press, 2001), 15–16, an excellent introduction to Yoder.

22. Yoder discusses Niebuhr in "Reinhold Niebuhr and Christian Pacifism," *Mennonite Quarterly Review* 29 (April 1955): 101–17; he analyzes the just war tradition in *When War Is Unjust*, and he examines both Niebuhr and the just war tradition in *Christian Attitudes to War, Peace, and Revolution* (Elkhart: Co-op Bookstore, 1983). For Yoder's own position, see especially *The Original Revolution*; *Nevertheless*, chap. 19 (and cf. chaps. 3, 8, 9, and 14); and *The Politics of Jesus*.

23. Yoder, "Reinhold Niebuhr and Christian Pacifism," 104–5; see also Yoder's essay, "The Political Axioms of the Sermon on the Mount," in *The Original Revolution*, 34–54.

24. Yoder, "Reinhold Niebuhr and Christian Pacifism," 111.

25. Ibid., 114.

26. Yoder, *The Original Revolution*, 18–26. In all, Yoder analyzes four possible options, besides the one Christ ultimately chooses. They include (1) the "realist" Herodian option of accommodating Roman rule, (2) the zealot option of revolutionary violence, (3) the Essenes' option of retreat to the desert, and (4) the Pharisees' option of emphasizing *personal* holiness while tolerating political compromise. One of the virtues of Yoder's essay is its allusion to many modern parallels to these options.

27. Ibid., 29.

28. Yoder, "The Pacifism of the Messianic Community," in *Nevertheless*, 133.

29. Ibid., 135.

30. Yoder, "Reinhold Niebuhr and Christian Pacifism," 116.

31. Yoder, *Body Politics: Five Practices of the Christian Community Before the Watching World* (Nashville: Discipleship Resources, 1992), ix; see also Yoder, *Christian Witness to the State* (Newton: Faith and Life, 1964), 10.
32. Carter, *Politics of the Cross*, 150, drawing upon Yoder's *Christian Witness to the State*, as well as his *Politics of Jesus*, 4–20. Carter's whole chapter on Yoder's "partially realized eschatology" is helpful to consult.
33. Yoder, "Reinhold Niebuhr and Christian Pacifism," 117.
34. Yoder, "The Political Axioms of the Sermon on the Mount," 40–42.
35. Yoder, "Reinhold Niebuhr and Christian Pacifism," 115–16.
36. Yoder, *Nevertheless*, 135.
37. Yoder sometimes takes his fellow Mennonites to task for espousing a form of dualism according to which there are two ethical standards, one based on Christ's teachings and applicable to Christians, another based on natural considerations and applicable to everyone else. The result is that what is "wrong for us" may be "right for the government." Yoder traces the source of this dualism precisely to the influence of Reinhold Niebuhr. Evidently, some Mennonites felt so affirmed by the affinities between theirs and Niebuhr's understanding of Jesus' ethic that they uncritically accepted Niebuhr's account of the alternatives (political responsibility or political irrelevance). See Yoder, *Nevertheless*, 80–82, 107–12, and 179, n. 3. Yoder's message to his fellow Mennonites is to "Reject the Niebuhrian compliment!" He claims to avoid this dualism himself by insisting that the ethic of Jesus *really is universal* (whether individuals recognize it or not) and that it really defines political relevance.
38. Though there are certainly Kantian qualities to the "ethic of Jesus" as Niebuhr and Yoder describe it, there are also certain characteristics of the ethic that are alien to Kant, and these are important to bear in mind. For Niebuhr and Yoder alike, the ground of the ethic is not a priori reason (as in Kant) but Christian experience and faith. And in Yoder's case especially, the ethic is also not universal *in the same way* that Kant's categorical imperative, for example, is universal; for while the ethic of Jesus may be universal in the sense of being the genuine law of life, it is not *universalizable* in the sense of being meaningful to nonbelievers. In spite of these important qualifications, it is useful, we think, to recognize the Kantian characteristics of the "ethic of Jesus" and especially the extent to which these are more consistently realized (in practical terms) in Yoder than in Niebuhr.
39. Yoder, *Nevertheless*, 137.
40. The classic texts of the just war tradition from which we draw generalizations include the following: Augustine, *City of God* IV.15 and 19.8, *Against Faustus the Manichaean* XXII.73–79, Letters 138 ("To Marcellinus") and 189 ("To Boniface"); Aquinas, *ST* II-II, Question 40; Luther, *On Secular Authority, Whether Soldiers Too Can Be Saved*, and *On War against the Turk*; and Calvin, *Institutes*, IV.20.
41. Mt. 22:37–40; cf. Mk. 12:28–34; and Lk. 10:25–38.
42. These are among the headings for Question 40, *ST* II-II (emphasis added).
43. See note 41.
44. See, e.g., Augustine's rejection of a literal interpretation of "turning the other cheek" in his Letter 138, "To Marcellinus"; see also Calvin, *Institutes*, IV.20.2.
45. For the analogy between parental and political force, see Augustine's Letter 138, "To Marcellinus."

46. Yoder, recognizing the problem, takes great pains in *Politics of Jesus* (pp. 42–43) to explain that the whip was likely used on the animals, not on the merchants, and that the verb "cast out" actually "posits no violence." We may grant him the *possibility* (and this is all he argues for) that the whip was not used on the merchants; yet it is hard to understand Christ's response to the money changers in general as anything other than force or "resistance."
47. See, e.g., Augustine, Letter 189, "To Boniface"; Aquinas, Q. 40, "*sed contra*"; and Luther, *On Secular Authority* §1. See also Hugo Grotius, *De Jure Belli ac Pacis* I.ii.7, who summarizes and synthesizes the earlier writers.
48. See Augustine, *Against Faustus the Manichean* XXII. 73–79.
49. Niebuhr was aware of these classic arguments against his own absolute ethic of Jesus. His response is simply to dismiss them with contempt. See, e.g., "Why the Christian Church Is Not Pacifist," 106: "It is very foolish to deny that the ethic of Jesus is an absolute and uncompromising ethic. . . . Nothing is more futile and pathetic than the effort of some Christian theologians [note: Augustine would have to be included here] who find it necessary to become involved in the relativities of politics, in resistance to tyranny or in social conflict, to justify themselves by seeking to prove that Christ was also involved in some of these relativities, that he used whips to drive the money-changers out of the Temple. . . ." Niebuhr's rejection of this aspect of Christian ethics should be borne in mind when considering the extent to which he is or is not Augustinian. He, of course, refers to his own realism as "Augustinian," but this claim should be qualified.
50. Paul Ramsey, "Justice in War," in *The Just War: Force and Political Responsibility* (Lanham: Rowman & Littlefield, 1983), 143.
51. Ibid.
52. "What good is it, my brothers and sisters, if you say you have faith but do not have works? Can faith save you? If a brother or sister is naked and lacks daily food, and one of you says to them, 'Go in peace; keep warm and eat your fill,' and yet you do not supply their bodily needs, what is the good of that?"

Acknowledgments

This book has been many years in the making, and the authors would like to express their gratitude to those people and institutions that supported it. Professor Corey is grateful to Baylor University for generous support of his research and for the opportunity to teach regular courses on the just war tradition. He is also grateful to the University of Tulsa and to Sharon Bell in particular for supporting him as the Visiting Bell Professor of Anglican and Ecumenical Studies during the fall of 2010. Professor Corey also thanks Professors David Clinton, Russ Hittinger, and Tim Fuller for reading and commenting on parts of the manuscript.

Professor Charles is indebted to Robert George, McCormick Professor of Jurisprudence and director of the James Madison Program at Princeton University, and Dr. Bradford Wilson, executive director of the James Madison Program, for extending the generous invitation to serve as 2007–2008 William E. Simon Visiting Fellow in Religion and Public Life at the university. There he had the luxury of incomparable resources, extraordinarily rich fellowship, and enormously stimulating discussions of culture, history, and political philosophy that were of inestimable value in attempting to probe the wider contours of the just war tradition.

Both authors are grateful to Professor George for commending the present volume to ISI's American Ideals and Institutions series. Some of the material herein has appeared in the volume *The West at War*, published by Lexington Books, and in the journals *Logos* and *Political Theology*. The authors are thankful for permission to reprint.

Index